P9-APH-435

FANTASY VACATIONS

FANTASY VACATIONS

JOURNEYS BEYOND YOUR IMAGINATION

STEPHANIE OCKO

CITADEL PRESS
Kensington Publishing Corp.
www.kensingtonbooks.com

CITADEL PRESS BOOKS are published by

Kensington Publishing Corp.
850 Third Avenue
New York, NY 10022

Copyright © 2003 Stephanie Ocko

All rights reserved. No part of this book may be reproduced in any form or by any means without the prior written consent of the publisher, excepting brief quotes used in reviews.

All Kensington titles, imprints, and distributed lines are available at special quantity discounts for bulk purchases for sales promotions, premiums, fund-raising, educational, or institutional use. Special book excerpts or customized printings can also be created to fit specific needs. For details, write or phone the office of the Kensington special sales manager: Kensington Publishing Corp., 850 Third Avenue, New York, NY 10022, attn: Special Sales Department, phone 1-800-221-2647.

CITADEL PRESS and the Citadel logo are Reg. U.S. Pat. & TM Off.

First printing: June 2003

10 9 8 7 6 5 4 3 2 1

Printed in the United States of America

Library of Congress Control Number: 2002116571

ISBN 0-8065-2435-9

Contents

Author's Note   vii

Introduction   ix

Chapter 1   ANTARCTICA   3

Chapter 2   THE ARCTIC   14

Chapter 3   ARCHITECTURE TOURS   21

Chapter 4   ART   26

Chapter 5   ASTRONOMY   40

Chapter 6   BALLOON EXCURSIONS   50

Chapter 7   CAMEL TREKS   55

Chapter 8   CARS: RACE, RALLY, AND ROAM   62

Chapter 9   THE CIRCUS   76

Chapter 10   COOKING AND WINE TASTING   81

Chapter 11   COWBOY FANTASIES   99

Chapter 12   EARTH AND WEATHER   107

Chapter 13   FISHING AND HUNTING   116

Chapter 14   FLIGHTS OF FANTASY   126

Chapter 15   HISTORY   136

Chapter 16 HORSES 152

Chapter 17 HOTELS WITH A CERTAIN EDGE 163

Chapter 18 LONG TRIPS 180

Chapter 19 MOTORCYCLE TOURS 188

Chapter 20 MUSIC AND DANCE 194

Chapter 21 RV CARAVANS 204

Chapter 22 SAFARIS 207

Chapter 23 SAILING 226

Chapter 24 SHARK DIVES 234

Chapter 25 SPACE: READY FOR LIFTOFF 239

Chapter 26 THE SPY TRADE 249

Chapter 27 SUBMERSIBLES 258

Chapter 28 SURVIVAL TRAINING 263

Chapter 29 TRAINS 268

Travel Safely 277

Index 283

Author's Note

The trips described in this book are naturally subject to change, and sometimes simply indicate the type of product that the companies offer. The book does not pretend to be a complete list. The material is presented in good faith without bias or preference. On many of these trips, travelers are warned that the weather can alter plans. Neither the publisher nor the author takes responsibility for a company's incompetence or for any accident or injury to any participant incurred while undertaking a project mentioned in this book.

Thanks to everyone who helped; and to Citadel's Ann LaFarge, Bruce Bender; Roger Archibald for his superb pictures; and Peter Ocko.

Introduction

Someone once said that in times of uncertainty, style is the one thing that helps bridge the unknown. Style helps define your identity now and puts a new stamp on your future. How do you get there? Fantasy opens the gates to possibilities.

The purpose of this book is to offer some options for your imagination. Because one person's fantasy is not necessarily another's, you have to hook into that part of you that hangs between memory and desire. That's where your fantasy lies, and that provides the passion to create the architecture of your imagination.

This takes experimentation. Sometimes it involves acting out old dreams, or combining old and new dreams, and accepting things that will never be. Following your curiosity allows you to take paths you never took before. Constantly testing what you know and do not know helps you to surmount worn-out boundaries.

Fantasy gives you the right to experiment. You try on different lifestyles and personalities, as you strategize the next step. It encourages you to refine your senses and cultivate grace, as if you were in love for the first time. It forgives you if you go too far. It sends you back—still you, but with secret exceptional inner abilities.

And the world awaits. Good companies stand, doors open, ready to help you fulfill your dreams. Some offerings are very expensive; others are amazingly reasonable; most are loaded with value. If you feel that you've been everywhere, try space or the deep ocean or the earth's phenomena such as storms and volcanoes.

Go beneath the North Pole in a submersible, swing on a flying trapeze, track the transit of Venus, break the sound barrier, circle the globe in a private jet, dive with sharks, balloon over the Alps, retrace the Northwest Passage, spend Halloween in Dracula's castle.

Or paint at the edge of a field of lavender in Provence, take a cloud tour, sail the Seychelles, spend a few minutes in zero gravity.

Henry James said that you're rich if you can meet the needs of your imagination.

This is a good place to start.

FANTASY VACATIONS

In Antarctica, the Ross Ice Shelf dwarfs the people below. This amazing wall of ice, the size of France, is the southernmost navigable point on the planet. (*Michael Van Woert, NOAA NESDIS, ORA*)

CHAPTER 1

ANTARCTICA

POLAR TOURISM

Thanks to Russian icebreakers, global-sponsored research, and tourism, the Poles have become familiar places. Huge vessels known as icebreakers, capable of 75,000 HP and able to carry a limited number of passengers comfortably, and ice-strengthened expedition ships have made safe polar access possible. As a guest on a polar ship, you can watch from the bridge as your vessel actually cuts through the dense pack ice. Onboard zodiacs ferry passengers ashore for short trips to explore unmapped islands or penguin nests.

These ships have libraries and lecture halls, and most expeditions are accompanied by scientists engaged in projects studying the earth's atmosphere, glaciology, and oceanography; or measuring the sun's cosmic rays which cause the northern (and southern) lights.

POLES APART

Until about 100 years ago, the Poles were the last undiscovered territory on earth, areas of unmapped and frozen fantasy, dark for half the year and hostile to sailors. In Antarctica, early whalers and fishermen met cold ends after chasing their prey and finding themselves pushed by fierce winds into furious storms with walls of ocean water and dense coastal fogs that shrouded icebergs.

The big difference between the Poles is that Antarctica is a continent, and the Arctic is an ocean. No matter how cold it gets in the Arctic, it never gets as cold as it gets in the Antarctic. Parts of East Antarctica are too cold even for research stations with the latest high-tech means of keeping people warm and keeping equipment at a functioning temperature.

Go North for Bears, South for Penguins

The subantarctic islands and Antarctica's 98 percent ice cover are home chiefly to birds: numerous penguin species and breeding albatrosses and other sea birds. All other wildlife lives in the ocean: seals, sea lions, and whales. In contrast, the Arctic area is full of caribou and polar bears, and small, furry Arctic foxes and hares, as well as walruses, seals, whales, and narwhals. The tundra of the Arctic Circle is a botanist's and bird-watcher's dream.

See Them While You Can

The Poles are the first to demonstrate signs of global climate change: The tear in the ozone layer above Antarctica is the largest ever recorded on earth; scientists have already found evidence of cellular changes in fish a few meters below the sea surface there. Huge, state-size chunks of ice now break off from the previously permanent ice shelves.

Global climate change is doing a number on the North Pole area, too: The Greenland ice cover and Alaska sea ice are melting at an alarming rate; and the pool of ice-free water at the North Pole in the summer is larger than ever before.

Antarctica, 90 Degrees South Latitude: Stark Polar Lands

The only "settlers" in Antarctica were there not by their own choosing; they were stranded or abandoned sailors, or explorers such as

Ernest Shackleton's men, who met each challenge as it came while they hoped help would come. Today the population varies from about 4,000 in summer to 1,000 in winter and is confined to researchers from twenty-nine nations.

The first research station in the Antarctic was opened in 1956, and since then, news of the frozen continent is all about life. Whole new life-forms have been found thriving in the cold; most recently, scientists discovered microbes living in total darkness two miles beneath the ice in a trapped freshwater lake (Lake Vostok).

In the Footsteps of Shackleton

Less than a hundred years ago Ernest Shackleton and his loyal crew chose life over death after they witnessed their sailing ship *Endurance* break into splinters after being squeezed in the pack ice of the Weddell Sea. The men packed their gear into three life boats, pulled them to the open ocean, and sailed north to Elephant Island. It was April 1916, the beginning of the southern winter. The wicked weather, currents, and sheer isolation in Drake Passage caused most of them to prefer to remain on Elephant Island.

Shackleton and four others, however, patched together the twenty-two-foot *James Caird* and set sail northeast to South Georgia Island to find help. There they landed in July 1916, on the wrong side of the island, separated from the Stromness Whaling Station—and help—by mountains and glaciers. They crossed by land with screws from the ship's fittings driven into the soles of their shoes for traction. They reached the station three days later, and got help to return to Elephant Island and rescue the men.

On a later trip to Antarctica, Shackleton suffered a heart attack and was buried in Grytviken, near the Whaling Station.

The Classic Antarctica Voyage

If tour managers today know anything about the Antarctic, it is this: Don't take passengers in the Antarctic winters.

The second rule is: Emphasize the flexibility that travel there demands. Ice and sudden storms keep planes on the ground or prevent them from landing; both weather and the unexpected thrill of seeing breeching whales contribute to changes in cruise itineraries. The ships are supersafe, and voyages are accompanied by experts who know the area. "We love adventure, but we're not fools," said Matt Drennan, expedition leader on Lindblad Expeditions.

Lindblad Expeditions   720 Fifth Avenue, New York, NY 10019. 800-397-3348 (toll free); 212-765-7740 (tel); 212-265-3770 (fax). E-mail: explore@expeditions.com; Web site: www.expeditions.com

In 1966 Lars-Erik Lindblad made the first nonscientific cruise to Antarctica. It was a decision reached after sitting with his tour leaders around a campfire in Mongolia, discussing where to go next and realizing that Antarctica was not even on their map. When Lindblad saw the pristine continent, the magnificent ice formations, and the number of species of penguins and seabirds, Antarctic tourism was born.

Lindblad trips travel on the *Endeavor*, a 295-foot, one-class "ice-strengthened" expedition ship which accommodates 110 passengers and has all the amenities, including individual climate control and a doctor onboard. A fleet of zodiacs ferry passengers to land to take closeups of penguins or sea lions or seals.

Most trips begin in Buenos Aires, travel to Ushuaia, pick up the ship, cross Drake Passage, then visit the islands enroute to the Antarctic Peninsula and the summer research stations at Paradise Bay. Passengers have time to swim in Deception Bay, the warm and steamy (sulphuric) waters of a volcanic caldera.

Ten days: about $7,500 to $9,700, depending on the deck.

Abercrombie & Kent, Inc.   1520 Kensington Road, Oak Brook, Illinois 60523-2141. 800-757-5884 (toll free for brochures); 800-323-7308 (toll free); 630-954-2944 (tel); 630-954-3324 (fax). E-mail: info@abercrombiekent.com; Web site: www. abercrombiekent.com

Abercrombie runs several trips to Antarctica on the 238-foot, ice-reinforced *Explorer*. The ship carries 100 passengers with all the amenities, and a host of natural history experts.

The schedule, which begins in Miami, flies to Santiago, Chile, and Ushuaia, before heading out on Drake Passage, stays deliberately flexible to avoid storms, as well as to take advantage of the unpredictable wildlife. Zodiacs are ready to take passengers one or two times a day to land in the four or five days the ship cruises the Antarctic Peninsula, including the rarely visited east side.

Fourteen or sixteen days, including airfare from Miami: about $8,000 to $11,300, depending on the deck.

Mountain Travel Sobek   6420 Fairmount Avenue, El Cerrito, California 94530. 888-687-6235 (toll free); 510-525-7710 (fax). E-mail: info@mtsonek.com; Web site: www.mtsobek.com

This adventure company has been providing trips to Antarctica for sixteen years and offers a variety, most of which include one or more of Shackleton's historic places. MTSobek travels in the 234-foot, forty-nine-passenger, ice-reinforced *Professor Multanovskiy*, with a highly experienced Russian crew and amenities including a sauna and an infirmary.

The ship carries a fleet of zodiacs for hiking on the volcanic slopes of Deception Island and observing flocks of penguins along the Antarctic Peninsula. Passengers can also kayak if they wish, depending on weather and ice. You might see glaciers calve at Paradise Bay.

Thirteen days from Buenos Aires: about $6,400 to $8,600, depending on berth.

Clipper Cruise Line   11969 Westline Industrial Drive, Saint Louis, Missouri 63146-3220. 800-325-0010 (toll free); 314-655-6700 (tel); 314-655-6670 (fax). E-mail: clipper@clippercruise.com; Web site: www.clippercruise.com

On the *Clipper Adventurer*, a 333-foot, 122-passenger, ice-reinforced expedition ship, Clipper Cruise Line takes you to Shackleton's grave at Grytviken, as well as to the same whaling station (now a museum) on South Georgia Island that Shackleton struggled to reach.

Their twenty-three-day trip begins in Buenos Aires and Ushuaia, cruises Drake Passage, the islands of the Antarctic Peninsula, then goes to South Georgia Islands and the Falklands. Zodiacs keep you in touch with land, wildlife, hikes, and museums. Onboard scientists and naturalists guide you through the amazing experience. (Call 800-227-4099 to take a look at a video of *Clipper Adventurer* filmed for "CNN Travel Now.")

Twenty-three days: about $10,500 to $15,700, depending on berth.

Photography

National Geographic Expeditions   P.O. Box 65265, Washington, D.C. 20035-5265. 888-966-8687 (toll free). Reserve online at: www.nationalgeographic.com/ngexpeditions

National Geographic photographer Gordon Wiltsie, who has climbed the big wall of ice in Queen Maud Land, Antarctica, and done ten expeditions to the seventh continent, leads a tour there with other *NG* photographers who guide passengers interested in good photography. The ship is the *Endeavor* (see Lindblad Expeditions, above, for a description), and it travels from Santiago/Ushuaia to the Antarctic Peninsula and back to Elephant Island and Ushuaia.

From the zodiacs, passengers can take photo walks among the penguins. Kayak expeditions allow picture taking from the level of the sea. Evenings, discuss and critique the pictures.

Thirteen days from Miami: about $8,000 to $9,800.

Shackleton's Famous Voyage

Fathom Expeditions, Inc.   146 Madison Avenue, Toronto, Ontario M5R 2S5 Canada. 800-621-0176 (toll free); 416-925-3174 (tel); 416-925-4219 (fax). E-mail: Dave@fathomexpeditions.com; Web site: www.fathomexpeditions.com

Fathom Expeditions is the company of the Antarctic explorers who were the key expedition leaders for the IMAX, television, and film (*Shackleton's Antarctic Adventure*) about Ernest Shackleton. Their Spirit of Shackleton Voyage is accompanied by President Dave German, who led the IMAX and *Endurance* crews to Antarctica; mountaineer Conrad Anker, who crossed South Georgia in a reenactment of Shackleton's crossing (and who also has climbed the formidable mountains in Queen Maud Land with the *National Geographic Magazine*); and Bob Wallace, an Antarctic explorer and master craftsman who built a replica of the *James Caird*.

Traveling on the forty-nine-passenger *M.V. Fathom Discovery*, Fathom Expeditions leaders work closely with each passenger to enact their Antarctic fantasy. Starting in Ushuaia, you cross the Drake Passage to the Antarctic Peninsula, where you experience the volcano in Paradise Bay, icebergs, plus the huge number of birds, whales, and elephant seals that roll around on the ice. Lectures by the leaders will vividly describe Shackleton's experience. There are also lots of opportunities to photograph from the zodiacs.

Then land on Elephant Island, where Shackleton left his crew while he set off in the *James Caird*. Lowering the replica into the icy waters, you can sail the *James Caird* as well, to begin to appreciate some of the incredible ingenuity explorers such as Shackleton have demonstrated.

Landing on South Georgia, you will be able to walk and hike or ski across parts of the arduous path that Shackelton and two of his men took to the whaling station.

Sixteen days, including everything except airfare: about $7,000.

Shackleton's South Georgia Crossing

Geographic Expeditions   2627 Lombard Street, San Francisco, California 94123. 415-922-0448 (tel); 415-346-5535 (fax). E-mail: info@geoex.com; Web site: www.geoex.com

It's not clear that Shackleton would have ever opted to do this again, and don't try it unless you are an experienced glacier climber.

But for all Shackleton groupies, this is a power-plus tour that will leave you deeply satisfied.

You begin in Buenos Aires with a short hop to Puerto Madryn, where the *Professor Multanovskiy* will be waiting. After three days at sea, you land on the rocky coast of South Georgia Island, where snowy peaks rise abruptly from the ocean.

For the next four days, you—with the best new stuff—will try to imagine how Shackleton and his companions ever did it. "The crossing is nontechnical but may be cold and wet," said GeoEx tour leader Al Read. They use ropes and glacier protocol. The weather is unpredictable; strong winds and whiteouts happen even in summer.

You can go on the trip without climbing over, if you want. There's a lot to explore on the island, a former whaling station, and the site of Shackleton's grave. Return through Ushuaia.

Twenty-two days: voyage only, from about $7,200; to cross the island's glaciers, add about $4,000.

Other Explorers to Antarctica

Captain James Cook saw Antarctica in 1777 and said "No thanks" to any further ventures into the snow and ice. In 1908 Robert F. Scott made a "Furthest South" record on a cruise with Edmund Shackleton, who later returned to try to better the record in 1914. Shackleton's failed expedition came within ninety-seven miles of the South Pole; and it was not until 1911 that Norwegian Roald Amundsen actually made it to the Pole by dogsled.

Scott arrived about a month later, dismayed to see that Amundsen had preceded him. He died, along with his entire crew, on the return voyage.

Richard Byrd flew over the Pole and dropped an American flag on it in 1929; and in 1935 Lincoln Ellsworth flew over the entire continent.

But many, whose names have been lost or forgotten, left behind dreams that got lost in whiteouts and huts in which they tried to keep warm.

Track Explorers in an Icebreaker

Quark Expeditions, Inc. 980 Post Road, Darien, Connecticut 06820. 800-356-5699 (toll free); 203-656-0499 (tel); 203-655-6623 (fax). E-mail: enquiry@quarkexpeditions.com; Web site: www.quarkexpeditions.com

The Great Explorers trip begins on Ross Island, where both Shackleton and Scott began their inland journeys. It is also a place of enormous walls of icebergs and wildlife.

Traveling in the Russian icebreaker *Kapitan Khlebnikov* with the company that was the first to take passengers on icebreakers, the voyage begins in Auckland, New Zealand, and cruises in the Southern Ocean past wildlife near New Zealand's Subantarctic islands, where it encounters icebergs. The ship then goes to McMurdo Sound, the U.S. Antarctic research base; spends several days cruising in the Ross Sea; and will try to land one of its onboard helicopters (used for ice reconnaissance) on top of the Ross Ice Shelf, the size of France.

Standing on the bridge and open deck, passengers have a chance to see the icebreaker do its work on thick ice floes. With the helicopters, passengers will be able to appreciate the remains of Scott's and Shackleton's old base camps and the huts of early explorers, as well as to fly over amazing glaciers, icebergs, and pods of whales. Experts onboard keep passengers abreast of wildlife, history, natural history, and geology.

Twenty-three days, Auckland to Hobart, Tasmania, with a stop at the wildlife sanctuary at Macquarie Island in the Southern Ocean: about $12,000.

This company also offers a circumnavigation of Antarctica, a trip they were the first to organize.

Fly to the South Pole

Adventure Network International 4800 North Federal Highway, Suite 307D, Boca Raton, Florida 33431. 866-395-6664 (toll free); 561-237-2359 (tel); 561-347-7523 (fax). E-mail: general@adventure-network.com; Web site: www.adventure-network.com

This is the only company offering private flights to the South Pole, a practice Adventure Network International began in 1987. Flying out of Punta Arenas to Patriot Hills, Antarctica, in a Ilyushin-76 takes about four and a half hours (about 2,000 miles).

From Patriot Hills, climb aboard a Cessna or Twin Otter and fly for six hours over Antarctica (about 600 miles), before setting down at the Amundsen-Scott Base, and the South Pole. Take a tour of the station, and realize that "beneath your feet, 360 lines of longitude collide, and the ice is almost 10,000 feet thick."

Return to Patriot Hills Base, and depending on the weather and your moxie, you can skidoo to the local mountains, do cross-country skiing, and camp (!) overnight in the Ellsworth Mountains for a truly remote experience.

Expert scientific guides keep you informed. You can shop for souvenirs at the South Pole station, and have your picture taken there. Ten days: about $25,000.

This company also sponsors an Antarctic Marathon (26.2 miles on ice and snow) and a Mount Vinson climb (16,000 feet).

Collect Meteorites

Some astrobiologists believe "life"—microbes—first came to Earth on a comet or asteroid several billion years ago. Most recently they have been interested in collecting meteorites from Antarctica, some of which are thought to be ancient and loaded with information about the formation of the universe. The controversial meteorite from Mars, which might contain evidence of life-forms, was found in Antarctica.

Space Adventures   4350 North Fairfax Drive, Suite 840, Arlington, Virginia 22203. 888-85-SPACE [857-7223] (toll free); 703-524-7176 (fax). E-mail: info@spaceadventures.com; Web site: www.spaceadventures.com

The first Antarctica Meteorite Expedition, in partnership with Adventure Network, took an international team of about a dozen people to Antarctica to help planetary geologist Paul Sipiera collect meteorites in January 2002. Their take totaled thirty-three; some of them were very rare on Earth. In the Antarctic summer light (with a never-rising, never-setting sun), meteorites stand out in the blazing ice "like blueberries on vanilla ice cream," according to an astrophysicist.

The twenty-two-day expedition is not for the faint of heart. You will live in remote base camps in 20-degree F weather, which often unpredictably turns cold and wild. Inside the tents the temperature is a comfortable 50 degrees; but the facilities—the "Ice Latrine"—can be a challenge, especially when storms send the temperature plummeting to minus 15 degrees. At the end of the trip, you must carry all your trash bags with you. And it's never dark, so you might suffer confusion about exactly when to sleep.

Since research groups to Antarctica share airplanes in the summer, plans must remain flexible. The first group spent a lot of time packing in anticipation of being airlifted to another base camp, then unpacking when the plane was a no-show, then packing when they received split-second notice that the plane was theirs.

Finding meteorites requires a lot of walking and looking, and oddly, not all meteorites are what they seem: small icy piles of black mud—what one participant called "meteor-wrongs"—masquerade as the real thing.

You will act as your own cooks, and can expect to consume about 3,500 calories a day and rarely bathe. But the thrill of actually being the first human to pick up a meteorite that flew through the sky hundreds of thousands of years ago and the amazing beauty of Antarctica with its walls and peaks of frozen snow and pools of blue ice are unforgettable. See www.spaceadventures.com/terrestrial/antarctica/index/html for an account of the 2002 trip.

Twenty-two days, including air from Punta Arenas, Chile: about $44,000.

CHAPTER 2

THE ARCTIC

At the North Pole, so the ancient Greeks believed, savage creatures lived in icy darkness, their battles sending ethereal lights into the sky. Greeks called the farthest north the *Ultima Thule*, which became the goal set by later explorers. But the shifting sea of Arctic ice and broad cobalt pools proved to be a navigational nightmare. In the winter the entire sea is frozen in pack ice which forms quickly, and many sailors and explorers found themselves locked into ice traps for the winter, with dwindling food supplies and inadequate clothing.

NINETY DEGREES NORTH LATITUDE: LAND OF THE MIDNIGHT SUN

At 90 degrees North during summer months, the sun rides the horizon from east to west, never directly overhead and never rising or setting. In the winter, polar bears leap from ice floe to floe, traveling as many as twenty miles a day searching for seals in the broken ice and clear pools. Huge dark walruses with long ivory tusks loll about on the ice, as do black and white seals, all of which barely acknowledge the presence of ships.

No one has ever settled or ever will settle at the North Pole, although the Arctic Circle (the area above 67 degrees North) is populated with about 2 million people in eight different countries

Lunch at the North Pole. The Arctic is an ocean and an area of ice that is home to polar bears. Here, an adult watches two young bears eat a seal, their main diet in winter. *(NOAA)*

(Russia, Finland, Sweden, Norway, Iceland, Greenland, Canada, and the United States).

Was Santa Claus the First?

Being the first person to find the Pole and claim it for his country was not easy because geographical recording instruments were inaccurate until recent times; and the ice in summer drifts. The first explorer to claim reaching it—Robert Peary in 1909—was challenged by later scientific analyses. So was Commander Richard Byrd in 1926, who believed he flew over the Pole on a flight from Norway, a feat that critics said could not have been done in his short-range Fokker trimotor.

Three days later, no one doubted the route of the flight of Roald Amundsen and Lincoln Ellsworth, who floated above the Pole in a blimp, the *Norge*.

Since then, a few dogsled expeditions have made it from Alaska to Norway, or the other way; nuclear submarines have cruised beneath 90 degrees North; and in 1977, the Russian icebreaker, the *Arkita*, was the first ship to sail across the compass point.

Explore Beneath the Pole

Deep Ocean Expeditions   64b Sunninghill Avenue, Burradoo NSW 2576, Australia. 011 +61 2 48623013 (fax). E-mail: info@deepoceanexpeditions.com; Web site: www. deepoceanexpeditions.com

The North Pole Dive will take you beneath the North Pole in a submersible *Mir I* or *Mir II*.

This seventeen-day trip, scheduled for 2005, begins when the group meets in Oslo, Norway, then flies to Longyearbyen, where passengers are helicoptered to the icebreaker *Yamal*. Cutting through pack ice, the ship cruises north to 90 degrees North—the Pole—where it spends five days.

From here approximately eight (depending on weather) submersible dives will descend to a depth of 14,500 feet to examine what's beneath the polar ice cap. Each descent will take about seven to eight hours, and will go around the clock, in the twenty-four hours of daylight. Onboard will be an extensive program of lectures by scientists discussing wildlife adaptation at the Pole, its geology, glaciology, and history of exploration. Video screens located throughout the ship will show live pictures from the deep, sent back from a remote operated vehicle (ROV).

On the return from the Pole, the *Yamal* will cruise south to Franz Josef Island, a contrast of volcanoes and glaciers. You are able to visit the hut built by Norwegian sailor and explorer Fridtjof Nansen, who, in 1896–97 with Hjalmar Johansen, was among those who came within a few degrees of the Pole. Helicopters and zodiacs will take you to the mainland for tours.

Celebrate the contrast! One night you will have an ice barbecue, and enjoy a black-tie classical musical recital.

Seventeen days, including lodging, meals onboard, lectures, and special expedition parka: for submersible divers: about $70,000; for nondivers: about $15,000.

In the Arctic Circle

Sail the Northwest Passage—The Amundsen Route: Pacific to the Atlantic

Quark Expeditions, Inc. 980 Post Road, Darien, Connecticut 06820. 800-356-5699 (toll free); 203-656-0499 (tel); 203-655-6623 (fax). E-mail: enquiry@quarkexpeditions.com; Web site: www.quarkexpeditions.com

From at least the 1500s, traders and explorers from Europe desperately sought a short route to the Orient. With patched-together maps and lots of sailors' yarns, Sebastian Cabot, Henry Hudson, and Martin Frobisher were some who ventured in vain, getting tricked by the jagged landmass that surrounds the Arctic Ocean or the fickle, ever-forming ice. In 1853–54, a brave soul named Robert McLure walked the Northwest Passage, but traders were not looking for a footpath. Finally, in 1903–16, fearless explorer Roald Amundsen pointed his bow east from the Beaufort Sea, and traced a route that was stable enough to put on a map. In recent years, the Passage has regained importance, as an alternative to the Panama Canal.

You can do the Northwest Passage in an icebreaker. Fly from Anchorage to Anadyr, Russia, and helicopter to the anchored 428-foot *Kapitan Khlebnikov*. Then head north through the Chukotka Peninsula and Bering Strait to the Beaufort Sea, where you cross the Arctic Circle at Point Barrow, and begin to deal with ice.

On the way to Amundsen Gulf, stop at the old whaling station of Herschel Island, a ghost town in the Yukon filled with Arctic wildlife and near a spot where Amundsen wintered over.

Through Amundsen Gulf with a stop at Victoria Island, home to 300 Inuit, you travel to Cambridge Bay and the remains of the three-masted schooner *Maud*, once one of Amundsen's ships in a voyage in the 1920s. Heading up through more ice toward the Boothia Peninsula, you pass the sites of previous failed Northwest Passage explorations, and the sad evidence—graves, sledges, naval artifacts—of John Franklin's lost expedition in 1859.

Through Lancaster Sound to Beechey Island, you pass amazing wildlife. This is the last night before you reach Resolute, and the airport where you catch a plane to Ottawa.

Eighteen days, including hotels ashore, meals, and excursions: from about $9,600 to $16,000, depending on size of berth.

Canoe the Soper River

Sunrise International 4 Union Plaza, Bangor, Maine 04401. 800-RIVER-30 [748-3730] (toll free); 207-942-9300 (tel); 207-942-9399 (fax). E-mail: info@expeditionlogistics.com; Web site: www.sunrise-exp.com

Baffin Island, in Nunavut Territory, is home to the Inuit, and Iqaluit is their art capital. Caribou—small deerlike animals with three-foot antlers (the domesticated version is known as reindeer)—and musk ox are Inuit staples, which feed, clothe, and inspire them to carve soapstone, for which they are famous.

Fly in to the Soper River from Iqaluit in a twin Otter tundra plane. Then spend five days canoeing down the river, running Class I and Class II white-water rapids, camping, and stopping along the way to explore, hike, and fish for Arctic char. The tundra is filled with wildflowers, and you will pass waterfalls plunging down mountain walls. The tour ends with everyone a guest of the Inuit families for dinner at Kimmirut.

This company has specialized in canoe trips around the world since 1973. Nine days, starting and finishing in Ottawa, including camping and canoe equipment, expert guides, some meals, and some accommodations: about $2,200 for one; $4,000 for two.

Botany on Baffin Island

Odyssey Learning Adventures 182 Princess Street, Kingston, Ontario K7L 1B1, Canada. 800-263-0050 (toll free); 613-

549-3342. E-mail: learning@odyssey-travel.com; Web site: www. odysseylearningadventures.ca

Accompanied by an expert research botanist from the Canadian Museum of Nature, this trip, Arctic Nature, goes to icy Baffin Island. Despite its extreme winters, Baffin Island is home to fantastic plant life, which you explore on hikes and in lectures, as you fly from place to place. It is also home to birds: 12 percent of North American birds breed here, among them eider ducks, gyrfalcons, and snowy owls.

See what the Inuit can do with stone and bone carvings, as you visit museums, such as the Uqqurmiut Centre for Arts and Crafts. The tour leader will take you to other studios and galleries as well. Seven days, including flights, meals, and hotel accommodations: $3,400 Canadian (about $2,200 U.S.).

Kayak the Arctic Ocean

Mountain Travel Sobek   6420 Fairmount Avenue, El Cerrito, California 94530. 888-687-6235 (toll free); 510-525-7710 (fax). E-mail: info@mtsonek.com; Web site: www.mtsobek.com

This trip is for experienced kayakers in love with the Far North. At 80 degrees North in the western fjords of Ellesmere Island, northwest of Greenland, join expert polar guide Ulrik Vedel in a kayak expedition to lands that have been visited only by a handful of people.

Weaving between pack ice, you will encounter and paddle past numerous icebergs, small bands of caribou, musk ox, polar bears, and maybe Arctic wolves. For ten days, paddling for eight to fifteen miles a day, your world will be mountains, glaciers, ice fields, and stark beauty. Camp on the tundra, and hike if you like, or climb a peak that is not on the map yet.

The trip starts in Resolute, Nunavut Territory, then flies to the Fosheim Peninsula on Ellesmere Island, where the expedition begins. Fly back to Resolute on Day 14.

Fifteen days, with nine to ten travelers: land: about $3,200; flights: about $1,600. Prices are slightly higher for a smaller group.

European Arctic Circle by Private Jet

TCS Expeditions   2025 First Avenue, Suite 500, Seattle, Washington 98121. 800-727-7477 (toll free); 206-727-7300 (tel); 206-727-7309 (fax). E-mail: travel@tcs-expeditions.com; Web site: www.tcs-expeditions.com

Meet your private Boeing 757 in Halifax, Nova Scotia, and take off for a day or two on Erik the Red's farm on Greenland, settled in 986, the first European settlement in the Arctic Circle.

Then jet to Bergen, Norway, the Brussels of the fourteenth century, where you board the Flam Railway on the top of one of Norway's peaks, and descend at an almost 45-degree angle from 2,600 feet to sea level through twenty-one tunnels, past waterfalls, and around hairpin curves.

Next day fly to Lapland and visit with the Sami people at a reindeer farm, before continuing on to Russia and Archangel, the port for Russian expeditions to the North Pole.

Your gateway will be Spitsbergen in the Arctic Ocean, where you board a Russian icebreaker, the *Orlova*, and spend three nights aboard, traveling through Arctic ice, with zodiac visits to glaciers for hikes.

And there's still more.

From Longyearbyen in Spitzbergen, fly to Reykjavik in Iceland for a geologic visit to some of the country's amazing hot springs, lava fields, and geysers. Helicopter over Surtsey, the volcanic island formed in 1963, and visit Heimaey, a still-smoking volcanic island, home to numerous seabirds.

Jet to Churchill, Manitoba, and helicopter over the annual migration of polar bears who gather to wait for the winter ice to form. Then catch a whale watching boat from which you can snorkel or dive among the whales—it is a safe and incredible encounter, and will reinforce your memory of the frozen Arctic as a place teeming with life.

Expert lecturers accompany the trip.

Seventeen days, including everything except round-trip airfare from home: about $28,000.

CHAPTER 3

ARCHITECTURE TOURS

In *The Fountainhead*, Ayn Rand chronicled the angst of the architect, but no one has ever addressed the angst of the architecture groupie. On the other side of the professional door, left to wander city streets on early Sunday mornings (the better to view the buildings), given only books, magazines, and a camera to satisfy his or her passion, the groupie now has help: in-depth, substantial architectural tours, the closest thing to total immersion. Guided by an expert and accompanied by a small group with similar feelings, tours not only visit significant architectural sites around the world, but recreate the ambiance in which they were conceived.

CZECH REPUBLIC

Archetours, Inc. 260 West Broadway, Suite 2, New York, New York 10013. 800-770-3051 (toll free); 646-613-1896 (tel); 646-613-1897 (fax). E-mail: info@archetours.com; Web site: www. archetours.com

In many ways, Prague is one of the most "European" cities of Europe, its ups and downs in history rendering it palpably layered in beauty. Archetours' tour to Prague encompasses buildings from the Romanesque to those of Frank Gehry.

Accompanied by Czech architect Martin Holub, you will spend seven days reveling in the banquet of civic, religious, and domestic

Architect Frank Gehry's amazing Guggenheim Museum in Bilbao, Spain. Designed on a computer and faced with titanium, the burnished building has been called one of the greatest architectural achievements of the century. *(Photo by Carrie Snyder, courtesy of Archetours, Inc.)*

buildings that crowd Prague streets, from the Old Town Hall to the fourteenth-century Karlstein Castle, to the Jewish Quarter; plus art nouveau, deconstructionist, and 1930s "Modern" buildings, where you will have private tours. Final night is dinner at Frank Gehry's "Fred and Ginger" office building.

Archetours has been running "intelligently hip vacations" since 1995. Created by architectural historian Gail Cornell, Archetours are accompanied by experts—an academic or an architect—and attract as many professional architects as interested participants. Eight-day tours are offered in Europe from Belgium to the Veneto, in Japan, and in Morocco. Hotels are deluxe and downtown; restaurants reflect the best of the locals.

The average price is about $3,000, including almost everything except airfare.

On all Archetours, your pretour package will brief you in architectural background; you will benefit from private showings and visits to the parts of buildings that the public rarely sees. The energy level among the group animates discussions over dinner; but Archetours guarantees you private time as well.

Be prepared to walk a lot.

SPAIN

Martin Randall Travel, Ltd.   10, Barley Mow Passage, Chiswick, London, W4 GF, UK. 011 +44 (0) 20 8742 3355 (tel); 011 +44 (0) 20 8742 7766 (fax). E-mail: info@martinrandall.co.uk; Web site: www.martinrandall.com

Martin Randall has been taking travelers interested in architecture, art, design, as well as music, to the best places with the best guides for many years. Some of their tours are exclusively for members of the Royal Academy of the Arts. Each tour examines the elements of the architectural climate, or penetrates the mind of the architect. Expect to walk a lot on city streets that are not always straight and smooth.

The Gaudi and the Guggenheim tour cuts through the heart of Spanish architecture. It looks at L.A. architect Frank Gehry's splashy burnished titanium Guggenheim Museum in Bilbao, called "the signature building of the twentieth century," a sinuous collection of shapes that mimic the bends in the Nervion river; and compares it with the work of Antoni Gaudi, "the father of postmodernism," whose art nouveau buildings that resemble dripped sand castles defied Barcelona's critics.

The tours take small groups, providing comfortable, accessible hotel accommodations and good restaurants. This trip is led by Gijs van Hensbergen, author of a biography of Gaudi. Seven days, including everything, from round-trip airfare from London to tips and drinks with meals: about £1,100 ($1,500).

Los Angeles

Architours, Los Angeles, California.   866-227-2448 (toll free);
323-294-5821 (tel); 323-294-5825 (fax). E-mail: architours@
aol.com; Web site: www.architours.com

This company, run by a husband-and-wife design team, gets to
the heart of Unique Americana, by looking at architecture that
probably could not exist elsewhere.

Architours' half-day driving tour, California Pop, examines some
of the icons unique to the twentieth century: monster-sized hot
dogs, doughnuts, and other expressive architecture that grew out of
advertising's competitive quest for our attention. Cost: $25 per hour.

Architours directors Rochelle and Jeffrey Mills give specialty
"boutique" walking and driving architecture tours in the Los Angeles area, including Food and Design tours that concentrate on
restaurant design. "So many people don't realize that architects had
a hand in designing restaurants," says Rochelle.

Architours also runs overnight and weekend tours; and small-
group tours to other American and Canadian cities, and Cuba. They
will custom design an architecture trip for you or your group.

Romania

Ace Study Tours, Cambridge, UK.   E-mail: ace@study-tours.org;
Web site: www.study-tours.org

From Cambridge to the Carpathians, you pass through a time
warp from the twenty-first to previous centuries. Once an outer
margin of the Roman Empire, Romania has developed a distinctive
culture over the centuries. In the fifteenth and sixteenth centuries,
monks built magnificent monasteries and painted wood churches,
some of them fortified, all rich in folk paintings. The monasteries
are blessed with frescoes untouched by political struggles.

This tour travels by van from Bucharest north through Transylvania for two weeks. You will visit fortified medieval towns with
gates and towers, sixteenth-century houses, Roman camps, Austrian

forts, and the monastery of Putna, Stephen the Great's resting place. At Brasov you can hear the 4,000-pipe organ in a fourteenth-century church, whose walls are hung with oriental rugs.

Accompanied by architectural historian Mark Powell, also a linguist, the tour is housed in hotels that vary according to the area, but always have private facilities. Cost, including air to and from Gatwick: about £1,100 ($1,550).

CHAPTER 4

ART

What you see is your own private fantasy, whether it's the sunset in your camera viewfinder, or the flowers you visualize blooming in your seeded garden. Art is seeing. Translating what you see for others to appreciate takes certain skills. Then it becomes a quest for the proper techniques. Here are some possibilities.

FAUX FINISHES

Faux, the French word for "fake" or "phony," is the imitation of something real, such as a view of the sky painted on a blank ceiling. In the United States, a handful of artists and artisans have mastered the techniques of faux finishes and stenciling that can turn your living room into a Pompeiian villa or your plasterboard walls into marble halls.

Trompe l'oeil is the ultimate art of surface deception. Done well, it can make passersby try to open the door painted on the wall, or lean out a window that isn't there. Murals will often incorporate three-dimensional items, such as a doorknob in the faux door. The secret of deception is the layering of finishes.

Around the country, you can find courses that, in one intensive week, more or less, will leave you a changed person, able to create miracles with your skills.

All is not as it seems. The Decorative Finishes Studio in Louisville, Kentucky, was not a Tuscan villa before Martin Alan Hirsch made it one. Everything except the front door is a trick rendered by this clever faux artist: the Corinthian columns, the engraved stonework and archways, the rusty railings, the verandah, and the "Michelangelo" frescoes. You, too, can learn to do this. *(Courtesy of Faux Finish School)*

The Faux Finish School   1905 Bardstown Road, Louisville, Kentucky. 800-598-FAUX [3289] (toll free); 502-452-1339 (tel/fax). E-mail: fauxfinishschool@fauxfinishschool.com; Web site: www.fauxfinish.com

Since 1987 located in a building that is an excellent example of the faux artist's power, the Faux Finish School gives courses for professionals and beginners and was the first school to teach the business side of faux painting. Founder Martin Alan Hirsch, following a stint in the Marines, became a faux artist after seeing an old craftsman turn a metal elevator door into a beautiful piece of mahogany.

Beginners' classes are offered in faux painting, marbling and woodgraining techniques, murals, stenciling, as well as advice about starting your own faux business. A course in trompe l'oeil begins with understanding "perspectives," since drawing skill is important with this technique. Hirsch and his staff teach a course in "perceptively correct" Italian tile floors, as well as arched doors and windows.

Seven days of intensive step-by-step instruction: about $1,500 to $1,800. The staff makes recommendations for lodging, often with discounts.

Kelly S. King Institute of Decorative Finishes   13308 Millard Avenue, Suite A, Omaha, Nebraska 68137. 888-560-FAUX [3289] (toll free); 402-896-1294 (fax). E-mail: info@in-faux.com; Web site: www.in-faux.com

Kelly King gives courses for both beginners and professionals at three places around the country: Omaha, Denver, and Seattle. At the end of your week, in which each day might stretch into night, you will come away with twenty-two samples and thirty-five techniques, no small accomplishment.

King offers three-, five-, and six-day courses. A three-day course in the art of faux finishes, including glazing, metallic, pearlescent, marble, brick, stone, and crackle: about $700. A five-day basic trompe l'oeil course, including drapery and architectural molding: about $1,800. The staff makes recommendations for local lodging.

For those who believe faux could be a career for them, King includes a business seminar. Many of his former students are now teachers.

Italy

Tania Vartan Academy of Trompe L'oeil Painting P.O. Box 2432, Palm Beach, Florida 33480-2432. 561-827-4848 (tel); 561-802-4456 (fax). E-mail: taniavartan@aol.com; Web site: www. taniavartan.com

At the Tania Vartan Academy, you will learn the basic lifelike rendering of marble, wood, and semiprecious stones, as well as glazing and gilding techniques for furniture and walls—all in Phase I. This is followed by Phases II and III, working with specialty finishes and understanding the particular problems involved in mural painting.

For trompe l'oeil, you will need some prior art experience. Vartan's mission is "to instill classical 'chic' and self-assurance in our artists."

Vartan gives courses in the summer in Siena for three weeks; in the fall, in Florence, over three-and-a-half months. Lodging is in a room in a castle in Siena or a villa in Florence.

Siena: about $3,600; Florence: beginners: $2,000; intermediate: $2,300; advanced: $2,500. (Each session is three or more weeks long.)

FRESCO

Real fresco works against time: The artist must have his drawing ("cartoon") in place, his colors mixed, and be able to work fast against the drying of the plaster that is applied at the same time. Working as a team, fresco artists must develop a superb harmony. Very few master the skills anymore, although it was often the preferred medium of Renaissance Florentine artists. Leonardo da Vinci's recently restored *The Last Supper* is a good example.

Ilia Anossov, True Fresco   1129 East 5th Street, Loft #8,
Los Angeles, California 90032. 310-337-2783 (tel). E-mail: fresco@
truefresco.com; Web site: www.truefresco.com

Moscow-born, award-winning fresco artist Ilia Anossov has set
his goal "to see fresco being painted in every town." To that end, he
and his staff offer two-day professional-level courses ($750) and a
one-day beginner's course, Introduction to Fresco Painting, in his
L.A. studio ($165, plus materials fee of $25).

A dynamic teacher, Anossov gives workshops around the country
and has made a video for kids called *Discover Fresco*. Join a chat-
room, "Café Al Fresco," at his Web site to learn more about the
world of fresco artists. Also take a look at his extraordinary 400-
square-foot Albuquerque mural.

POTTERY

The Southwest USA—The Ancient Pottery of the Anasazi

Crow Canyon Archaeological Center   23390 Road K, Cortez,
Colorado 81321. 800-422-8975 (toll free); 970-565-8975 (tel);
970-565-4859 (fax). Web site: www.crowcanyon.org

Mesa Verde Black-on-White Pottery Workshop, taught by two
art educators, will introduce you to the characteristics of the clays in
the Southwest that help trace the whereabouts of the Anasazi, who
lived in the area until about A.D. 1300.

During a week of lectures, field trips, and workshops, construct
and decorate a replica coil black-on-white pot, and fire it in an
Anasazi-type kiln. Sleep in a Navajo-style hogan (eight-sided log
cabin) at Crow Canyon and feast at the lodge.

One week: about $1,000.

Anguilla

Anguilla Arts Festival   Marge Morani, Organizer, Box 928,
The Valley, Anguilla, BWI. 264-497-4229 (tel). E-mail: marge@
masonc.com; Web site: www.loblollygallery.com

Spend a week in Anguilla in the late fall during the annual Arts Festival, studying pinch pottery with Jimmy Clark; and painting lovely tropics in watercolors with Sihn Ja An, an academy teacher. Lodging is at a beach hotel (www.arawakbeach.com). One week, including lodging, instruction, breakfast, and lunch: under $1,000.

PAINTING

French Polynesia

Art Trek   P.O. Box 1103, Bolinas, California 94924. 888-522-2652 (toll free); 415-868-9558 (tel); 415-868-9033 (fax). E-mail: carol@arttreks.com; Web site: www.arttreks.com

Paul Gauguin died in the Marquesas, leaving behind a banquet of canvasses in hot pinks and oranges and a record of the lazy, lovely lifestyle in the South Pacific. This trip will enable you to paint in the same style, or in your own, while you get closer to the passionate spirit of Gauguin.

Art Trek sponsors study painting classes in the south of France, Tuscany, and the South Pacific. Watercolor in Tahiti includes painting classes with artist Sally Robertson, and doing hatha yoga on the beach, a beautiful combination.

Twelve days, including airfare from Los Angeles to the South Pacific: about $5,000.

France

Languedoc

ICSCIS, Inc.   44, Vieux Chemin Val-des-Monts, Quebec City J8N 4A9, Canada. 800-611-4789 (toll free); 819-457-1892 (tel/fax). E-mail: icscis@painting-workshops.com or icscis@ cyberus.ca; Web site: www.cyberus.ca.

Monet is the inspiration of this trip. Studio Languedoc will take you into the heart of the Impressionists on the trail of Monet. Stay in a large house (*maison bourgeoise*) with a private bath, and spend the days around Montpelier understanding the "painters of light."

Take side trips to the garden at Giverny and to Paris, where you spend a day painting on the Left Bank.

Small group, eight days: about $2,300 per person.

Provence

Painting in Provence   30 Ipswich Street, Number 306, Boston, Massachusetts 02215. 617-859-0282 (tel). E-mail: jryanartist@msn.com

"Forget what you are painting, and think only about color, shape, and value, and the painting will paint itself," advises Judy Ryan, an instructor at the Museum of Fine Arts, Boston, who teaches landscape oil painting in Provence in the summer.

Stay at an imposing old house in the lush area of Drome Provencale with no more than six others, as you experience the light and life of the Impressionists and Post-Impressionists, amid sunny fields of lavender, sage, and rosemary.

Two weeks: about $2,000; nonpainters: $1,300.

Canada

Arts in the Wild   800-668-2746 (toll free). Web site: www.artsinthewild.com

Grab your paintbox and head for the hills.

The inspiration of fresh air and breathtaking vistas, rivers rough enough to keep your adrenalin high, wild animals never far away, can lead you to the nub of your core.

Artist Cory Trepanier will accompany a small group kayaking through Neys Provincial Park (full kayaking instruction provided). You maneuver the river until you come to the right scenic spot; then you stop and paint.

Arts in the Wild, a coalition of Canadian artists and artisans, art schools, and tourism organizations (to make sure you sleep and eat well) takes you and your art gear to the rugged ends of Ontario,

Canada. You can study everything from soapstone carving, willow furniture making, to woodcarving, as well as painting, and combine it with the kayaking and camping.

One week, including everything: about $2,500 Canadian (about $1,600 U.S.). Offered through Naturally Superior Adventures (www.naturallysuperior.com).

Bermuda

Hudson River Valley Art Workshops   P.O. Box 659, Greenville, New York 12086. 518-966-5219 (tel); 518-966-8754 (fax). E-mail: info@artworkshops.com; Web site: www.artworkshops.com

Dramatic skies, crazy tides, pink sands, and inspiration from Winslow Homer make a week of watercolors and pastels in Bermuda with teacher Alan Flattmann a rich experience.

You will be able to paint by day and enjoy a first-class Bermuda beach resort in the evenings. Seven days, including five days of workshop, seven nights in a hotel, all meals, and local transport: about $1,900, double occupancy; $2,250, single; nonpainting companion: $1,700.

In the summer, try out the workshops at home base, a hotel with a porch and rockers, in the Hudson River Valley.

Scotland

Edinburgh

Edinburgh Artbreaks   12 Muirend Avenue, Edinburgh EH14 5BD, Scotland. 011 +44 (0) 131 466 4356 (tel); 011 +44 (0) 131 478 1805 (fax). E-mail: info@edinburgh-artbreaks.co.uk; Web site: www.edinburgh-artbreaks.co.uk

Edinburgh is full of art surprises, from modern galleries to superb old buildings. Edinburgh Artbreaks offers art instruction with professional artists. Choose your medium, then work in the studio, on city streets, or in the countryside.

Five days (a total of twenty hours of art instruction), including hotel lodging, most meals, and materials: about £450 to £650 (about $675 to $975).

The Isle of Mull

Inniemore School of Painting   Carsaig, Isle of Mull, Scotland. 011 +44 (0) 1681 704 282 (tel). E-mail: innimor@btinternet.com
Scotland's islands are full of fresh winds and draped in legends. No cell phones, no television, no traffic at this castle give art a real place in a week's vacation. The Isle of Mull, a forty-minute boat ride from the mainland of western Scotland, is surrounded by rocky coasts, pounding surf, and steep cliffs.

At the school, run by artists Julia Wroughton and Bruce Killeen since 1967, find the spot that inspires you the most, then paint.

Breakfast is big (eggs, tomatoes, sausage, haddock, baked beans, and toast); then the day is yours until tea at four, after which artists meet to discuss each other's work before the three-course evening dinner.

One week in Mull: about £500 ($750).

NEEDLEWORK

Ireland

Madra Dubh Fabrics and Threads, Ltd.   Madra Dubh House, Ballinaboola, New Ross, County Wexford, Republic of Ireland. 011 +353 51 428771 (tel). E-mail: madradubh@tinet.ie; Web site: www.madradubh.com

At this crafts center located in the south of lush and mystic Ireland, you can stay at a B&B, eat homemade Irish food, and choose from a banquet of needlework courses from zigzag Bargello to Jacobean embroidery to trapunto quilting.

In three-day and weekend courses, you will receive a minimum of twelve hours training. That leaves time for walks, sightseeing, shopping in nearby Waterford, or driving to the sea, about thirty minutes away. All materials are provided. The Trapunto Quilting course (cross-stitching an outline, then filling it with padding) costs about €20 (Euros) a day (about the same in U.S. dollars). Lodging is €25, and the evening meal is €7.50.

SILVERSMITHING

Ireland

Horizons to Go   P.O. Box 2206, Amherst, Massachusetts 01004. 413-549-2900 (tel); 413-549-5995 (fax). E-mail: horizons@horizons-art.com; Web site: www.horizons-art.org

Horizons to Go will provide artists and artisans on week-long trips in the United States, Central America, Europe, and the Far East the chance to learn crafts unique to specific countries.

In Dublin you can learn the ancient, intricate art of Celtic silversmithing. These trips are very popular, so book in advance.

One week, including instruction, some food, and lodging: between $1,400 and $2,000.

WEAVING

Guatemala

Art Workshops in Guatemala   *In the United States:* 4758 Lyndale Avenue South, Minneapolis, Minnesota 55409-2304. 612-825-0747 (tel); 612-825-6637 (fax). E-mail: info@artguat.org; Web site: www.artguat.org. *In Guatemala:* Callejon Lopez #22, Antigua, Sacatepequez, Guatemala, Central America. 011 +502 832-6403 (tel); 011 +502 832-6925 (fax).

Women in the two tiny villages of San Antonia Aguas Calienta and Santa Catarina Bahahona, fifteen minutes outside the city of Antigua, have been weaving all their lives in the tradition of their female ancestors. Art Workshops introduces you to the weavers so you can join them in their own homes, sitting on the floor with your own backstrap loom.

Throughout the week, learn natural dye techniques for wool, cotton, and hard fibers by actually collecting the plants and boiling them for their colors. Guides will take you to visit hidden villages in the Mayan highlands with weaving cooperatives.

One week, including lodging in a large colonial house or nearby small hotels, local transport, breakfast, materials and tuition, plus airfare from the United States: about $2,000.

ART TOURS IN THE UNITED STATES

Las Vegas

Smithsonian Study Tours   P.O. Box 23293, Washington, D.C. 20026-3293. 877-338-8687 (toll free); 202-357-4700 (tel); 202-633-9250 (fax). E-mail: tours@tsa.si.edu; Web site: smithsonianstudytours.org

In the past decade, Las Vegas has evolved into one of the hottest art centers in the country. In addition to the flashing decorative art of the Strip, world-class architects and art dealers have found a comfortable home in Las Vegas.

On this five-day excursion, stay at the beautiful Bellagio Hotel; take a behind-the-scenes guided tour of the Venetian Hotel with one of its architects, Bob Hlusak; visit the Guggenheim-Hermitage Museum there; then have lunch with contemporary artist Robert Beckmann. The tour ends with a visit to West Las Vegas and its Michael Graves library, among other significant buildings.

Five days: about $2,400.

The Southwest

Martha Hopkins Struever   P.O. Box 2203, Santa Fe, New Mexico 87504. 505-983-9515 (tel); 505-983-9517 (fax). E-mail: info@marthastruever.com; Web site: www. marthastruever.com

Martha Struever, a specialist in American Indian art and a former curator of Southwest art at a private gallery in Chicago, gives an eleven-day traveling comprehensive seminar.

In addition to lectures by professors, you will have rare visits to studios and homes of practicing Navajo and Hopi artists and artisans at their mesas, watching them work silver into jewelry, weave tapestries and blankets, carve kachina figures, and paint and fire pottery.

The tour also includes visits to some of the spectacular vistas of the area, such as a private tour of breathtaking Canyon de Chelly.

Eleven days, including lodging, some meals, and local transport: about $3,500.

Art Tours Abroad

Tuscany

Tuscany Tours: Welcome to the Renaissance! 40 Fourth Street, Suite 122, Petaluma, California 94952. 707-794-0722 (tel). E-mail: info@tuscanytours.com; Web site: www.tuscanytours.com

Tuscany Tours offers small-group seminar tours finely calibrated to the independent, traveling art lover and specifically to the art lover of Renaissance Tuscany. They arrange lodging in a small, interesting hotel in Florence, suggest the best trattoria, and will act as informed guides to the collections and buildings that define the Renaissance.

Pamela Mercer and specialist in the quattrocento Samuel Hilt have been spending summers in their home in Tuscany since 1991, to expand their appreciation of Siena and Florence. They are joined by poet Nils Peterson from San Jose State College, who acts as a guide. You will have plenty of time to converse over dinner with like-minded travelers.

Six days in Florence, including food and lodging: about $1,500.

Vienna

Martin Randall Travel Ltd. 10 Barley Mow Passage, Chisick, London W4 4GF, United Kingdom. 011 +44 (0) 20 8742 3355; 011 +44 (0) 20 8742 7766 (fax). E-mail: info@martinrandall.co.uk; Web site: www.martinrandall.com

Vienna 1900 was the city of Freud and Mahler as well as Klimt and Kokoshka. Beneath a suffocating bureaucratic political structure lay a simmering nest of artists and thinkers whose works have influenced the world.

Accompanied by an expert guide, this walking tour of Vienna will take a look at some of the buildings of Max Fabiani and Adolf Loos, as well as friezes by Klimt; plus all the art museums. Hear a performance of Franz Lehar's *Merry Widow*, to evoke the era musically. Lodging is in a four-star hotel.

Four days, including some meals, admissions, and round-trip air from London: about £1,000 (about $1,600).

Ancient Art From France to Ethiopia

TCS Expeditions 2025 First Avenue, Suite 500, Seattle, Washington 98121. 800-727-7477 (toll free); 206-727-7300 (tel); 206-727-7309 (fax). E-mail: travel@tcs-xpeditions.com; Web site: www.tcs-expeditions.com

The Human Odyssey gets to the very root of human expression by visiting everything from Olduvai Gorge in Tanzania to Frank Gehry's Bilbao Museum.

What lines can be drawn from Lucy, our 3.2-million-year-old *Australopithecus* ancestor (in an Ethiopian vault, where you will have an exclusive viewing), to Ice Age cave art in the Dordogne Valley, France (visit many caves as well as Lascaux II, a perfect replica of the original), and in Northern Spain (the cave paintings of Altamira), to Roman architecture and decoration in Tunis, Carthage, and Dougga, as well as Taormina and Siracusa in Sicily, an ancient Greek outpost; to the stone temples at Malta? Accompanied by three premier university professors, the voyage will explore some wonderful examples of human expression.

By private jet, the trip begins and ends in London with a night at the Berkeley Hotel, then travels by private Boeing 757, with a full European crew of sixteen, and first-class service throughout.

Nineteen days, including first-class hotels and lodges, from London: about $33,000.

CHAPTER 5

ASTRONOMY

What is the fascination of the night sky? Places like Stonehenge, Machu Picchu, and hundreds of other sites around the planet testify to the incredible time and energy our ancestors put into building temples that chart celestial phenomena. Early shepherds created blockbuster myths by connecting stars into people and plots.

From the 1950s on, space organizations such as NASA have united technology and science to probe exactly what is out there. We know Jupiter's red spot is a perpetual storm composed of hot swirling gases, and quasars mark the end of our universe and the beginning of time, but what is it that draws us back to marvel at meteor showers and eclipses, and even with all our scientific knowledge, to stare in awe at their beauty?

ECLIPSES AND OTHER CELESTIAL PHENOMENA

The first total solar eclipse expedition cruise that took "interested parties" was in 1970. Since then, interest has spawned trips to view lunar eclipses, partial solar eclipses, the Leonids, and the more arcane events, such as the transit of Venus and the passage of asteroids across the larger planets.

The "diamond ring" effect of a total eclipse of the sun results as the shadow of the moon moves across its face and signals the end of totality. *(The Museum of Science, Boston)*

The Transit of Venus

Venus will cross the sun on June 8, 2004, and on June 6, 2012. Astronomers are excited about these transits, because no one on Earth today has seen this phenomenon. Used by early astronomers to measure our distance from the sun, the last transit occurred in 1882.

The six-hour transit in 2004 will be visible with the naked eye and a solar filter. (For terrific graphics of Venus and Mercury crossing the face of the solar globe, see: eclipse.span.ch/transit.htm.) If you miss these transits, there won't be another until 2117.

Astronomical Tours   913-432-4636 (Shawnee Mission, Kansas) or 816-554-0547 (Lees Summit, Missouri).
E-mail: astronomicaltours@astronomicaltours.net;
Web site: www.astronomicaltours.net

This company organizes tours to view solar and lunar eclipses, star parties, and other celestial events. Their plans for viewing the transit of Venus in Switzerland in June 2004 are being formulated at this writing. Call for details or check their Web site.

Innovations in Travel, Inc.   1203 West Street, Suite D, Annapolis, Maryland 21401. 800-733-3361 (toll free); 410-268-2883 (tel); 410-268-3530 (fax). E-mail: info@innovationsintravel. com; Web site; www.innovationsintravel.com

Innovations in Travel will take you to Egypt, where you will be able to view the transit of Venus from the deck of a luxury cruise ship, anchored off Aswan. Lecturer Dr. James Huddle, from the U.S. Naval Academy, will explain the history and astronomy of the phenomenon, which begins shortly after 8:00 A.M. and can be tracked through one of the onboard solar-filtered telescopes. The transit ends about 2:20 P.M., after which the ship will continue on to Edfu.

The transit of Venus fits in beautifully with the rest of this tour, which covers the major monuments and places from Cairo to Karnak of a people for whom the heavens determined the course of events and astronomical events were loaded with meaning.

Your understanding is deepened with nightly lectures by Egyptologists, and a "Native Egyptian and Pharaonic style" costume party while at Luxor. The final day is spent at the famous Cairo Museum of Antiquities.

Ten days, including international airfare from the U.S. East Coast (more from other cities), lodging (double occupancy), and meals: about $3,600.

Solar Eclipses

The big draws are total eclipses of the sun.

A *total* solar eclipse occurs when the sun is completely covered by the moon's shadow. Stars become visible in the dark sky, birds bed down for what they think is night, and a faint aura of light plays around the dark disk in the sky.

A *partial* solar eclipse occurs when the moon's shadow does not completely cover the sun, and the sun gradually shrinks into a crescent.

An *annular* eclipse occurs when the moon's shadow is slightly smaller than the sun, and the sun is surrounded by what looks like a diamond ring. *Bailey's Beads* are the little "diamonds" in the light, created by the sun shining through the mountains and valleys of the moon.

Solar eclipses occur only at the new moon; the shadow cuts a swath across the earth that is only about 75 miles wide and moves about 1,000 miles per hour.

Eclipse afficionados count the days until the long total solar eclipses—the ones that last six or more minutes, time enough to get good photographs.

For best viewing, you will need clear air (the kind usually available on the ocean or at the Poles), flexibility, and forgiveness—the weather might not cooperate.

Most important, never look directly at an eclipse of any kind. Shield your eyes with specially made glasses or undeveloped 35mm film. Never look at a partial eclipse either, even if it remains bright—watch it move across a smooth sidewalk or on a piece of paper.

November 23, 2003, is the date of the last total solar eclipse (visible within the Antarctic circle) until March 29, 2006.

Solar eclipses are also predicted for successive years, as follows:

Total

March 29, 2006 (Africa, Turkey, Russia; about 4 min.)
August 1, 2008 (Arctic Circle; about 2 min.)
July 22, 2009 (India, China, Hawaii; about 6 min.)
July 11, 2010 (Easter Island, Chile, Argentina; about 5 min.)

Annular

October 3, 2005 (Portugal, Sudan, Kenya; about 4 min.)
September 22, 2006 (Guyana, Suriname, Antarctica; about
    7 min.)
February 7, 2008 (Antartica, Australia, New Zealand; about
    2 min.)
January 26, 2009 (South Africa, Antarctica, Borneo; about
    7 min.)
January 15, 2010 (Central Africa, India, China; about 11 min.)

See sunearth.gsfc.nasa.gov/eclipse

Lunar Eclipses

Three total lunar eclipses are predicted for the next few years:

November 8–9, 2003 (visible in the southern hemisphere near
    Antarctica)
May 4, 2004 (Asia, East Europe, Africa, Indonesia, Australia,
    part of Antarctica)
October 28, 2004 (Switzerland and other parts of Europe, the
    Arctic, North America, Central and South America, part of
    Antarctica).

The following companies specialize in astronomical tours; check
with them for details of trips not mentioned here.

TravelQuest International   305 Double D. Drive, Prescott,
Arizona 86303. 800-830-1998 (toll free); 928-445-7754 (tel); 928-
445-8771 (fax). E-mail: tours@tq-international.com; Web site:
www.tq-international.com

TravelQuest teams up with editors from *Sky and Telescope* magazine to create tours that let you travel with experts. Aram
Kaprielian, the president of TravelQuest, has been leading astronomy tours since 1986, and is used to settling diplomatic situations
that might arise in countries not accustomed to eclipse viewing.

For the two-minute total eclipse in Antarctica in November 2003, TravelQuest and *Sky and Telescope* editor-in-chief Richard Fienberg will set up camp at Eclipse I, a space on the barren icefield of Dronning Maud Land (not named until 1930), about a thousand miles from the South Pole on the continent of Antarctica. Remote, in other words.

The eclipse will take place about 9 degrees above the horizon in the beginning of the southern winter in air completely unobstructed by city lights or pollution, in the middle of the darkest part of the shadow.

This two-week tour flies out of Punta Arenas, Chile, on the sturdy Ilyushin-76 for the seven-hour flight to an area of blue ice, where you will be met by a DC-3 and Twin Otter to take you on a short hop to Eclipse I. The camp is outfitted with the latest in Antarctic tents. Cooking and eating will be in a separate tent.

For amusement in the days in which you set up instruments and cameras for the two minutes of glory, you can travel around on ski-doos and explore, or look for meteorites. Lectures bring you up to speed: astronomy in the polar atmosphere, weather, human history, how to communicate with the rest of the world, the challenges of navigation, safety in the frozen wasteland, survival, as well as using compasses, GPS, and sextants.

TravelQuest provides $1 million emergency medical insurance; but highly recommend buying trip cancellation insurance. You will need a physician's good health report, and you must realize that the viewing depends on the weather.

Two weeks, including everything except travel to and from Punta Arenas, a sleeping bag, and Antarctic clothing: from $35,000 to $46,500, depending on the size of the group.

Mayhugh Travel   701 Perdew Avenue, Ridgecrest, California 93555. 888-412-5317 (toll free); 760-446-0050. E-mail: roy@mayhugh.com; Web site: www.astronomyvacations.com

Mayhugh links up with the appropriate ships for eclipse cruises around the world. For the November 2003 Antarctica eclipse, Mayhugh will book passage on the Russian icebreaker *Kapitan Khleb-nikov* and sail from Port Elizabeth, South Africa, to a place in the Davis Sea, west of the Shackleton Ice Shelf.

Onboard lecturers include Dr. Fred Espenak, a NASA astronomer with the Goddard Space Flight Center and a specialist in planetary atmospheric infrared spectrometry, and Professor John Parkinson of Sheffield Hallam University in England, who has led numerous eclipse cruises and done documentaries for BBC-TV.

The trip ends in Hobart, Tasmania. Enroute, before and after the eclipse, passengers will be able to take zodiac hops to penguin nests and helicopter over amazing ice shelves.

One month, including everything except airfare to and from South Africa and Tasmania: from about $19,000 to $32,000, depending on berth.

Hole in the Sky Tours   E-mail: holeinthesky@earthlink.net; Web site: www.holeinthesky.com

This company will also host a group on the *Kapitan Khlebnikov* for the Antarctica 2003 eclipse, *and* will include observation of a total lunar eclipse on November 9 as the ship steams toward Antarctica. Onboard lecturers, in addition to Dr. Fred Espenak (see above), include Jay Pasachoff, Oliver Staiger, and Vic Winter.

One month: about $19,000 to $32,000, depending on berth.

Hole in the Sky does other trips, including the transit of Venus.

Iceland

Ring of Fire Expeditions   Future Travel Inc., 1085 Hercules Avenue, Houston, Texas 77058. 281-480-1988 (tel); 281-480-2587 (fax). **Contacts:** *for brochures:* George Weller 800-929-9004 (toll free); E-mail: wellerg@carlsontravel.com; *For eclipse planning:* Paul Maley, 281-244-0208 (tel); E-mail: pdmaley@yahoo.com. Web site: www.eclipsetours.com

Paul Maley from the NASA Johnson Space Center Astronomical Society (JSCAS) has been offering eclipse tours around the world since 1970. He also does tours to view other space phenomena, such as comets, lunar eclipses, asteroids passing in front of stars, and satellite reentries.

His nine-day tour to view the dawn annular eclipse (about three minutes) of the sun in Iceland, for example, includes tours of the geologic wonders of Iceland, such as geysers and fumaroles, and trips to the Faroe Islands to hike the spectacular sea cliffs, some 750 meters above the ocean.

Nine days, including roundtrip airfare from Boston: about $2,500.

AURORA BOREALIS

We may feel isolated in the universe, but we are extremely connected to everything that happens in space. Nothing brings space closer to earth than the aurora displays around the North Pole. (The aurora australis attracts fewer visitors because it occurs over Antarctica in the winter.)

Fiery explosions in the central meridian of the sun shoot charged particles at hyperspeeds across the solar system toward the earth, which deflects the bombardment with its magnetosphere. The particles break into oxygen, hydrogen, and nitrogen ions, which then perform fantastic dances across the dark sky, shaping into veils and flowing arms of yellow-green, red, blue, violet, and yellow that float and dip from 60 to 600 miles up.

The whole event, which occurs about 250 times a year around the Arctic Circle, is dependent entirely on sunspot activity. Tours to the clear and mostly dark northern polar regions are very popular; you can find specially built aurora viewing huts, with glass roofs and sides. But there are no guarantees on the weather or the display; what the sun chooses to do, said a tour director, "is up to the gods."

Canada

Inn on the Lake   P.O. Box 10420, Whitehorse, Yukon Y1A7A1. 867-660-5253 (tel); 867-660-5259 (fax). E-mail: info@ exceptionalplaces.com; Web site: www.exceptionalplaces.com

From December to April, the Inn on the Lake offers a special three-night stay at its luxury resort to view the aurora. This log structure, built on Marsh Lake in the middle of some of the most pristine country in Canada, offers a first-class menu, with organic vegetables, local meats and fish, such as Arctic Char, and a wide selection of wines. A state-of-the-art fitness center, in-room Jacuzzis, fine linens, and the coziness of an inn at the edge of the universe combine with toboganning, ice fishing, snowshoeing, and a superheated outdoor hot tub, from which you can watch the aurora in the crisp night air.

Three nights, including airport pickup: from about $950 Canadian (about $625 U.S.).

Alaska

TravelQuest International   305 Double D. Drive, Prescott, Arizona 86303. 800-830-1998; 928-445-7754 (tel); 928-445-8771 (fax). E-mail: tours@tq-international.com; Web site: www.tq-international.com

Capture the Aurora is a five-day trip that starts in Fairbanks, Alaska, then drives to Chena Hot Springs Resort, next to Spring Creek Mountain to be as close to the display as you can. In-depth lectures will explain the phenomena of the lights, and the connection between the sun and the earth.

In Fairbanks, you visit the University of Alaska museum and meet with award-winning photographer Dennis Mammana, who will teach you the best techniques for getting good photographs of the aurora. The tour provides a daily pickup and drop-off film run, which will give you instant feedback on your pictures.

On the drive to the Chena Hot Springs Resort, you stop for lunch at the Chatanika Gold Camp and take a tour of the high-altitude rocket range at Poker Flats Research Range—full Alaska experiences. Each night watch and photograph the aurora.

The Chena Hot Springs are natural and a perfect end to whatever you choose to do during the day while you spend two days at the resort—dog sledding, skiing, ice skating, or riding in a horse-drawn sleigh. You can even watch the aurora from outside your room or in a viewing hut. But the tour provides passes on the bus up Spring Creek Mountain, where the view is unimpeded.

Six nights, including ground transportation, some meals, and lectures: about $1,300. TravelQuest will rent Arctic clothing if you send them your sizes in advance.

CHAPTER 6

BALLOON EXCURSIONS

Balloon travel is perfect for dreamers who wish they could float. Beyond the fantasy of drifting, ballooning has always been accompanied by aesthetics—balloon designs would be as compelling in a gallery as the sky—and ritual—the staff bring out the best china and silver when you land, whether you're in the Loire Valley or the Namibian outback. Otherwise, it's you and the wind, and the skill of your trained pilot.

Buddy Bombard Balloon Vacations   The Bombard Society, Inc., 333 Pershing Way, West Palm Beach, Florida 33401. 800-862-8537 (toll free); 561-837-6610 (tel); 561-837-6623 (fax). E-mail: travel@bombardsciety.com; Web site: www.bombardsociety.com

Or book through **Rex Travel**, 100 North Lasalle, Suite 2010, Chicago, Illinois 60602. 800-777-7739 (toll free); 312-641-6633 (tel); 312-641-6641 (fax). E-mail: vacations@nextravel.com; Web site: www.rextravel.com

On Bombard's nine-day Winter Swiss Alps adventure, you cruise quietly over the icy peaks of the Alps, aided by the lift of the cold air. Elegant picnic lunches are served aloft as you float for three and a half hours each day. Each night descend to your four-star hotel and enjoy a well-deserved dinner party. On the fourth day, join a fleet of sixty-five other balloons at the International Balloon Festival in Chateau d'Oex, and take part in a precision-flying competition.

Balloons against the clear morning sky are as beautiful as they are peaceful.
(Stephanie Ocko)

Nine days: about $12,000.

Buddy Bombard has been ballooning for three decades, making sure that his guests enjoy the safe, first-class "aerial nature walk" experience and the comity of their group. A licensed airplane pilot, Bombard has a background as a transatlantic sailor and crew member on several America's Cup yacht contenders. Today his Bombard Society, dedicated to providing luxury service to balloon vacationers, has twelve programs in six countries.

Try a five-day art and architecture tour of Prague, for example, mostly on the ground, except for the magical balloon ride each morning. Drifting quietly above city streets just stirring to life, you can see the sun play over the ancient stones and spires before you have breakfast.

Five days: about $8,000.

Bombard's favorite flights go over villages and farms, low enough to engage people on the ground in conversation. On flights over the Loire Valley, you can see the spectacular former medieval fiefdoms straight out of a *Book of the Hours* as you cruise over estate vineyards and their chateaux. Each night stay in a castle, including the romantic eleventh-century tower of Chateau Sinq Mars la Pile, dining by candlelight. Visit vintners and their wine cellars, especially the huge Côtes de Nuits, and taste some of the many burgundies.

Eleven days: about $13,000.

Air Ventures Hot Air Balloon Flights, Inc. P.O. Box 711, Paoli, Pennsylvania. 800-826-6361 (toll free); 610-827-7203 (fax). E-mail: airvenhab@earthlink.net; Web site: www.air-ventures.com

From the quiet, unobtrusive level of a balloon drifting at dawn above the Serengeti, you see grazing herds of wildebeest or zebra, crocodiles lazing on lakeshores, and hippos taking morning swims. The only sound is the advance on your camera.

Air Ventures offers one major excursion a year, sometimes at balloon festivals and rallies. Their eighteen-day trip to Tanzania and Kenya, for example, starts in Philadelphia, flies to Nairobi for a night at a five-star hotel, then drives to the Great Rift Valley and a lodge to get acclimated to Africa and its unique rhythms.

Then you hop in the Land Cruiser and travel in tandem with another cruiser hauling the gas cylinders and a trailer with the balloon, and head down to the Serengeti Plain and the Masai Mara or to Lake Navaisha. Here you will spend three to five days ballooning every morning at 5 A.M., over spectacular game, some of it on private game ranges (with permission). Nights, camp under the stars or stay at lodges.

"This is a hands-on trip, but you'll never be far from a hot shower," said a spokesman.

Then you work your way back to Nairobi, where you separate from the balloon, and take a quick flight to the coast and Watanamo Resort. One hundred yards from the Indian Ocean, you spend three days at the beach, where you can swim, dive, snorkel, and collect your thoughts.

Eighteen days, including meals, transport, lodging, park fees, and international airfare: $3,500–$4,500. Airfare (about $76) and meals at the resort are extra.

Be sure to bring items to trade with the Masai, who have a hankering for sneakers and T-shirts.

Montgolfiades Internationales de Tunisie 51 bis, rue Chazière, 69004 Lyon, France. E-mail: contact@air-ballon.com; Web site: www.air-ballon.com

This is a chance to join an international balloon fiesta that crosses the entire Sahara Desert, north to south.

You begin in Genoa, Italy, by catching an overnight boat, where you will have first-class accommodations and be briefed by a representative of Aeroasis, the company that sponsors the fiesta. You spend the first night at a first-class hotel in Tunis, your last touch with civilization before you head out into the desert.

For the next five days, the Dergine Oasis is your camp, where you will eat and sleep in desert luxury. With the right winds, you could spend the better part of the next four days aloft, ballooning over the amazing shapes of shifting sand and rock that the Sahara comprises. With inclement winds, you will explore the territory on camelback or in four-by-four vehicles.

For the next five days, drive to Tataouine, where you will balloon over the hills. Then travel to Douiret in the Sahara for breathtaking flights above the Grand Erg Mountains. Two final days are spent in Kairouan, with sunrise and sunset flights over the city, before returning by boat across the Mediterranean to Genoa.

Fourteen days, including boat, land transport, four- and five-star hotels, desert safari camps, food, and balloon flights: about €5,000 (Euros; approximately the same in U.S. dollars).

DuneHopper P.O. Box 5048, Windhoek, Republic of Namibia. 011 +264 61 234 793 (tel); 011 +264 61 259 316 (fax). E-mail: info@naturefriend.com.na; Web site: www.dunehopper.com

Balloon over the Namib Desert, watching the colors change as the sun grows higher; follow the game just getting up or going to bed: springbok, zebra, hyenas, leopards, babboons, ostriches, and eagles.

You leave close to sunrise, float silently over game, savannah, and desert filled with breathtaking colors, its dunes more than 300 meters high. Then land safely, enjoy a champagne breakfast, and return to your desert lodge.

In conjunction with NatureFriend Safaris, a company that provides fly-in tours to various destinations in Namibia, or arranges private charter flights and self-drive tours, DuneHopper will fly you in to the dunes in the Namib Desert or the wilderness of the Namib-Rand Nature Reserve. They also arrange lodging in a variety of luxury camps there, and will set you up with a hot-air balloon flight high over the desert.

Or walk the Tok-Tokkie Trail, used for centuries by Bushmen, for two or three days, camping under the amazing sky. A guide will lead you; the company sees to it you have a hot bucket shower at the camp, as well as picnic lunches and two-course dinners.

The lodges and camps in the area vary from luxury safari tents built on wooden platforms at the Wolwedans Dunes Lodge, to the brick and canvas, solar-powered Sossusvlei Movenpick Lodge, decorated with Bushmen art. The Sossusvlei Mountain Lodge has a star-gazing facility with a computerized telescope to take advantage of the absolutely clear night skies. Per day, including flight, balloon, lodge, and food: about $700 to $1,500.

CHAPTER 7

CAMEL TREKS

Ever since *Lawrence of Arabia*, camels have become synonymous with the romance of slow movement across vast stretches of sand as empty as the ocean. Wrapped in flowing robes with burnished cheeks, one knee thrown around the camel's hump, you plod your steady course without regard for time.

Out of the desert rise otherworldly vistas, mirages, horizons that vaporize, mountains that melt, as if the world recreates itself with every slow and rhythmic step. T. E. Lawrence said that all men dream dreams by night; but only dangerous men dream dreams by day and act them out.

CAMELS

Perfectly adapted to extreme dry conditions, camels have been used as pack animals probably for as long as humans have had something to pack. Some feral camels roam Central Australia and the Sahara (Napoleon used them for his North African campaigns in 1798), but for the most part, camels buddy up nicely with nomads, who use them to carry the camp, in return for which the nomads share well water with them. Because they store fat in the hump, camels can go for months without eating and drinking. They conserve water by raising their core temperature and not sweating. When they do drink, they can absorb more than a hundred gallons of water at one time.

An expert rider shows how it's done, with a swift kick and a flick of the little finger. *(Roger Archibald)*

Are they sweet? Wrong question. They are capable of giving off terrible whining groans and flashing dentist-perfect rows of teeth in a menacing grimace. If a camel is your mount for a while, you will learn to negotiate.

TEXAS

David Alloway's Skills of Survival P.O. Box 1777, Alpine, Texas 79831. 877-371-2634 (toll free). Web site: www. skillsofsurvival.com

Texans say Texas has everything, and that may be true. They even have desert and camels and a Camel Corps. Doug Baum and the Texas Camel Corps invite riders to participate in desert camel treks that reenact parts of the original exploration and mapping of the Big Bend area of Texas. Imported to help builders open up the Far West, camels were suited to the arid conditions and used during the Civil War.

Baum's treks take you along the routes laid out by Brevet Lieutenant William Echols, laid down in 1859 and 1860. If you have never ridden a camel before, Baum will teach you the gentle art of positioning your body comfortably, how to parcel out your water, and the best way to camp. Expert guides will explain the history of Big Bend and the Camel Corps. You will cover about seven miles a day.

Big Bend is magnificent, rugged country, once home to pterodactyls. The camels here are pussycat-sweet, coddled from their bottle-fed babyhood. Baum says they are affectionate. Texas does have everything.

One-day overnight treks: about $690.

THE SAHARA

Dreamweaver Travel 1185 River Drive, River Falls, Wisconsin 54022. 715-425-1037 (tel); 715-426-0829 (fax). E-mail: Dudley@ dreamweavertravel.net; Web site: www.dreamweavertravel.net

Saharan Dream is a two-week trip that incorporates camel travel with lots of opportunity to meet some of the Tuareg and Fulani nomads who ply the Sahara.

Start in Niamey, Niger, with a day at the museum and zoo. Then fly a short distance to Agadez to see truly exotic and ancient architecture, as well as to pay a visit to the Sultan of Agadez. Travel by Land Cruiser to the Air Mountains and Tenere Desert, a magnificent spread of deep gorges, vast stretches of golden dunes, and fascinating things like dinosaur graveyards, rocks with perfectly fossilized fish, petroglyphs, even artifacts from the last Saharan civilization 7,000 years ago.

In the desert, saddle up for a three-day trek to examine any or all of the above. On Days 11–12, you have the choice of continuing the camel trek or staying with a Fulani family. The final two days are spent in Niamey, with visits to the amazing marketplace to shop. In September and October, the Tuareg and Fulani hold festivals, and you have a chance to see both the Cure Salé and the Gerewol. Tuaregs' respect for the camel extends to giving camels as a wedding gift, decorated and accompanied by lots of music and dance.

Dreamweaver donates a portion of each trip to aid local Niger communities. Director Dudley Parkinson, who has spent eight of the last twenty-five years in Niger, believes that cultural exchange is the only way to travel, and will arrange an overnight stay with a Fulani family in a small village, if you choose. Those who have done so found their Fulani hosts solicitous and hospitable, and got to know much more about life in the Sahara.

Develop the habit of "listening and observing, rather than hearing and seeing," Parkinson advises.

Fifteen days, including lodging, camping, hotel, food, camels, and local transport: about $2,800.

Morocco

The Best of Morocco   London office: 011 +44 (0) 207 3535589 (tel); 011 +44 (0) 1380 828630 (fax). E-mail: morocco@morocco-travel.com; Web site: www.morocco-travel.com

Three hundred and fifty-two kilometers southeast of Marrakesh at a tiny desert town called Zagora is where you start. Check into a hotel for the first night, wrap yourself in the Moroccan mystique, and begin your holiday in the sands of the Moroccan Sahara. The next day saddle up and head north through the desert, carrying your Berber tent, while other camels carry provisions, including mineral water.

This company provides everything and runs a series of trips, all beginning in Zagora and proceeding north through sand plains, casbahs, oases, long dunes, steep-walled gorges, and green clusters of acacia trees (what once made the Sahara green until they were harvested widely to be used in the manufacture of gum arabic). Camels love to eat acacias, thorns and all.

Camping is either in the tent or under the vast canopy of stars in the cool desert nights. A cook prepares dinner while you sip mint tea at the end of the day.

Meals and mineral water are provided in addition to tent and camel; bring your own sleeping bags, first-aid kits, and water purification filters, plus a broad-brimmed hat. Treks are accompanied by a French-speaking guide. Expect really cold night temperatures (20 degrees F) if you go in winter. All treks end with a taxi ride back to Zagora.

Start with the one-overnight trek, sleeping in a Berber tent among the dunes: about £40 ($60). Work up to five nights, with treks across stony hills and through deep gorges: about £250 ($375).

Finish this with a trip to Casablanca.

Mountain Travel Sobek   6420 Fairmount Avenue, El Cerrito, California 94530. 888-687-6235 (toll free); 510-527-8100 (tel); 510-525-7710 (fax). E-mail: info@mtsobek.com; Web site: www. mtsovbek.com

Date palms once lined the route plied by camel caravans that crossed from the Red Sea to the Atlantic. Spend a few days in exotic Marrakesh before taking a Land Rover through Berber country across empty terra-cotta dunes to the small town of Zagora. Here, saddle up on camels for a four-day trek into the Sahara to Erg Chebbi, a huge dune several kilometers to the northeast.

From here, indoctrinated into desert life, you take the Land Rover again through the Atlas Mountains to Fez, a trading center for beautiful blue tiled ware, jewelry, skin dyes, as well as spices and dates.

Fifteen days, including camping gear, hotel, meals, camels, and guides: about $3,300 to $3,700, depending on the size of the group.

Kenya

A Camel-Assisted Walking Safari

Wild Frontiers   Contact: Helen Douglas-Dufresne, P.O. Box 15165, Nairobi, Kenya. 011 +254 (2) 884258/9 (tel); 011 +254 (2) 891394 (fax). E-mail: wildfrontiers@pyramide.net; Web site: www. pyramide.net

Long-time Kenya resident Helen Douglas-Dufresne and her Samburu crew, all experts in the area, will lead you on a walking safari, accompanied by camels which you can ride if you wish, but which are happy to haul your camping gear. The trek will take you into the hilly and largely unexplored region of the Matthews and Ndoto Mountain Ranges in northern Kenya. The only other people you will meet are the nomadic Rendille and Samburu shepherds. The place is so remote that even the wildlife is unused to being looked at, and is as curious about humans as you will be about them. Exotic birds abound.

Since each trip is custom-designed, depending on the season and how much time you have, Douglas-Dufresne recommends planning to be there during the full moon—"a bonus." You will walk out early, covering anywhere between eight to twenty kilometers; breakfast midmorning; see wildlife and breathtaking scenery; then set up camp after midday when the heat settles in. A cook will prepare dinner, while you explore the area. Sleep in mosquito-proof beds in tents or under "a billion stars as bright as diamonds."

Guides carry a radiophone and medical kit; laundry service is provided, as are hot camp showers. Douglas-Dufresne asks that you have comprehensive travel insurance and photograph only the Samburu guides, not members of local tribes. Price depends on the trip. Her expertise is in "folklore, botany, ornithology, and astrology."

AUSTRALIA

Explore the Outback   via Port Augusta 5710, South Australia, Australia. 011 +61 (8) 8672 3968 (tel); 011 +61 (8) 8672 3990 (fax). E-mail: explore@austcamel.com.au; Web site: www.austcamel. com.au

The Australian desert has preserved numerous relics from Australia's first settlers in the 1850s, including mines, stone huts, forges and kilns, copper transport roads, the overland telegraph, and an original wagon trail.

During the day, you will move in camel caravan through the outback, stopping to see historical artifacts and unusual plants and animals; nights you will camp out. The camels are "very friendly and personable." Your safety is ensured with a competent staff and communication with the Royal Flying Doctor Service.

Explore the Outback is a nature-based, educational camel safari operator in seasonal operation since 1987. They run four- to ten-day camel safaris throughout the year into wild central Australia, with the primary objective to discover and map the cultural heritage sites in the Denison Range and contribute to a flora and fauna survey of the area.

Four days, including all meals, camel, and camping gear except your sleeping bag: about AU $650 (Australian dollars) for adults (about $350 U.S.). Extra days on safari, if you choose: about AU $160 (about $90 U.S.). If you bring the family, for each member the cost is about AU $500 (about $280 U.S.).

CHAPTER 8

CARS: RACE, RALLY, AND ROAM

If you buy a car with triple digits on the speedometer and a transmission that urges Go, go, go, while you are waiting at a stoplight, how can you reconcile the need for highway safety with the burning need to know what the engine can really do?

One answer: Take a course on a racetrack. Bring your car, and let it do what you dream it can do.

Cale Yarborough's Executive Racing School P.O. Box 90487, Lakeland, Florida 33804; 839 Massachusetts Avenue, Lakeland, Florida 33801; 800-316-6985 (toll free); 863-682-7500 (tel); 863-687-2996 (fax). E-mail: gofast@executiveracingschool.com; Web site: www.executiveracingschool.com

For about $400, a half-day of Yarborough's Spirit of Racing will give you not only the safe space in which to test your car (the USA International Speedway in Lakeland, Florida), but the subtle techniques to coax it to greatness. Tour the shop facilities first, get some instruction, and take a trial passenger run with a pro in a stock car for ten breathless laps. Then grab a helmet and a radio, strap yourself in to your own car, and go solo at fantastic speeds for the fifteen laps included in the price.

Stock Car Racing

If you like the taste of speed and want to venture farther into the world of stock car racing, give your own car a rest and try out a late-model stock car.

Cale Yarborough, three-time NASCAR cup winner, runs two stock car programs: one for beginners who want to know what it's really like to be in a stock car race; and one for serious students who plan to become stock car racers.

Spend the whole day on the Circle Track Challenge program, with one classroom session, ten laps next to a professional driver

Two orange Cobra Mustangs use some of their 320+ horsepower as they tear along the Bob Bondurant School track in the Advanced Road Racing Course. *(Photo by Rick Scuteri, courtesy of the Bob Bondurant School)*

white-knuckling at 140 mph, then take the car yourself for fifty laps solo.

One day, including breakfast and lunch: about $1,000.

For a list of companies offering programs like these, see www.racingschools.com.

Open Wheel Race Cars

After you gain confidence doing stock car laps, try a Formula One race car. This open-wheel race car looks like a banana with a hole in it, and goes like sixty (as it were).

Track Time, Inc.   Stock Car School at Michigan Speedway, 1104 North Meridian, Youngstown, Ohio 44509. 330-759-1868 (tel); 330-759-7189 (fax). E-mail: info@tracktime.com; Web site: www.tracktime.com

Track Time's The Super School offers a unique one-day program driving late-model stock cars in the morning, and open-wheel race cars in the afternoon on the Michigan International Speedway.

Full day: about $1,000; two days: about $1,800.

Driving 101   6915 Speedway Boulevard, Las Vegas, Nevada 89115. 702-651-6300 (tel); 702-651-6310 (fax). E-mail: info@ driving101.com; Web site: www.driving101.com

Driving 101 offers experience behind the wheel of an open-wheel race car for beginners on up to champions. One day of orientation, safety instructions, and six laps up to 145 mph: $375. Or you can start by doing six laps as a passenger in the pace car. You might reach speeds flirting with 180 mph, but the driving is left to the pro.

One day: $99.

If you find that open wheel is for you, work your way up to the Advanced Racing Experience. This three-day program, with one-on-one instruction, gives you the technical training you need to ride in a six-car side-by-side or nose-to-tail grouping at unreal speeds.

Sixty-six laps in all: about $3,000.

HIGH-PERFORMANCE VEHICLES

NASCAR, Formula One (Europe), and Indy 500 all race high-performance vehicles, cars familiar to everyone off the track and on the road. The trick, as far as nonracers are concerned, is to match your driving skills with the technical near-perfection of the high-performance vehicle. The goal is to become one with your one-and-a-half tons of motion, in the same way a rider bonds with his horse. It takes knowledge and practice.

Bob Bondurant School of High Performance Driving

20000 South Maricopa Road, Gate 3, Chandler, Arizona 85226. 800-842-RACE [7223] (toll free); 602-961-0143 (tel); 520-796-0660 (fax). E-mail: inquiry@bondurant.com; Web site: www. bondurant.com. Contact: Greg Fresquez.

Paul Newman studied here, as have several tens of thousands of others over the years.

Bondurant's High Performance Driving Course is designed to improve the way you handle a car on streets and highways. In one of their high-performance Mustang GTs, you will become sensitive to a car's abilities; learn proper positioning of your body, hands, and feet; and get to know what to do in bad situations. In car-control exercises, you will avoid skids and accidents, and sharpen your visual skills to avoid both.

One day: about $1,900; three days: about $2,900.

You can also try Bondurant's one-day Highway Survival Training, an apt course for the times, which uses an accident avoidance simulator, practice in skid cars on a handling oval, and a slalom course. Learn true defensive driving.

Training is in a Mustang GT, but the techniques apply to everything from a Mini to a Hummer. This course will leave you a more self-confident driver.

One day: about $900.

For a list of driving schools, try www.racesearch.com and www.commondriver.com. If you know any teenagers, check out the safe-driving courses offered for them.

The National Auto Sport Association sponsors high-performance driving events on the track and road for members in their own cars. Contact NASA: 510-232-NASA [6272]; Web site: www. nasaproracing.com.

ROAD RACING

Yes, you can work up to the Monte Carlo, which follows the curvy Corniche that skirts the cliff above the Mediterranean then winds through the tiny crowded streets of Monaco.

Or something like it. Road racing is an art in which the driver is in maximum control of his car and himself under all circumstances. If your car is a dynamo that murmurs with possibility when you downshift, road racing is for you.

Instruction begins with an understanding of what a car can do—usually a GT on which you will practice. You will also learn the basic vocabulary of the road race, what the flags mean, and how the race is scored.

On the track, practice is on the Skid Pad, a permanently wet surface on which you will drive at maximum speeds, learning to use the throttle and brake, and proper steering techniques.

You will learn threshold braking, the art of braking for smooth slow-downs at fast speeds; and trail braking, which is braking smoothly while turning.

Then on the Autocross, a course determined by pylons requiring sudden turns, you practice driving for consistent control, using heel-and-toe down shifting with the stick shift, steady, balanced steering, and proper braking.

Not easy. It takes a lot of practice.

Panoz Racing School   5290 Winder Highway, Braselton, Georgia 30517. 888-282-4872 (toll free); 770-967-1220 (tel);

770-967-1226 (fax). E-mail: shartiner@panozracingschool.com; Web site: www.panozracingschool.com

Panoz has four facilities: Road Atlanta Raceway; Sebring International Raceway, Florida; Texas Motor Speedway, Fort Worth; and Mosport, Ontario, Canada.

You can learn all of the above techniques on their Panoz GT-RA in one-day road racing: about $900; three days, with extra instruction in track lead and follow the instructor, the art of passing at high speeds: about $2,800; and two-day advanced road racing: $2,400.

Completion of the three-day course will make you eligible for the Sports Car Club of America (SCCA) license, which means you will be able to compete regionally. Add two lapping days ($875 per day) to that, and you will be eligible to race Panoz GTs.

Bob Bondurant School of High Performance Driving   20000 South Maricopa Road, Gate 3, Chandler, Arizona 85226. 800-842-RACE [7223] (toll free); 602-961-0143 (tel); 520-796-0660 (fax). E-mail: inquiry@bondurant.com; Web site: www.bondurant.com

Bondurant teaches an Introduction to Road Racing, during which you learn heel-and-toe downshifting, trail braking, keen visual smarts, and other techniques on a Mustang GT, all of which allow you to move with ease around obstacles, up and down hills, and through twists and turns at a constant speed.

Move on to Grand Prix Road Racing with three days in a Mustang GT and one day in an F-1 style Formula Ford, racing against classmates. This will qualify you for a SCCA (Sports Car Club of America) license, which will open doors on the car racing world. Four days: about $3,800.

Advanced Road Racing in a Mustang Cobra or F-1 Style Formula Ford helps you fine-tune your skills. You ride with an instructor, who will evaluate your performance as you negotiate different track configurations. One day: about $1,500; two days: about $3,200; three days: about $4,900.

Rallies

If you want to know how your car performs against others in its class, take it on a rally. This competitive race can last for a day or a month and cover a few miles or half a continent.

A driver and a navigator with a road map and local maps, and any other aids, such as a GPS, computer, or odometer, travel on regular public roads with dirt or asphalt paving. Each navigator is given a detailed route book, which describes every bump and sharp turn on the course, so he can help the driver anticipate the next move.

Leaving in one-minute intervals, each car races in segments called special stages. Timers with stopwatches at checkpoints record each car's progress. On closed-off roads, many of them rough logging trails or desert tracks, cars open up and engage in full racing, not always aware of standing puddles, thank-you-ma'ams, the perils of gravel, and the number of spectators.

Between special stages, cars travel at normal speeds through regular traffic, obeying regular traffic laws, still keeping on schedule so that they arrive at the next special stage exactly on time.

At the end of the rally back at the staging area, the times are tallied up, and the fastest is the winner.

Warning: Rallies can be addictive. Some drivers lurch from rally to rally.

SCCA Performance Rally Dept.   9033 East Easter Place, Centennial, Colorado 80112. 303-779-6622, ext. 316 (tel); 303-694-3654 (fax). E-mail: performancerally@scca.org; Web site: www.scca.org

The SCCA ProRally Championship sponsors ten events in the United States; and the ClubRally Championship, fifty events. This is a good place to start and learn all about the various classes of rally cars, some of which include huge modifications to your car and cost big bucks.

Ivor Wigham's European Rally and Performance Driving School   7266 Airport Road, Keystone Heights Airpark, Starke, Florida 32091. 877-872-5593 (toll free); 325-473-2999 (tel). Web site: www.gorally.com

Professional instruction and hands-on experience over a course for a full day will let you know what is expected in rally driving.

The introductory course briefs you on safety, then puts you on the Slalom, where you must use throttle control and hand-brake turns. Then drive on the one-mile skill pad, and try to control your slide, with four-wheel drifting. In the afternoon, you will perform two 2.1-mile special stages. After each drive, the instructor will give you time to assess what you have learned back in the classroom.

One day: $625; weekends: $675.

The advanced one-on-one course gives you five hours of "seat time," interspersed with assessment sessions. After this, you will be ready to rally.

One day, standard car (two-wheel drive): $1,250; weekends: $1,400.

For an index of worldwide rallies, see www.goss.com.

For all of these courses, you will need to be at least eighteen, have a valid driver's license, bring a helmet, and be ready to accept extra liability insurance. Repair of any damage to the cars you use is your responsibility. If you use your own vehicle, it must be in good working order, with fresh oil and clean brakes.

OFF-ROAD FOUR-WHEEL DRIVES

Can your Jeep, Hummer, Land Rover, or Four-by-Four Whatever actually do what it's built to do—roam at ease through woods and desert over rocks, hills, dips, mud, sand, streams, deep underbrush, and other impossible terrain? Find out by joining up with others and venturing as a group into the wilderness.

It's not exactly like the fantasy TV commercials, in which the four-wheel drive winds up atop a desert mesa. Bouncing around in the wilderness can mean broken headlights, dents in the doors, dents in the underpinnings, and a flat tire or two. But after the experience, you will look at your prized possession with great respect and pride. Surviving an off-road experience is a great way to bond with your car.

Start first with some instruction on how to protect your underpinnings from rocks, how to dig out, and how to perform repairs that might be immediately necessary.

United Four-Wheel Drive Association has a list of local clubs. Telephone: 800-448-3932 (toll free); Web site: www.ufwda.org

4-Wheeling America   307 North Ash Street, Fruita, Colorado 81521-2316. 970-858-3468 (tel). E-mail: bbwa4@bb4wa.com; Web site: www.bb4wa.com

This company offers group and private courses in off-road driving. It also sponsors back-country trips and training events in other states. The off-road training event in the Moab Desert, Utah, is open to all types of vehicles.

Entry fee: about $500 for three days, plus $75 for each passenger twelve years and older. This includes training, lunch, dinner, and T-shirts.

Overland Experts   112 Hemlock Valley Road, East Haddam, Connecticut 06423. 877-931-3343 (tel). E-mail: bruce@ overlandexperts.com; Web site: www.overlandexperts.com

Overland Experts founder Bruce Elfstrom is a biologist who learned something about four-wheel drives traveling around the world as a scientist. The company offers beginners and advanced four-wheel-drive training at their private course in Connecticut, which includes log steps, rock climbs, side-slide traverses, downhill slaloms, controlled water courses, and a variety of situations similar to those you are likely to meet in the woods. Overland also offers four-wheel-drive trips in Africa and snowy Iceland. Contact for prices.

JEEPS

Jeep Jamborees occur around the country. Bring your Jeep and ride in a kind of caravan in the wilderness. The best part is the other folks you meet; everyone shares Jeep knowledge and will help out if you have a problem.

At Camp Jeep, a summer weekend get-together for Jeep families, you can do four-wheeling, and learn more about your Jeep and how to make back-road adjustments. Plus, there is a lot for the entire family: concerts, kayaks, swimming, barbecue, fireworks, and meeting other Jeep owners. Go to Camp Jeep at www.jeep.com. Or call 800-789-JEEP [5337].

For both the camp and jamboree events, go to the Web site, www.jeepjamboreeusa.com, and click on Events for the schedules.

For Land Rovers: 800-864-9180; Web site: www.4x4center.com. See also www.classic4x4.net.

Off-Road Tours

Wide Open Baja Off Road Adventures   888-788-2252. Web site: www.wideopenbaja.com

Leaving from San Diego or Cabo San Lucas, this company provides a total package in beautiful Baja California that includes their off-road race vehicle, luxury accommodations in resort hotels, a chase crew, a professional guide, safety equipment, and spare parts. You bring your driver's license and driving cool. Scuba is possible during downtime. They will also handle the details if you want to enter the Score Baja 1000 desert endurance race.

Four days, with three days of driving on empty beaches, forests, and canyons, from Cabo San Lucas: about $3,500. Other options from $2,500 to $5,500.

TANKS

Steve Parker Off Road Entertainments Ltd.
44 Wood Hey Grove, Syke, Rochdale, Lancashire OL12 9UA,
United Kingdom. 011 +44 (01) 706 854222 (tel). Web site: www.
militaryvehicledrive.co.uk

If you are in England, between the ages of twenty-one and
seventy, and have a driver's license, meet Steve Parker on the first
Sunday of every month from April to October and drive on a special course in any of the following off-road vehicles: a twenty-two-
ton AEC Militant Tank, a Volvo Snowcat, an Abbot Self-Propelled
Gun, a six-wheeled amphibious Alvis Stalwart, and a Land Rover
with a difference. Parker specializes in Land Rovers, and has an
unusual collection of large, decommissioned military vehicles.

One full fun day, including breakfast, snacks throughout the day,
and lunch at the local pub: £130 (about $195).

Guided Tours

Grand Prix Tours   1071 Camelback Street, Newport Beach,
California 92660-3228. 800-400-1998 (toll free); 949-717-3333
(tel); 949-717-3344 (fax). E-mail: information@gptours.com;
Web site: www.gptours.com

Grand Prix Tours will guide you to all the big ones—NASCAR
in Daytona, Formula One in Monaco, the Indy 500, Le Mans, and
lots of other important races around the world. Your guides will be
former champions, such as F-1 World Champion Phil Hill,
NASCAR legend Buddy Baker, and sportscar champion Derek Bell.
Get great tickets to events, go behind the scenes and hear the
insider stories, and attend parties with racing celebrities. Let Grand
Prix take care of lodging and meals, too.

Prices range from about $300 to $7,000, depending on the race.

Roadtrips   800-191 Lombard Avenue, Winnipeg, Manitoba,
R3B OX1, Canada. 800-465-1765 (toll free); 204-957-1241 (fax).
E-mail: info@roadtrips.com; Web site: www.roadtrips.com

Roadtrips will take care of all your needs to attend an auto-racing event, as well as other sports events throughout the world.

EXPENSIVE CARS

Mille Miglia Tour

Posh Journeys   530 East Patriot Boulevard, #172, Reno, Nevada 89511. 775-852-5105 (tel/fax). E-mail: contact@poshjourneys.com; Web site: www.poshjourneys.com

This tour incorporates the best of Italy interwoven with views of the Mille Miglia, a race with some of Italy's most spectacular expensive, vintage cars.

The Mille Miglia was run annually from 1927 to 1957. Revived in 1977, it now comprises about 370 of the world's most dazzling vintage sports cars that race a route through village, town, and city, from Brescia to Rome to Tuscany and back to Brescia—about a thousand miles in two and a half days. The cars gather to begin the race in the Brescia Piazza.

Your tour starts in Brescia, about sixty miles east of Milan, where you stay at one of the official Mille Miglia hotels. Traveling in a sixteen-passenger, custom-built Mercedes-Benz coach, from there your tour goes to Mantua and Florence, where the cars will pass through the crowded streets. Then drive up through the Tuscan hills to Siena, and follow the Mille route across the Futa and Raticosa passes, where drivers are greeted with a great hoopla. Travel then to Modena, where you will visit the Lamborghini and Maserati factories.

Next morning visit the workshops and museum of Stanguellini, Italy's famous custom-car builder; and in the afternoon, drive to the fourteenth-century country castle of Mario Reghini for a special appointment to view his collection of 300 prized cars.

The next two days you visit the Galleria Ferrari in Maranello and the Alfa Romeo Museum in Arese. (Factory tours are dependent on their being open.)

If that's not enough cars, spend some time at the Monza racetrack.

Nine nights, including deluxe accommodation, meals, and grandstand tickets for the start of the Mille Miglia: about $3,500.

Smithsonian Study Tours   P.O. Box 23293, Washington, D.C. 20026-3293. 877-338-8687 (toll free); 202-357-4700 (tel); 202-633-9250 (fax). E-mail: tours@tsa.si.edu; Web site: smithsonianstudytours.org

This seminar takes a serious look at the development of the technology and design of Italy's spectacular sports cars.

Start in Turin with a tour of the Museo dell'Automobile and a visit to the auto design studio of Pinintarina. In Milan, visit the museum of Lancia, one of the first—1906—race cars ever made.

In Arese take a private tour of the Alfa Romeo factory museum. Next day drop in at the Monza racetrack, then drive over to Ferrari for a guided tour of the Galleria, before meeting up with the Mille Miglia in Modena. In the evening you will have a chance to meet some of the Mille drivers.

Spend the final day in the Lamborghini Factory Museum in Bologna, an amazing experience.

Ten days, including airfare from Newark, hotels, meals, lectures, and museums: about $5,200.

Ferrari Weekend

Whether or not you are contemplating buying one, try one out for the weekend.

Bespokes Classic Limited   West Barns, Fairclough Hall Farm, Halls Green, Weston, Nr. Stevenage SG4 7DP, United Kingdom. 011 +44 (0) 1462 791100 (tel); 011 +44 (0) 1462 790775 (fax). E-mail: info@bespokes.co.uk; Web site: www.bespokebreaks.com

This company has the best collection of the high-end automobiles on the planet. Graciously, they will arrange weekends with the car and the country cottage or hotel of your choice, for you to slip away enveloped in leather and luxury on your way to pure fantasy.

For example, take an Aston Martin or a Ferrari 328 GTS, and cross the moat to enter one of Queen Elizabeth I's castles (Amberley Castle, www.amberleycastle.co.uk), now made into a four-poster-bedded inn, each room outfitted with a Jacuzzi. (Gems like this abound for the cognoscenti; try www.english-country-cottages. co.uk.) But you can spend most of your weekend in the car, driving the countryside, or just sitting in it, marveling at details like the windshield wipers and door handles.

The above fantasy is about £1,200 (about $1,900 U.S.).

In the United States, try the Ferrari Club of America for ideas of what to do with your Ferrari: www.ferrariclubofamerica.org.

CHAPTER 9

THE CIRCUS

THE NEW CIRCUS

Nothing portrays fantasy as well as the New Circus. Not your father's Big Tent, the New Circus incorporates gymnasts, trapeze artists, actors, and musicians in situations that "transform the ordinary into the extraordinary." A combination of stage design, lighting, and the talent and willingness to experiment gives New Circus performers the ability to tricycle over the moon, turn into butterflies from caterpillars, and swim in imaginary oceans.

If nothing else, a course at the centers below will teach you how to play.

Circus Center of San Francisco   755 Frederick Street, San Francisco, California 94117. 415-759-8123 (tel); 415-759-8644 (fax). E-mail: sfsca@sfcircus.org; Web site: www. circuscenter.org

Chinese acrobatics use poles, teeterboards, and hoops, and give students the necessary focus, strength, and control to balance hand-to-hand and "walk" up poles. You can learn all levels as a prepro-fessional or recreational circus performer at the Circus Center. And that's not all. They will teach the intricacies of the flying trapeze in a curriculum-based program, all aspects of Russian aerial arts, as well as dance, movement, the trampoline, and juggling.

It can be done. The trapeze artist-to-be on the left made a few practice swings before connecting with the pro trapeze artist on the right. It was his first lesson. *(Photo by Anthony W. Jones, courtesy of Circus Center of San Francisco)*

One fascinating course is the Neutral Mask. Wearing a neutral mask, you must learn to leave behind all of your habitual methods of self-expression, and learn "economy of gesture and stillness in activity."

A twelve-week program might induce you to compete for a spot in the Center's New Pickle Circus: about $220 to $400. Drop-in juggling on Sunday nights: $2. Youth programs as well.

The Circus Space Coronet Street, London N1 6HD, United Kingdom. 011 +44 (0) 20 7739 9522 (tel); 011 +44 (0) 20 7729 9422 (fax). E-mail: info@thecircusspace.co.uk; Web site: www.thecircusspace.co.uk

At this transformed former power station in downtown London, acrobats tumble, aerialists fly, and jugglers juggle. Mimes and unicyclists practice, all preparing for their BA (Hon) in Circus Arts, an intensive two-year program.

Aside from serious pros preparing for the circus, "Absolute Beginners" are welcome (next up is "Beginner") to join classes, as are families and corporations. The Circus Space believes that the corporate team that flies together on the trapeze bonds, and they give a popular three-hour trapeze/acrobatic balance/clown workshop that teaches so much trust the team has its "graduation" picture taken in a human pyramid.

If you're in London, drop in for the Saturday morning Introduction to Circus Skills, and fly the trapeze, juggle, and do acrobatic balancing to your heart's delight. Three hours: £40 (about $63 U.S.). Other classes are on a drop-in basis: about £9 (about $15 U.S.) a class.

CLOWN SCHOOLS

California

The Clown Conservatory   Circus Center at San Francisco, 755 Frederick Street, San Francisco, California 94117. 415-759-8123 (tel). Contact: Peggy Ford. E-mail: paganrites@aol.com; Web site: www.circuscenter.org

This unique one-year program is the only professional clown training program in the country. Send a letter stating your interest, with a photograph, a résumé, and three references. Auditions for entrance are held in the spring. About $8,000, with opportunity for work/study.

Throughout the year, Circus Center gives workshops in clowning. Some offered in the past include The Clown Chakra, taught by Mister YooWho (Moshe Cohen). Drawing on a variety of clown traditions, including Native American and Japanese, Cohen explores "the physical and spiritual elements" of expression. Leslie Felbain has taught Le Jeu, in which students explore neutrality and expressiveness in "the essence of theatre, which is play."

A youth program for clowns is held in the summer.

Minnesota

Moosecamp P.O. Box 700, Maple Lake, Minnesota 55358.
E-mail: priscilla@mooseburger.com; Web site: www.
mooseburger.com

Tricia Bothun (aka Priscilla Mooseburger) and her experienced clown staff offer a week-long summer camp for clowns at all stages of their careers, professional and casual, to help you develop "your unique clown self." Joining an international group, clowns take classes in clown skills, movement, sight gags, ventriloquism, balloons, costumes, wigs, and magic, and have a chance to develop and present their own skits.

Price depends on your choice of lodging at Moosecamp, near Lake Sylvia in the Minnesota woods: about $450 to $650.

If you can't make it to the camp, catch Priscilla Mooseburger on the road. She and her staff give weekend workshops around the country. Check for schedule.

Clowning, says Priscilla, "is about the joy you bring to others."
Three days: about $100.

RODEO CLOWNS

Sankey Rodeo Schools 3943 Sycamore Church Road, Branson, Missouri 65616. 417-334-2513 (tel); 417-332-0676 (fax). E-mail: info@sankeyrodeo.com; Web site: www.sankeyrodeo.com

Rodeo clowns are about the closest thing to bullfighters in the Western arena. Despite red noses and curly blond wigs, clowns must divert the attention of the raging bull after its rider has quit, to keep the rider from being trampled.

Aside from distracting the bull, the clown must be adept at amusing the crowd by taking on a bull alone in the arena. Wearing track shoes, the clown uses all of his athletic skills to avoid the bull, including jumping into a barrel, which the bull will attack and sometimes throw around, thrusting its horns in anger.

Often a rodeo clown will ride a horse dressed as a man, who will suddenly lean forward or sit down or roll over, a true comic partner with the clown. In fact, rodeo clown horses are among the most highly trained in the West, capable of performing movements that only dressage horses are trained to do.

At Sankey Rodeo School's centers around the country, three- and four-day courses are offered in rodeo clownship. They will teach you everything from protection from the bull to entertainment clowning to "working the barrel." Sankey also sells protective everything, including a jaw-joint protector.

Three or four days: $350 to $450.

JOIN THE CIRCUS

Cirque du Soleil Montreal, Canada. E-mail: casting@ cirquedusoleil.com; Web site: www.cirquedusoleil.com

The Canadian Cirque du Soleil has five global touring and three resident circuses, and is always looking for onstage premier athletes, circus artists, musicians, dancers, clowns, and singers.

Send an application to their e-mail site, and if they are interested, they will hire you immediately or ask for an audition, during which you will be asked to perform alone and with a group and in improv situations. Average age is twenty-eight; the oldest is sixty-nine, and the youngest is five. Once hired, you sign a two-year contract and receive a competitive salary and insurance.

Performers give an average of ten performances a week, with the Dralion, the Quidam, the Vareka, the Saltimbanco, or the Allegria companies. In Las Vegas, performers are a part of O at the Bellagio Hotel or Mystère at Treasure Island Hotel. La Nouba performs at Disney World Resort in Orlando.

The Cirque has a need for the backstage crowd, too, everything from riggers, costume makers, even shoemakers, and lacemakers. Visit their site to connect.

CHAPTER 10

COOKING AND WINE TASTING

Whether your culinary desire is to whip up flawless *amuses bouche*, or catch olives in your apron shaken from a tree by a young farm-hand, it is possible to fulfill your cooking fantasy, probably more easily than any other. All over the world, chefs open their doors to students eager to learn not only about food, but about the people who catch the fish, collect the shellfish or the truffles, and cultivate the vines, bees, garlic, wheat fields, cheeses, and olives that supply the elements for most menus.

Because the operative word is *fresh*, the basic thing you need to ask is when the harvest occurs and what is the best season. Most harvests take place from late September to early November, and are usually variable within a couple of weeks, depending on local weather.

STUDY WITH A MASTER CHEF

Le Cordon Bleu   Director of Admissions, 8, rue Leon Delhomme, Paris 75015, France. 800-457-CHEF [2433] (from the U.S. and Canada). 011 +33 (0) 1-53-68-22-50 (tel); 011 +33 (0) 1-48-56-03-96 (fax). E-mail: info@cordonbleu.edu; Web site: www.cordonbleu.edu

On a four-day workshop, you work with master chefs. Wearing a

Learning the art of fine chopping with a chef's knife is as challenging as learning how to throw a sword. Accuracy counts. In bright red aprons, chef and student practice at the Ecole de Cuisine of Le Manoir aux Quat' Saisons, Oxford. *(Courtesy of Le Manoir aux Quat' Saisons)*

compulsory uniform, you join a dozen other students for a cooking demonstration in an amphitheater, followed by a tasting to develop the palate.

Then students retire to their individual work stations, where they must reproduce what they have seen. Each station is outfitted with a refrigerated marble surface, four-burner stove top, plus an oven and refrigerator. At day's end, your product is evaluated by the chef.

The recognized acme of cooking schools, the esteemed Cordon Bleu opened its Parisian doors in 1895 with the express purpose of training cooking staff for the rich, in the culinary traditions of the legendary French chef Auguste Escoffier (inventor of dishes cleverly named after famous patrons, such as *pêche melba*).

Today Le Cordon Bleu maintains cooking schools around the world, including Orlando, Florida, where food enthusiasts study to become professional chefs or simply to refine their understanding of good food. French cooking is still considered the best place to start to become a true gourmet.

Gourmet Sessions, courses intended for the amateur and non-professional cook, are offered for a half-day to four days at Le Cordon Bleu in Paris. One-day sessions, for example, include a visit to an open-air market, where you will buy fruits and vegetables "coaxed from the earth," and whose true flavors you must learn to "coax" from them. In the afternoon, you will learn how to make one dish, such as a cheese *soufflé, salade de coquillages, profiterolles au chocolat*, among others.

Start with the basics, for example, bread baking. For three days you learn the "secret techniques of the sacred processes" of making bread, from choosing the proper yeast, distinguishing from among various flours, learning how to shape and bake a loaf, and the subtle rhythms involved in coaxing the volatile ingredients into bakable shapes. You make crusty *baguette, pain de campagne, pain de mie, pain decoré*, and a lot of other types.

On the fourth day, light the fire under a pot of chocolate and create *Viennoiserie*, delicate pastries such as Napoleons.

Four days, including all instruction and the food that you actually make (for which they provide an airtight container): about 765 Euros (about US$765).

COOK WITH A PREMIER CHEF

Italy

Scuola Del Pettirosso, Abruzzo.   Book through:
The Parker Company, 152 The Lynnway, Seaport Landing, Lynn, Massachusetts 01902. 800-280-2811 (toll free); 781-596-8282 (tel); 781-596-3125 (fax). E-mail: pettirosso@theparkercompany. com; Web site: www.adventures-in-culture.com

Master Chef Angelo Chiavaroli, known to the Italian media as *Lo Chef del Buongusto*—the Chef of Good Taste—cooks at the Pettirosso Restaurant of the luxury hotel Montinope in Spoltore, Abruzzo, known as the gourmet capital of Italy. There, for six days, settle in and join the chef to learn a thing or two about food.

It starts with instruction at the market, where you learn to understand good from bad on the vegetable and fruit stands, how to pick the best cheeses, and how to choose the freshest fish and the best herbs. Then visit Mario Tortella's award-winning olive groves with sampling.

For the next three mornings you are in the kitchen for some serious hands-on study of sauces, desserts, great pasta, breads, and fine roasts. Afternoons, you visit wineries, a *pastifici* (where pasta is made), vegetable farms, and olive groves. Evenings, dine in splendor on five-star gourmet cuisine at the restaurant.

On Day 6, thoroughly acquainted with what Chef Chiavaroli knows as good food and newly skilled in culinary techniques, you and members of your small class will create, cook, and serve dinner in the Pettirosso Restaurant, with great fanfare, ending with the awarding of diplomas. Graduates get a chef's hat and apron.

Seven days, including lodging, food, cooking instruction, and excursions: about $2,800 per person, double occupancy; about $3,000, single.

United Kingdom

Le Manoir Ecole de Cuisine   Le Manoir aux Quat' Saisons, Church Road, Great Milton, Oxford OX44 7PD, United Kingdom, 011 +44 (01) 844 278881 (tel); 011 +44 (01) 844 278847 (fax). E-mail: lemanoir@blanc.co.uk; Web site: www.manoir.com

Master Chef Raymond Blanc opens the kitchens of his Manoir aux Quat' Saisons in Oxford to students at all levels of expertise and teaches them to create. "Give a pianist two other notes, or give a painter two complementary colors. Then you have the power to create a new world," says Blanc.

In a school located next door to the kitchens that service the Michelin two-star restaurant, Blanc and School Director Stephen Bulmer give one- and two-day courses that teach everything involved with giving a good dinner party, or in serving a traditional Christmas dinner, as well as the basics of vegetarian cooking, fish and shellfish, and two new courses, La Nutrition et la Cuisine Moderne (good nutrition despite a lack of time to really cook) and Fusion Cuisine (a blend of the best of Asian cooking, e.g., crab and lemongrass bisque or roast duck with tamarind, which is fast, attractive, and healthful).

The Dinner Party course, for example, will teach you how to prepare and serve *Tartare* smoked salmon, *Carre d'Agneau, Gateau d'Aubergine,* as well as *soufflés,* Thai fish soup, and for dessert, roast bananas and lychee nuts.

Prices vary, and include the room. The two-day Vegetarian course: £830 ($1,245) per person, £1,500 ($2,200) for two sharing the room. The one-day Christmas Dinner course: £450 ($675) per person, £810 ($1,215) for two.

The price includes accommodation at the Manoir and Blanc's seven-course Menu Gourmand evening dinner.

TRAVEL WITH A CHEF

Bike Riders   P.O. Box 130254, Boston, Massachusetts 02113.
800-473-7040 (toll free); 617-723-2355 (fax). E-mail: info@
bikeriderstours.com; Web site: www.bikeriderstours.com.

Bike Riders' hallmark Guest Chef Series combines intimate cooking and tasting classes, plus the presence of a chef accompanying
bicycle tours in France or Italy. These relaxed tours allow you to
shop in farmers' markets, learning from the chef what to buy, then
spend the afternoon cooking. In Provence, for example, your Relais
et Chateaux inns are never more than thirty-five miles apart.

As you bike through the sensuous air of Provence, you stop at
vineyards for lunches with delicacies like asparagus wrapped in
jambon cru and fresh *tartes des abricots*. Visit an escargot farm and
learn how to prepare the perfect garlic butter to serve the snails in.
Tour wine caves in Côtes-du-Rhone villages; and stop for a salt tasting, where you will actually be able to detect the differences among
sea salts of the Camargue.

Then, your palate refined, your skills honed by the chef, your
body toned by the bicycling, you prepare feasts for the evening
dinner, sumptuous meals such as roast lamb with wild mushrooms
and purple artichokes, replete with garlic and the herbs of Provence.

Seven days, Level B (moderate), fifteen to thirty-five miles a day,
including first-class lodging and meals: about $3,000 per person.
Bike rentals: $150. Begin and end in Avignon.

COOK AROUND THE WORLD

Venice, Italy

The Venice Carnivale

Bev Gruber's Everyday Gourmet Traveler
5053 NE 178th Street, Seattle, Washington 98155. 888-636-1602
(toll free); 206-363-1602 (tel/fax). E-mail: bev@gourmetravel.com;
Web site: www.gourmetravel.com

Carnivale in Venice in late February displays the glories of Renaissance pagentry with costumes and white ceramic masks, street magicians and musicians, jugglers, party givers, and partygoers.

Bev Gruber, who gives behind-the-scenes cooking tours in France, Italy, and North America, takes a small group to Venice. On two afternoons, you join a ninth-generation Venetian lady for cooking classes in her Venetian palazzo, and learn how to make perfect tiramisu. In addition to visits to pastry makers, you see artisans making masks, paper, and glass.

But the Carnivale! You witness the Grand Opening Costume Parade, the Flight of the Doves in St. Mark's Square, fireworks, and for the great finale, attend the Grand Costume Ball.

Nine days, including lodging and meals: about $3,000, double occupancy. International airfare is not included.

Sicily, Italy

Cook Like a Grandmother

To Grandmother's House We Go   Sue Baldassano. 718-768-6197 (tel); 212-645-5170, ext. 111 (tel). E-mail: info@tograndmothershousewego.com; Web site: www. tograndmothershousewego.com.

In Palermo, Nora Pottino, a Native Sicilian, invites you into her kitchen to help prepare dinner with items such as basil and anchovy pesto, pasta with sardines, and salad with fresh Sicilian olives. Learn the tricks as you help to cook, then light the candles on the terrace and carry your glass of wine to the table to join the family for dinner.

Legacy cooking, or traditional home cooking, is a dying art, says New Yorker Sue Baldassano, who pays tribute "to the unsung cooks (mostly grandmothers) who have managed to keep it alive." These days, legacy cooking comes under the heading of comfort food.

In small groups to Oaxaca, Mexico, and Palermo, Italy, To Grandmother's House We Go introduces you to the women in their kitchens, where food traditions are passed from generation to generation.

In Sicily, native Marcella Croce, educated in the United States, accompanies the trip and will give a slide lecture on the twenty-five centuries of Sicilian food. Over seven days, Croce, Giovanni Matranga, and Sue Baldassano take you to ancient temples and modern cannoli and carob candy factories. Taste spicy seafood couscous, part of Sicily's Arabic past. Visit (and shop at) the colorful ceramics workshops, see pastry-making demonstrations, and take tours of a tuna fishery, a winery, a saltworks museum, as well as monasteries and cathedrals. Each evening, head back to Nora's kitchen.

You will know Sicily after this tour, and you will have a deep feeling for the warmth of its kitchens and its people.

Seven days, including hotel lodging, meals, cooking classes, and excursions: about $2,000 per person, double occupancy.

Spain: The Basques

Cobblestone Small Group Tours   757 Saint Charles Avenue, Suite 203, New Orleans, Louisiana 70130. 800-227-7889 (toll free); 504-522-7888 (tel); 504-525-1273 (fax). E-mail: info@ cobblestonetours.com; Web site: www.cobblestonetours.com

Tucked in the mountains in the north of Spain, Basque cooking has clung to ancient styles of cooking; and the vines that produce the grapes for the acclaimed La Rioja and Navarra wines predate the Romans.

This trip with native-born or resident guides introduces you to dishes such as prawns and morels cooked together in scented olive oil, or clams and artichokes in parsley sauce. You visit a private gastronomic society in which Basque men gather to cook for their friends.

On trips from Haro to San Sebastien, visit ancient bodegas and one designed a couple of years ago by Frank Gehry. You eat at world-famous restaurants and see little-known museums. From Guernica to Bilbao, you will concentrate on the amazing combination of red peppers, seafood, cheeses, and artists such as Henry Moore, Pablo Picasso, and Frank Gehry.

Seven days, including deluxe hotels, food, and guides: about $3,000, double occupancy. Airfare is not included.

Ouro Preto, Brazil

Cuisine International   P.O. Box 25228, Dallas, Texas 75225. 214-373-1161 (tel); 214-373-1162 (fax). E-mail: cuisineint@ aol.com; Web site: www.cuisineinternational.com

Cuisine International presents food/culture travel around the world. At the Brazilian Academy of Cooking in Ouro Preto, a seventeenth-century Colonial town in the mountains of Minas Gerais, you study with expert cook Yara Castro Roberts, a host for the PBS/WGHB cook show series and a second-generation chef educated in Boston and in Paris.

In classwork, learn the art of Minas Gerais and Bahai cooking and Brazilian cakes and pastry making, candy and candied fruits. Visit a Brazilian coffee plantation and sugar cane distillery; and hear lectures on Brazilian culture. Each night, dinner is at a gourmet restaurant. Lots of Brazilian music and fun.

Seven days: about $3,000, double occupancy.

Santorini, Greece

Rosemary Barron's Greece. Please contact by E-mail: rbgreece@ aol.com; Web site: www.rosemarybarronsgreece.com

The author of the best-selling book *Flavours of Greece*, Rosemary Barron gives cooking classes on Santorini that have been voted one of the Top Ten Cookery Courses by *Condé Nast Traveler*. Introduced to the Minoan civilization on Crete while on an archaeological dig several years ago, Barron realized the food was essentially unchanged today.

Santorini is a whitewashed island a few miles north of Crete in the blue Aegean, where occasional winds and rough seas affect the seasonality of the fruits and vegetables and often keep fishermen's boats at the dock. Within these parameters, nevertheless, Santorinians have produced superb menus.

In the five-day workshop Ancient Wisdom, Modern Tables, for example, you learn how to make dishes such as bay-scented chicken with figs, or brine-cured bonito with capers. You will taste the best of farmhouse cheeses, local wines, and olive oils with local experts.

Workshops are taught at the Selene Restaurant by the owners of the restaurant and by Rosemary Barron.

Six days, including lodging in a small pension-style hotel, meals, and local transport: about £1,300 ($1,950), double occupancy.

Koh Samui Island, Thailand

Tasting Places Limited   Unit 108, Buspace Studios, Conlan Street, London W10 5AP, United Kingdom. 877-695 2469 (toll free in the U.S.); 011 +44 (0) 20 7460 0077 (tel); 011 +44 (0) 20 7460 0029 (fax). E-mail: ss@tastingplaces.com; Web site: www.tastingplaces.com

Southern Thailand is graced with white beaches, coconut palms, and a turquoise sea full of the fish you will learn how to prepare Thai-style. Imbued with subtle spices and exotic vegetables, much of southern Thai cooking derives from Malaysian immigrants.

In a shaded cooking place, each day you will cook things such as Gai Tom Ka (chicken coconut cream and galangal soup) or Tod Man Pla Gung (hot spicy fish and prawn cakes with cucumber and shallot dressing). On a special tour, visit the market, and special handicraft and furniture shops. During free time at your five-star resort, the Laem Set Inn, enjoy snorkeling or diving.

Eight days, including lodging, meals, classes, but not international airfare: from about £1,400 to £1,700 per person ($2,100 to $2,550), depending on the room.

New Mexico, the United States

Jane Butel Cooking School   125 Second Street NW, Albuquerque, New Mexico 87102. 800-472-8229 (toll free);

505-243-2622 (tel); 505-243-8297 (fax). E-mail: info@janebutel.com; Web site: www.janebutel.com

The author of sixteen cookbooks, Jane Butel unravels the mysteries of chilis in her courses on Southwestern cooking. Butel will explain the most commonly used of the 7,000 varieties of chili, how to judge a chili's "heat," and how to keep from being burned by chili seeds. Recipes include blue-corn tamales, and dishes such as grilled clams with green chili, chipotle garlic mashed potatoes, and chicken tortilla chowder.

Held in the kitchen of La Poseda Albuquerque, Conrad Hilton's first hotel, courses take place in the morning, with afternoons reserved for visits to local pueblos, shopping in boutiques in Old Town Albuquerque, sightseeing, and visiting some of the magnificent vistas in the high desert. Balloon Week in October is a spectacular time to be there, when thousands of private- and corporate-owned hot-air balloons take to the skies. Courses range from one day or weekend to one week. You will leave Albuquerque with a great respect for Southwestern cuisine.

Seven days, including instruction, lodging, and meals: about $2,000.

PICK OLIVES

Tasty Tuscany Patrizia and Paolo Vecchia, Via Agliati 123, 56036, Agliata—Palaia, Pisa, Italy. 011 +39 0587 622 531 (tel); 011 +39 0587 622 186 (tel/fax). E-mail: patrizia@tastytuscany.com; Web site: www.tastytuscany.com

Olive Oil, The Tuscan Gold gives you one day to experience olive picking with the local olive growers. At the olive mill, you learn how olive oil is made and graded, and receive two bottles of fresh extra virgin olive oil. In cooking classes you learn how olive oil is integral to Italian cooking as you prepare Tuscan dishes; a class in oil tasting will teach you to distinguish different grades.

Patrizia and Paolo Vecchia combine tours of the archaeology, architecture, and art of Tuscany with gastronomic courses, interspersed with visits to abandoned villages, Etruscan tombs, and antiques markets, as well as wine tastings and truffle hunts. "Food tastes like the place it's made and the people who prepare it," the Vecchias say. "It has the same color and the same music."

Seven nights, including lodging, classes, and some meals: about $2,000.

HUNT TRUFFLES

Les Liaisons Delicieuses. 877-966-1810 (toll free); 202-966-1810 (tel); 202-966-4091 (fax). E-mail: info@cookfrance.com; Web site: www.cookfrance.com

With Chef Pierre Corre of the Auberge de la Truffe in Sorges, the Dordogne, spend a winter week hunting truffles and tasting fois gras, at the height of the season.

On the first morning, visit the fois gras market in Perigueux, and spend the afternoon learning to make your own fois gras. Next morning, visit the Truffle Museum (it exists); then join the man who's been doing it all his life, the truffle hunter, and head off into the woods, where his dog knows where and how to root about to find the tiny fungus. Holding the warty little balls in your hand, you learn how to tell good truffles from bad. Next day, make truffle dishes.

This cooking tour takes you to a fourteenth-century walnut mill, where you see walnut oil produced, to the vineyards of Bergerac, a cheese farm, and the Lascaux cave paintings. And if you would like to have it arranged, join pheasant hunters for a day.

Seven days, including lodging at the Auberge, meals, and classes: about $2,300 per person. Group size limited to eight.

HUNT MUSHROOMS

Mexican Mushroom Tours   APDO #73, Tlaxcala, Tlax. 900000, Mexico. 011 +52 246-461-8829 (tel/fax) E-mail: erik@ mexmush.com; Web site: www.mexmush.com

No, this is not about *those* mushrooms; this is a serious trip to collect some of the hundreds of varieties of mushrooms that grow in various regions of Mexico.

Originally a tour for the North American Mycological Society, the mushroom-picking tour caught on when several participants asked to repeat it and brought their friends. Foraging in fields at 7,000 feet and above, participants learned to identify mushrooms, heard presentations and lectures, learned how to cook them, and enjoyed them cooked into recipes at gourmet restaurants.

According to Gundi Jeffrey, who with Erik Portsmouth, Canadians living in Mexico, organized Mexican Mushroom Tours, amateur and professional mycologists will be able to hunt mushrooms at other locales in Mexico, such as the jungle in Veracruz, combining it with white-water rafting. They will also hunt for mushrooms among archaeological ruins, and stay in two sixeenth-century coffee-producing haciendas. (Check their Web site—a mushroom tour to Copper Canyon is in the works.)

Trips include visits to indigenous local villagers and markets to understand the impact of mushrooms on Mexicans.

Seven nights, including lodging, meals, and instruction: about $1,400.

THE GREAT GARLIC COOK-OFF

Gilroy Garlic Festival Association, Inc. P.O. Box 2311, Gilroy, California 95020. 408-842-1625 (tel). E-mail: clove@gilroygarlicfestival.com; Web site: www.gilroygarlicfestival.com

Creamy Cancun Roasted Garlic Soup with Fiery Garlic Shrimp and Garlic Spring Rolls with Garlicky-Lime Sauce are some of the previous winners of the day-long competition that takes place every July in Gilroy, Garlic Capital of the World.

Send in your garlic recipes in February, and if the panel chooses them, you are invited to cook them on Festival Day. Celebrity judges will decide the winner, after tasting. If you win, you are crowned with—guess what—a wreath of garlic. And you receive a few dollars as well.

Wine Tasting

Wines depend on what French vintners call *terroir*, which means not only the soil where the vines take root, but all the influences that encourage the grape on the vine, from the weather to when grapes are harvested. A successful wine has something good going on in its *terroir*.

Italy

Palio Tours   1825 Ponce de Leon, 438, Coral Gables, Florida 33134. 888-495-8502 (toll free). E-mail: webmaster@paliotours.com; Web site: www.paliotours.com

Etruscans were the first to cultivate vines and crush grapes into wine in the Chianti region of Italy more then 2,500 years ago. Chianti Classico reached markets for the first time in 1924 after a group of thirty-three producers formed the Consorzio del Marchio Storico. Today the smooth deep red wine is composed of four grape varieties, mostly Sangiovese, which is harvested in September.

Palio's Wine Celebration Tour introduces you to the real meaning of a wine during harvest season in a region where it has been important for hundreds of years. For seven days in Tuscany, visit local wineries in castles in Chianti and take part in village street celebrations with theatrical productions and fanfare, some going back to the Renaissance. Palio will customize your tour for you as well.

Seven days, including lodging, and some meals: about $1,900.

South Africa

Cape Wineland Tours   3263 Juniper Lane, Falls Church, Virginia 22044. 888-868-7706 (toll free); 703-532-8820 (tel/fax). E-mail: info@capewinetours.com; Web site: www.capewinetours.com

In the 1600s Dutch farmers introduced muscat grapes to the steep hills and valleys sloping above the Atlantic near Cape Town. South African Constantia wine became a favorite of many Europeans, including Napoleon (who probably had easy access to it during his exile on Saint Helena). Attacked by a mold in the late 1800s, the vines perished, but Constantia wine remained a legend, until 1980 when the old estate was bought, and the industry was rekindled by planting three acres with new *muscat de Frontignac* vines.

Constantia put South Africa on the wine map, but today several wine districts produce wines that are the new and vigorous kids on the block.

Cape Wineland's Wine Lover's Tour takes you to tastings on fifteen premier wine estates in five wine districts. If you love wine and are interested in its cultivation, this is a chance to be guided deeply into it. Five days of "experience-based learning" with wine experts include a chance to taste more than 200 wines.

The estates are relaxed, and the guides are well informed. You spend two days in Cape Town, as well as a day in Hermanus on the Overberg coast, where southern right whales breed; and (for $1,400 for two for three days) at the Bushmans Kloof Wilderness Reserve in the Cederberg Mountains for game drives and hiking.

Nine days, including lodging, some meals, and airfare from the East Coast of the United States: about $5,300. Cape Winelands will also arrange a pre- or post-tour "Wine Lover's" excursion on the *Queen Elizabeth II* out of Cape Town: five nights: about $2,800 per person, double occupancy.

California: Napa and Sonoma Valleys

Bicycle Adventures   P.O. Box 11219, Olympia, Washington 98508. 800-443-6060 (toll free); 360-786-0989 (tel); 360-786-9661 (fax). E-mail: office@bicycleadventures.com; Web site: www.bicycleadventures.com

Even without vineyards, the Napa and Sonoma Valleys, with their easy hills and broad fields with craggy trees, are beautiful places to visit. California Wine Country, Bicycle Adventures' six-day tour, starts and ends in Bodega, California, and bikes through redwood forests, past fields of lavender to Sonoma, the oldest wine district on the Spanish missionaries' route north, where you visit the oldest wine estates of Sebastiani and Buena Vista.

Biking into Napa, you lunch at the estate of Clos du Val, then spend two days at a spa in Callistoga, the site of natural healing springs, a favorite of Russian visitors in the early 1900s.

The next night, head to the Napa Valley Culinary Institute of America *Wine Spectator* Greystone Restaurant, where Chef Pilar Sanchez offers up seven courses, each served with different wine tastings. Then, bike back to Sonoma Valley and private visits with estate owners, with a stop at Korbel Champagne Cellars.

The tour averages about forty miles a day, and is open to all levels of biking ability. Bicycle Adventures will rent you bicycles.

Six days, including luxury accommodations, meals, and van support: about $2,000.

STOMP GRAPES

You do have to wear shoes, so you can't have the pleasure of feeling the grapes squish through your toes. But if you want to get down and dirty with grapes, and learn a lot about vines, grapes, and wines, try these places:

Texas

Messina Hof Winery & Resort   4545 Old Reliance Road, Bryan, Texas 77808. 979-778-9463, ext. 34 (tel). E-mail: event@ messinahof.com; Web site: www.messinahof.com

Deep in the Hill Country of Texas, 90 miles west of Houston, 160 miles north of San Antonio, is a touch of Italy. The descendants of winemaker Paul Bonarrigo carried six generations of wine-making from Messina, Sicily, to Texas, where they produced their first vintage in 1983.

Harvest time is celebration time at Messina Hof, when they open the vineyards to anyone interested in first picking grapes, then stomping grapes at the crush pad. (Your final stomp is on a white T-shirt, which is yours to prove you crushed grapes.)

Gather after that for a sumptuous harvest luncheon, followed by a wine-and-cheese-pairing seminar.

You begin at 8:00 A.M. with a brief orientation. Reservations are imperative. Shoes are "highly recommended."

The whole enchilada: about $60.

Oregon

Cherry Hill Vineyard and Wine Camp   7867 Crowley Road, Rickreall, Oregon 97371. 503-949-8805 (tel). E-mail: info@ cherryhillvineyard.com; Web site: www.cherryhillvineyard.com

Owners Jan and Mike Sweeney cooked up the idea when they bought the property in Oregon's esteemed Pinot Noir district, and then realized the hardest thing about their wine camp was explaining it. One suggestion was "a silver-spoon summer camp for wine-lovers," and that captures the nine brand-new, air-conditioned rustic cabins in which grape pickers are housed.

Between June and November, you can be part of the wine team. The best part is that you get to choose what to do: learn about viticulture or which food goes with which wine; or hit the fields ("labor camp") and tend the vines, pick off insects, or at harvest, help pluck the grapes (and become a paid worker).

If you get tired, try fly-fishing in their seven-acre lake, or bike along some breathtaking trails, or get more serious training in vine-yards. Meals are held in the community lodge, followed by discussions about wines of the Eola Hills in the Willamette Valley.

Cabin, one night: $250 for two people (two-night minimum).

TAKE A CULINARY TRIP

TCS Expeditions   2025 First Avenue, Suite 500, Seattle, Washington 98121-2176. 800-727-7477 (toll free); 206-727-7300 (tel); 206-727-7309 (fax). E-mail: travel@tcs-expeditions.com; Web site: www.tcs-expeditions.com

The History of Food & Wine is one of those landmark tours that happen when people dream big dreams. Based on the belief that food is "nutrition, medicine, aphrodiasic, and offering," TCS presents a tour by private jet that seeks to understand the historical interplay of culture and eating and drinking.

From London, the tour flies to France and the Champagne, Burgundy, and Beaujolais regions, where wine has been cultivated since before the Middle Ages. Then passengers are flown to Marrakesh to dine at Yacout, a world-renowned first-class restaurant serving traditional Moroccan food, and take tours of Moroccan markets.

From there, fly back to Porto, Portugal, and explore the region from which Henry the Navigator sailed to explore the West, and port wine was barreled and exported. Then fly to Umbria for tavernas, vineyards, and a presentation by Dr. Carlo Urbani, whose family has exported truffles for several generations. On to Istanbul, where East meets West; then to Saint Petersburg, with dinner in Peter the Great's palace.

Fourteen days, including jet, lectures by distinguished experts, lodging, and meals: about $28,000.

CHAPTER 11

COWBOY FANTASIES

Part of the American West fantasy is that the red rock hills, high desert scrub, canyons, and valley steams are for the most part as empty as they were when cowboys, Indians, outlaws, and sheriffs rode across them. For the most part, they are still empty. Wild horses toss their manes and fly over ridges and meadows; cowboys still herd their cattle and sleep under the stars. What you learn here is that it's a big world where the wild must be both tamed and maintained.

BE THE SHERIFF OR THE OUTLAW

Posse Week, New Mexico. Contact: Hidden Trails, 202-380 West 1st Avenue, Vancouver, British Columbia V5Y 3T7 Canada. 888-9-TRAILS (toll free); 604-323-1141 (tel); 604-323-1148 (fax). E-mail: info@hiddentrails.com; Web site: hiddentrails.com

You can act out your wildest Pat Garrett or Billy the Kid fantasy for a week in western New Mexico, using "fancy horsemanship, nerves of steel, and a crafty mind."

Fly into Albuquerque, then travel four and a half hours to a working ranch in the high country near the Gila National Forest. The first night you draw straws to pick your team and decide whether you're going to be a sheriff or an outlaw for the week. Sleep well. In the morning, pack up your horse.

Roundup Time: A cowboy kicks up dust in a roundup as the herd thunders into a corral. *(Roger Archibald)*

Outlaws leave first, with a few hours' gain on the sheriff's posse. But you both carry maps that cover the 125-square-mile area in which the outlaws have stashed six piles of gold. Trouble is, your map shows only five of the stashes; and the other team's map has the missing one. The goal: Get their map; get the six piles of gold; and if you're the posse, capture the outlaws. The first person back gets $500 (which is shared among teammates).

But it's not as easy as it sounds.

Outlaws are no good, so don't trust your partners. Yes, they might try to compromise your whereabouts to be the first back.

Through forest and canyon, you have to hurry. Nights you must sleep quietly, not letting the other team know where you are. This can mean no fire, just canned food, and cold nights. The weather will do anything, from sudden storms to snow squalls. One person must stand watch to make sure no one steals the horses, which of course the other team will try to do.

There is at least a half-day's riding between stashes, and you have to be able to read the land to know where you are. A ranch guide will never be far away, to make sure you stay on the right track. You can't quit in the middle of the hunt (unless you are sick or injured). If you need to sleep in a bed, you can stay in one of the two ranch camps on the range.

But how can you sleep? You're a target for ambush.

If nothing else, after this week, you will learn why the West was wild, and how difficult it was to survive either as a crook or a sheriff. But you will also increase your capacity for vigilance, strategizing, staying alive, and using all your smarts.

Orienteering experience is a great help in this adventure, as is tracking. Bring your steady nerves and sharp eye. If you were a middling rider before the game, you will be above average when you return. Most important, you need endurance.

Six nights, including transfer from Albuquerque, all meals, horse, and tack: about $1,000.

GO TO COWBOY SCHOOL

Arizona Cowboy College   Lorill Equestrian Center, 30208 North 152nd Street, Scottsdale, Arizona 85262. 888-330-8070 (toll free); 480-471-3151 (tel); 480-471-3530 (fax). E-mail: info@ cowboycollege.com; Web site: www.cowboycollege.com

If you are serious about wanting to be a cowboy, this is the place to experience the real thing. In a full and challenging week, you work side by side with real cowboys, helping them do what they do, which is get down and dirty with horses and cattle.

To start the week, you spend time working on your own riding ability and increasing your understanding of horses. By the end of the first day when you ride out for the evening, you will have learned how to rope and horseshoe.

By the end of the second day, you will participate in team-roping cattle, learn more horseshoeing, and at the end of the day, riding and roping. By the third day, you are deemed ready to go round up the cattle, which you will do for the next three days, spending the nights in a camp, taking care of your own horse.

On the final day, when you bring the herd back to the ranch, you will help brand the calves, and inoculate and dehorn the cattle (they will teach you how). No easy stuff here, but fully rewarding, and you will know if the smell of leather and dust and the feel of riding a horse beween six to ten hours a day are in your blood.

Six days, including lodging, camp equipment, horse, tack, meals, sun, and stars: about $1,500.

Learn Extreme Horsemanship

Blackhawk Adventures, Inc.   4337 East Fanfol Drive, Phoenix, Arizona 85028. 800-346-8717 (toll free); 602-996-5114 (tel). E-mail: info@cdiamondc.com; Web site: www.flapjack.com

At the C Diamond C Ranch on the Santa Fe Trail in northern New Mexico is the National Training Center for Extreme Horsemanship. Here you will learn more about horses than you thought possible with trainer Gary Clay and his staff. Open to all levels of riders, this training will teach you how to communicate with your horse, the different levels of a tamed horse ("broke" to trained-for-tricks), as well as the nuances involved in the union of human and horse.

Three days (minimum), including lodging at the beautiful ranch, where you can trail ride at your leisure: about $300 a day.

Join the Cattle Roundup

Cattle spend the summer in the mountains, or wherever they can keep cool. Throughout the West in the spring, cowboys gather up their cattle and corral them to the high country; and in the fall, round them back up for the trip back to the ranch. Except for keeping mavericks with the herd, the riding is generally easy over the long stretches, although you might spend six or more hours in the saddle. In the movies, Roy Rogers usually sings during cattle roundup rides.

As night falls, you pitch camp to cook over a fire, tell stories, play the harmonica, or recite poetry, before sleeping in tents or under the stars, listening to the occasional distant braying of the cattle or the snorting of your horse (your new partner) as it chews on the grass in the camp.

Back at the ranch, you might be called on to help brand the calves or castrate them (somebody has to provide Rocky Mountain oysters), or dehorn some bulls. It's all in a day's work.

Wyoming

Equitours P.O. Box 807, 10 Stainaker Street, Dubois, Wyoming 82513. 800-545-0019 (toll free); 307-455-3363 (tel); 307-455-2354 (fax). E-mail: Equitours@wyoming.com; Web site: www.ridingtours.com

At the Bitterroot roundup in Wyoming, join cowboys taking their herds to the mountains in July or bringing them back in September. The trick is, the cattle are spread out over fifty square miles, and those miles include high mountains, river valleys, or forests. Riding is slow, but you must be a good rider to negotiate varied terrain.

Wild game—lots of elk, deer, an occasional moose, and the ever-present (but when and where exactly?) grizzly bear—live here. Eight days, seven nights of camping, including all meals, horse, and beauty: about $1,800.

New Mexico

Copper Creek Cattle Round Ups, New Mexico. Hidden Trails, 202-380 West 1st Avenue, Vancouver, British Columbia V5Y 3T7, Canada. 888-9-TRAILS [987-2457] (toll free); 604-323-1141 (tel); 604-323-1148 (fax). E-mail: info@hiddentrails.com; Web site: hiddentrails.com

This trip takes place high in the Gila National Forest. First acclimate to 5,000 to 8,200 feet, where you will be gathering up members of the herd and riding with them through forests, grasslands, and canyons. In the distance are snowy peaks 11,000 feet high.

Spring roundup takes place in April and May; fall roundup in September to November. On the 75,000-acre range, you will stay at a 100-year-old cowboy ranch (no electricity or running water, but good food cooked in Dutch ovens). Days you will spend branding calves.

On the fall roundup, you will have to ride around the weather, which will be unpredictable. Riding can be more rugged; the cattle have to be branded, and the herd, sorted and cut (chosen to sell), before they go to the pens. Seven days, including camping, meals, horses, but no frills: about $1,000.

Wyoming

Off the Beaten Path   7 East Beall Street, Bozeman, Montana 59715. 800-445-2995 (toll free); 406-586-1311 (tel); 406-587-4147 (fax). E-mail: travel@offthebeatenpath.com; Web site: www. offthebeatenpath.com

In the middle of this week-long guided trip, you will spend two days on horseback and drive the cattle near Cody, Wyoming. Off the Beaten Path specializes in in-depth tours that allow you to understand the people and place. Staying at a working cattle ranch in Crow country, you can visit historical sites as well as Crow artists, and experience the colorful ritual, dancing, and games at the annual Crow Fair. Seven days, including everything: about $2,500.

BULL RIDING

Fantasy Bull Riding Adventure   c/o Sankey Rodeo Schools, 3943 Sycamore Church Road, Branson, Missouri 65616. 417-334-2513 (tel); 417-332-0676 (fax). E-mail: info@sankeyrodeo.com; Web site: www.sankeyrodeo.com

The difference between this bull adventure and running with the bulls at Pamplona is attitude. In Spain, you run like the wind to stay out of the bull's way; in this one, you take on the bull, muscle for muscle.

Sankey Rodeo Schools have been bringing people and bulls or horses together for more than two decades, so they know something about all three.

Outside of rodeos, bull riding is not in high demand as a skill (or as a fantasy). Bulls are big, a solid ton of muscle. Those who have ridden them say the first thing you notice is that the hump you are behind is almost as big as you are. The second thing is that a bull's skin fits like a slipcover, rather than upholstery. The third thing is the adept way the bull will spin in addition to bucking to get rid of the rider.

Originally, bulls were ridden until the bull got tired or the rider fell off. Now rodeos sound the buzzer at a merciful eight seconds; and clowns and horsemen will distract the bull while its former rider gets out of the arena. You need a lot of strength to do this.

The Fantasy Bull Riding Adventure teaches what has been called "the most dangerous sport" in one to four days at its Rose Hill, Kansas, facility. Group size minimum is fifteen. All professional equipment, including ropes and spurs, is provided, and your bull experience is captured on video (which you have the option to buy). Sankey will make recommendations for local lodging.

One to four days: about $300 to $400. Private lessons, minimum two people, in Rose Hill, Kansas: $600 to $700 for two days.

Bucking Broncos

At Sankey Rodeo facilities located around the country from California to Florida, you can learn the skill of staying on, controlling, and gracefully falling off a bucking bronco (an untamed but not wild horse). Once you learn the ropes, you can do it bareback or in a saddle.

Lyle Sankey qualified for the National Finals Rodeo in not just one but three rodeo skills: bareback and saddled broncos as well as bull riding. He knows full well the jingle you will hear around rodeos: "There isn't a bronc that can't be rode. There isn't a cowboy that can't be thrown."

Three- and four-day courses give you access to unlimited bucking broncos, training drills, video tape replay, and a couple of lectures on the business of rodeos: between $300 and $400. Accommodations are extra.

CHAPTER 12

EARTH AND WEATHER

Fantastic celestial events shaped the earth, and the evidence is everywhere: in the deep craters left by meteorites, asteroids, or comets; and in undersea trenches, including the one in the South Pacific that might mark the place where the moon was drawn off by gravitational forces and flung into orbit.

Tides and wind and terrible storms are constant reminders of our place in space. So are volcanoes, spewing lava out of the fiery core, and layers of minerals in rocks, and their jewels, left by a cooling planet.

This is a small sampling of ways to experience the earth.

HAWAII

Space Adventures   4350 North Fairfax Drive, Suite 840, Arlington, Virginia 22203. 888-85-SPACE [857-7223] (toll free); 703-524-7176 (fax). E-mail: info@spaceadventures.com; Web site: www.spaceadventures.com

Space on the Beach is Space Adventures' tour to Hawaii, currently one of the earthiest places on the planet. The Kilauea volcano has been shooting rich lava into the sea (and forming a new island in the chain) for decades, in the same way ancient volcanoes shaped other planets in the solar system. Mauna Kea, one of the highest points in the Pacific, at 13,500 feet, is home to the world's largest cluster of observatories, because the skies are so clear. And surrounding the Big Island, an 18,000-year-old coral reef is home to an amazing variety of life that swims in the sea.

Guided by astronaut Guy Gardner, the tour explores vulcanism as a planetary process at Volcanoes National Park and on a two-hour helicopter flight over the lava vents at Kilauea.

On the peak at Mauna Kea, the tour group visits the observatories and, after sunset, hosts its own star party with portable telescopes.

The following day, tour members go underwater and glide by the reef and its amazing colorful life for an hour in a forty-eight-passenger submarine. The trip is not all work: you have lots of time to relax on the beach and hike through tropical rainforests.

Six days, including everything except international airfare: about $3,500.

NEW MEXICO

Kayenta Scientific Investigations   2000 Ridgewood Road, Suite 317, Chapel Hill, North Carolina 27516. 866-222-0777 (toll free). E-mail: rgiral@kayentasci.com; Web site: www.kayentasci.com

Geologically, the American Southwest is an archive of some of the changes Earth went through when it was a still-forming part of the solar system.

If you love finding minerals and looking for clues in the earth to the past, Kayenta's Circle-A Jemez Tour in New Mexico is for you. The tour begins near Albuquerque with a ride in the aerial tram up 10,000 feet to Sandia Peak (once covered by ocean), then spends the evening at Circle-A Ranch looking at stars through a Meade telescope in the clear and undisturbed high desert air north of Albuquerque, at an elevation of about 7,000 feet. Geologist Ruben Giral, who has been leading tours to the area for the past six years, says it is the "ethereal nature" of the place that keeps his participants coming back. "There is a spiritual quality here that's hard to describe," he says.

The next eight days are spent exploring the Colorado Plateau, which shows evidence of plate migration over a volcanic hotspot, with Mesozoic sedimentary beds thrust into vertical position, areas of exposed petrified wood, copper, gypsum, travertine, and fossil beds with ancient seashells.

Drive north to see the Jemez Caldera, remnant of a fiery ring of volcanoes that once exploded in the Southwest, visit a Triassic dinosaur site, and then compare the geology of the Sangre de Cristo Mountains with that of the Nacimento Mountains and map the events that created both. The tour also visits Los Alamos, the site of the development of the atomic bomb, and spends time in Santa Fe. Hiking is moderate to strenuous.

Ten days, including ground transport, lodging, and meals: about $3,000. Partners receive a 10 percent discount.

PATAGONIA

Patagonia Research Expedition   c/o Dr. Morty Ortega, Department of Natural Resources Management and Engineering, Unit 4087, University of Connecticut, Storrs, Connecticut 06269-4087. 860-486-0161 (tel). E-mail: morty.ortega@uconn.edu; Web site: www.canr.uconn.edu/paine

This is a chance to spend eighteen days in Patagonia, the southernmost tip of South America in the Chilean Torres del Paine (pronounced *pine*) National Park, among amazing ancient volcanic peaks and extensive grasslands populated by mammals that rarely appear in city zoos: huemuls, small antlered deer; guanacos, vicuna-like animals of the camel family; and the lesser rhea, which looks remarkably like an ostrich. Little research has ever been done here, even though it is designated a World Biosphere Reserve, because the park managers have no mandate to make inventories of birds, mammals, or even maps of wetlands. Dr. Morty Ortega has been leading groups here for the past five years collecting data of the fragile ecosystems.

Living in an area that early explorers likened to another planet, you have a total immersion experience of Patagonia. "Some people when they come are timid at first," said Dr. Ortega, "but then they love it."

With its towering 9,000-foot snowy peaks and flat grassland and lakes, Torres is a beautiful place to study the harmony between mammals and their habitats—ever-changing wetlands and how the interplay with its inhabitants alters both.

Conditions are "rough," said Dr. Ortega. You will live in a tent camp with a cook and eat "in a shack," and take showers every three or four days. Participants are expected to be able to walk as many as ten miles a day.

Taking a team of about ten people each January, a relatively mild month in the Southern Hemisphere, Dr. Ortega instructs everyone in the collection of data, which the team roams through the park to do during the day. At night, everyone meets to discuss the finds.

Eighteen days, including lodging, meals, and ground transport: $2,500. Airfare to Patagonia from the United States: about $1,000.

VOLCANOES

Russia

Sokol Tours. *In the U.S. and Canada:* 800-55-RUSSIA [557-8774] (toll free); 617-269-2659 (tel/fax). *In Russia:* 011 +7 95 424-7988 (tel/fax). E-mail: sokol@sokoltours.com; Web site: www. sokoltours.com

The Volcanoes of Kamchatka Tour mountain bikes around nine volcanoes in the Peninsula, some of them as recent as twenty years ago. Biking for ten days through the tundra and around volcanoes, you experience all aspects of volcanic activity. In the shadow of the highest volcano in Eurasia, Kluchevskoy (about 4,900 meters high), bike up to a lava flow, then to the place where Soviets tested their lunar roving vehicle because it resembles the moon's landscape. Visit vent cones and a dead forest. Explore lava caves and soak in thermal hot springs.

The Sokol Tours Team, composed of Canadians and Russians based in Boston and Moscow, organizes tours to Central Asia and

Russia, in which they are expert. They will mix and match tour elements to suit your needs.

On the final day of the Kamchatka tour, you actually climb an active volcano, Mutnovsky, to look down into its deep crater lake. Its 1999 eruption is still present in merged craters, its hissing vents, jets and plumes of superheated water, and sulphurous smoke. Standing there amid Earth's most powerful experience, you hear and feel "the deafening roar of volcanic madness and exhilarating rumbles underfoot."

Lodging is in hotels, cabins, and tents. The trip spends parts of five days mountain biking, supported by a six-wheel-drive van. Fly into Moscow, wait a day; fly to Vladivostok, then to Petropavlovsk-Kamchatsky. Its level of difficulty is "strenuous."

Sixteen days, including everything except international airfare: about $1,300.

Costa Rica

Lindblad Expeditions   720 Fifth Avenue, New York, New York 10019. 800-397-3348 (toll free); 212-765-7740 (tel); 212-265-3770 (fax). E-mail: explore@expeditions.com; Web site: www.expeditions.com

In the middle of the mountain chain that runs along Costa Rica rises Arenal, the poster child of volcanoes. Its perfect cone juts out of the tropical rainforest like something out of a movie, and it shoots out plumes of smoke, rocks, and lava every half hour or so, some as high as a kilometer. Part of the "Ring of Fire" volcanoes that erupt along the Pacific coasts from Chile to Alaska to Russia to New Zealand, Arenal was dormant until 1968 when it suddenly erupted, and it hasn't stopped since then.

This Lindblad trip begins in Miami with the sixty-two-passenger *Sea Voyager*, which cruises through the Panama Canal and turns north to Herradura, Costa Rica, where you disembark and drive up to the Monteverde Cloud Forest for a couple of days looking for quetzals and walking forest trails.

Descend to the tropical rainforest to spend some time on a working cattle ranch, complete with rides on a tractor to the hills to see the sun set.

Then get ready to spend two nights at the Arenal Observatory Lodge, located at the foot of the volcano, which is about as close to it as anyone can safely get. You will learn what it is like for many people who live in the shadow of an active volcano, and how completely unpredictable volcanoes are. This one slept like a giant for almost five hundred years.

Fifteen days, including everything except international airfare: from about $4,600 to $5,650 (double occupancy), depending on berth.

WEATHER

Storm Chasing

Tornadoes rip across the central plains of the United States in May and early June with some displays of the tremendous power of wind, one of the effects of the planet's spinning in space. Fed by heat, the unsettled air funnels up into columns hundreds of feet high that roar with terrifying randomness and speed across roads and towns. The film *Twister* captured some of the manic zeal that drives storm chasers, those who track and get as close as possible to the behemoths as they rip across the land. Photographers, videographers, and TV cameras document tornadoes' horrific beauty.

Storm Chasing Adventure Tours   P.O. Box 150812, Lakewood, Colorado 80215. 303-888-8629 (tel). E-mail: Todd@stormchasing. com; Web site: www.stormchasing.com

This company, composed of meteorologists and technologists, who operate two fifteen-passenger vans, outfitted with equipment that provides real-time satellite weather information, lightning detection, access to the Weather Channel, and radar, has been running storm-chasing tours for seven years.

The vortex of a huge tornado bears down east of Dimmitt, Texas, in June 1995. One of the most thoroughly and closely tracked tornadoes, this storm demolished cars, blew up transformers, and tore off the asphalt highway as if it were a blanket on a bed. *(Photo by Harald Richter, NOAA Photo Library, OAR/ERL/National Severe Storms Laboratory)*

Start in Oklahoma City or Denver (depending on the activity) and head out each day, with six passengers to a van (everyone with a window seat), analyzing the weather and trying to predict where the next tornado will erupt. Severe weather is the theme of this trip. Onboard experts will educate you on weather; downtime, when tornadoes are not a possibility, visit the National Severe Weather Center in Norman, Oklahoma, and other weather data stations.

Caution: You must be comfortable spending long hours in the van; in the five-day tour, you will cover 2,500 miles; in the ten-day tour, 5,000 miles. Nights are spent at motels such as the Hampton Inn or Holiday Inn Express; restaurants feature barbecued spareribs and homemade pies. Minimum age: eighteen.

Five days: about $1,700; ten days: about $2,900. Food and airfare are extra.

Silver Lining Tours, L.C.   David Gold, Manager, P.O. Box 420898, Houston, Texas 77242-0898. 281-759-4181 (tel); 281-759-5261 (fax). E-mail: stormtours@earthlink.net; Web site: www.silverliningtours.com

If you have a special interest in the formation of tornadoes and severe weather, this company will appeal to you. Led by professional meteorologists, it will teach you how to make your own weather forecasts as well as how to plot and forecast the potential path of a storm. Guides Roger Hill and David Gold teach you how to collate and interpret not only data available on the Internet but signs in the sky from careful observations. Bring your own notebook computer.

Tours start in either Oklahoma City or Denver; travel six to a fifteen-passenger van equipped with GPS, and an LCD screen for video playback; stay at motels such as the Holiday Inn Express. Minimum age: eighteen.

Six days, including everything as well as daily bottled water and a highlights video: $1,900; ten days: $2,600. Food and airfare are extra.

Cloud 9 Tours   P.O. Box 3631, Shawnee, Oklahoma 74802. 405-214-0320 (tel). E-mail: cedwards@cloud9tours.com; Web site: www.cloud9tours.com

Meteorologist Charles Edwards and veteran storm chaser Jim Leonard cover the area from Mexico to Canada, the Rockies to Indiana, identifying storm systems, which they then follow. Bring your camcorder.

Seven days: about $1,500; fourteen days: about $2,300.

Tempest Tours   P.O. Box 121084, Arlington, Texas 76012. 817-274-9313 (tel). E-mail: info@tempesttours.com; Web site: www.tempesttours.com

Tempest Tours concentrates on forecasting supercell thunderstorms in Tornado Alley. A supercell storm has a long-lived updraft, and is most likely to breed tornadoes. As soon as one is spotted, the vans will carry you closer to see them (safely).

Eleven nights in May (for storm lovers): about $2,500. Seven nights in early June (for people with little time to spare): about $1,700. Eight nights in mid-June (lecture tour by noted meteorologist Dr. Charles Doswell, and severe-weather workshop): about $2,200.

CLOUDS

Rapid Weather's Guided Weather Expeditions
1601 Mount Rushmore Road, #4-217, Rapid City, South Dakota 57701. 605-718-3613 (tel); 605-718-3614 (fax). E-mail: metcenter@rushmore.com; Web site: www.rapidwx.com

Rapid Weather, a company that provides weather updates to businesses and government, offers a menu of courses, seminars, and weather trips for people interested in weather.

Their Cloud Excursions tour spends twelve days in the West and Central United States (from the Dakotas to Texas), seeking cloud formations, which guides will identify and explain. They look for everything from "standing lenticular to valley fogs." You will be able to photograph clouds at your leisure, or simply gaze at them, and learn everything you need to know about their formation, the meaning of their shapes, and their dissolution.

This trip is good, they say, for people who have no definite itinerary in mind and who don't mind traveling the back roads. The tours are in September. There are no guarantees about the weather.

Twelve days, including lodging, meals, and transport: about $2,300.

CHAPTER 13

FISHING AND HUNTING

FISHING

The Holy Grail of fishing is a virgin river, lake, or ocean that other fishermen don't know about, that is accessible by boat or plane, and ideally, that has a comfortable lodge nearby. In this aquatic paradise, fish are big, numerous, and ready for a fierce fight; the lures are perfect; and the others staying at the lodge appreciate long and detailed fish stories.

What follows is a tiny sampling of some places that are still considered to be at least slightly virginal.

Deep Water Trophy Fishing

Zane Grey Reef, Panama

Tropic Star Lodge, Pinas Bay Resorts   635 North Rio Grande Avenue, Orlando, Florida 32805. 800-682-3424 (toll free); 407-843-0125 (tel).

Fifty minutes by plane from Panama City and a short boat trip from Pinas Bay airstrip is the Tropic Star Lodge and a Robinson Crusoe beach. The lodge is luxurious, and you can kayak, swim, and explore.

But you are here to fish.

Hooking and playing with a twelve-foot, several-hundred-pound blue marlin is one thing; landing it in the boat is another. A charter boat returns with its trophy caught off Kona, Hawaii. *(NMFS File Photo)*

It begins at 6:30 every morning, as you hop aboard the thirty-one-foot Bertram yacht and head out to Zane Grey Reef in the warm Pacific waters, where big black marlin cruise not far beneath the surface.

Mapped by diver Guy Harvey, the Reef has three solid rock peaks about 150 feet below the surface. Over these and in the valleys of the reef, about 205 feet deep, are huge numbers of fish. The little ones eat the plankton that comes up from South America; the middle ones, like snappers, groupers, and jacks, eat them; and the feeding goes on up the food chain to some world-record marlin. In fact, this company owns 170 IGFA world records.

You can also fish for striped and blue marlin, sailfish, yellowfin tuna, and mahi mahi.

Seven nights, two people fishing January through March, including lodging, meals, boat, captain and mate, and first-class fishing tackle: $4,000 per person. Room tax: $20 per person per week. Add round-trip airfare from Panama City to Pinas Bay: $315 per person.

Tropic Star also offers four-night programs. Rates are less April to September, and December.

Marlin University

Marlin University   888-281-5720, ext. 4800 (toll free). E-mail: fishingschools@worldpub.net; Web site: www.marlinmag.com

Marlin own their piece of the ocean, and fishing for them is not like fishing for other blue-water big fish, which is probably why Hemingway preferred them: they're the bulls of the sea. In addition to their muscle, they have been known to use their pointy bill as a weapon.

Marlin University provides hands-on classroom seminars in four great marlin locations: Costa Rica (March), Saint Thomas (July), Venezuela (September), and Australia (November).

In five to eight days, they will teach you everything you need to know about fishing marlin: bait, lure, and fly techniques; how to bring them in; and how to deal with their muscled fights in the boat. They also teach the duties of first and second mates and how to handle the boat while a marlin is on the line. Marlin University makes sure there are interesting activities landside as well, because "if the wife's not happy, nobody's happy."

Five to eight days, including instruction, tackle, boat, lodging, and meals: about $5,000.

Shallow Water Fly Fishing

Next to the thrill of hauling in a prize mount from blue water is the excitement of the subtle fight that shallow-water ocean fish provide. Sometimes hiding in the grass, sometimes racing to your lure in completely clear water, fish like bonefish, permit, and tarpon never disappoint a serious angler.

The Seychelles

Some European fishermen have found this place, but so few people have ever lived or visited there, as a French sports angler noted, "The fish still have their original aggressiveness."

The Seychelles is an archipelago of about 115 islands a thousand miles off the coast of Kenya, just above Madagascar. Long known to naturalists for their abundant rare birds and hawksbill turtles which come here to breed, the Seychelles never attracted a lot of settlers and today has a population of only 75,000.

Fishing International, Inc.   1824 Fourth Street, Santa Rosa, California 95404. 707-542-4242 (tel); 707-526-3473 (fax). E-mail: fishint@fishinginternational.com; Web site: www. fishinginternational.com

Didier Van der Veecken has been fishing off some of the Seychelles Islands since 1978, when they were even more remote than they are today. He discovered incredible fishing on the 15,000 acres of flats around the coral islands of the Amirantes: bonefish (5 to 8 pounds) that come in with the tide, the southern Indo-Pacific fish giant trevally (one was 121 pounds) and golden trevally (30 pounds), as well as grouper, jacks, job fish, and barracuda.

The best way to fish is to sail on Van der Veecken's forty-foot Royal Cape Catamaran out to the islands, then to take the zodiac onto the flats, where you can wade and cast. All fishing is catch and release, so barbless hooks are advised.

The shallow warm water is exquisitely blue, the same color as the sky. The fish are wildly abundant, and you can see them play shyly with your bait. Deciding what flies or lures to use can be a challenge, as the fish may not respond to what they are supposed to grab. Once hooked, however, they give anglers a run for their money.

Van der Veecken has two lodging options: live aboard the catamaran or in a thatched reed hotel bungalow on Alphonse Island,
once a coconut farm.

Living aboard: six double cabins, each with hot and cold fresh-
water showers and head, seven nights, all meals, and daily transport
by zodiac for nonguided fishing: about $2,900 per person (in a
group of four).

Alphonse Island Hotel: seven nights double, all meals: about
$5,600.

Fly to the main island Mahe in the Seychelles and take a chartered fifty-minute flight to Alphonse Island. Van der Veecken will
give advice on tackle and take you to island flats not on maps.

Note: You must have medical insurance with medical evacuation
coverage if you go to Alphonse Island.

Arctic Char Fishing

Nunavut Territory, Canada

This brave and hardy fish lives in the waters of the Arctic Circle
except during the last month of the midnight sun, when it takes to
lakes and rivers to mate. It enters calmer waters a modest gray-
green with orange spots, but turns black with an orange belly when
it spawns. Growing to about three feet in length, it weighs upward
of twenty-five pounds. Once hooked, it will give you a ferocious
fight.

Learning Adventures   182 Princess Street, Kingston, Ontario
K7L 1B1, Canada. 800-263-0050 (toll free); 613-549-3342.
E-mail: learning@odyssey-travel.com; Web sites: www.
odysseylearningadventures.ca

Accompanied by the Director of Research from the Canadian
Museum of Nature, this Arctic Char fly-fishing trip takes place in
Lake Merkley around Victoria Island in Inuit country, Nunavut
Territory.

The lake is crystal clear and practically pristine, 300 miles north of the Arctic Circle, and it's a place where line class records are regularly made. If you get tired of fishing the lake, the pilot, who knows the waters intimately, will find a virgin stream or river where you can cast your fly.

Lodging is at the High Arctic Lodge, reachable only by float plane. For two of your seven nights, you can overnight at the lodge's remote outpost camps, even farther north, where even fewer fishermen have ever gone.

Fishing is catch and release. Extras include seals, caribou, polar bears, Arctic fox, loons, owls, swans, and maybe the aurora borealis.

Eight days, including boat, pilot/guide, lodging, meals, flight from Edmonton to Victoria Island, and from there to the High Arctic Lodge: about $7,100.

HUNTING

Regardless of how you feel personally about hunting, it is in our blood. Early man did not live by nuts and berries alone. For Cro-Magnon, hunting was the Big Thing. They chased and killed the beast, and the women helped to skin and gut it. Once on the fire, the roasted beast supplied important calories for the whole tribe, as well as a chance to celebrate with a feast. But as cave paintings attest, it was more than that. Priests and artists also performed rituals to pay homage to the animals that sustained them. Over the years, our attitudes about who is really at the top of the food chain might have changed, but some instincts still lie sentient.

Wild Boars in Hungary

You can capture a whiff of some of these ancient rituals that surround the hunt by chasing boar in the woods of Hungary, where there is a long tradition of hunting. Medieval aristocrats hunted with much formal ritual, sustained by long tradition. Under Communist rule, party leaders were encouraged to carry on the hunt, after confiscating aristocrats' estates. Today, hunters from around the world hunt on state-owned property, with the opportunity to stay in some of the former landowners' lodges.

The rituals of the ancient hunt linger in hundreds of superstitions. For one, the hunters pause for a prayer over the slain beast before sounding the hunting horn that tells the kitchen how many of which species of beast have been killed. Back at the lodge with trophy heads hung above the grand fireplace, the air redolent of wild game dishes, you, too, can experience in the feast the ancient spiritual comity among hunters.

Hunting Navigator.com   P.O. Box 1508, Camarillo, California 93011. 805-383-2795 (tel); 805-388-0485 (fax). E-mail: info@ huntingnavigator.com; Web site: www.huntingnavigator.com

Most of the hunting grounds in Hungary are owned and managed by the state, which carefully controls the numbers; and there are a lot of boars, some of them behemoths. The largest caught to date was 500 pounds, but four-hundred-pound boars are not unusual. Because taking a trophy boar involves fees and permits, it is best to travel with a company that takes care of that for you.

Hunting Navigator will take you to the Gemenc Forest and Game Company, which controls 75,000 hectares of oak forest that straddles the Danube River in the south of Hungary. The woods teem with game. In the middle of the forest is the former hunting castle of Royal Archduke Albrecht, a "neo-baroque" lodge built in the late 1800s. Here, you have access to carriages and coaches, and the skills of beaters, who accompany guest hunters to the blinds, then make a racket that sends the boars scattering.

And scatter they will, grunting and squealing, unbelievably fast for their massive size, tiny feet, and not very good eyesight. Staying cool enough to place a well-aimed shot in these conditions can be a real challenge. Shooting is not hunting, as they will tell you.

Depending on the area, wild boar beating is done in either November or December, with about seven to ten other hunters in the group. An average of forty to fifty boars are slain in a day. You can also hunt individually with a guide, best done at twilight, for a full wild boar experience. Red deer stag also abound in these woods.

Your trophy fees depend on its size and the length of the tusks. Expect to bring it home or pay an extra 25 percent VAT to the Hungarian Hunting Agencies. You must bring your own gun, because Hungarian hunting regulations do not allow rented guns.

Hunting Navigator offers a package for two hunters with a professional guide. The price includes trophy fees for two wild boars, with 18-centimeter (about 7 inches) tusks, license and insurance fees, airport transfers from Budapest (about a three-hour drive), first-class lodging, and meals. Please reserve at least a month in advance, as the hunts are very popular.

Three nights, four days: about $3,500.

WING SHOOTING

Made famous in films such as *Gosford Park*, in which men in tweeds, attended by barking hounds, head off with servants to shoot birds scared out of their nests, wingshooting is a tradition of the English country estate, attended as much by ritual as by the number of game birds taken. The country weekend requires formal dinner dress, a capacity for gossip, and ideally, enough staff to pluck the feathers and dress the birds for lunch or dinner.

If you would like a taste of this, and have graduated from skeet and trap shooting and want to try shooting at flying objects that rise unpredictably from the brush and dip or swing alone or in pairs through the sky to the left, right, away from you, or toward you, then wingshooting is your game. It is an expensive sport—guns run sometimes in the tens of thousands of dollars. And it's addictive. Your spouse or partner will probably feel widowed.

That's why most wingshooting operations offer trips with two agendas: one for the shooters, another equally appealing for nonshooters.

Orvis Travel   Historic Route 7A, Manchester, Vermont 05254. 800-547-4322 (toll free); 802-362-8790 (tel); 802-362-8795 (fax). E-mail: Orvistravel@Orvis.com; Web site: www.orvis.com

Wingshooting Safari, Southern Africa is a classy trip through South Africa from Pretoria, through the Kalahari Desert, the Drakensberg Mountains, and a variety of other places on a private train.

Traveling on rails laid about a hundred years ago, the restored antique train carries ten shooters. The interior is lushly wood-paneled, and staterooms have private bathrooms. A dining car serves the best of South African cuisine in excellent style.

In forests and fields that are hunted only once or twice a year, 150 beaters flush the francolin, guineafowl, partridge, and sandgrouse from their hidden nests, and shooters have between five and nine opportunities a day to take game. Nonshooters and nonshooter companions can join some hunts; and those with little interest in shooting birds have the options of visiting the De Beers wildlife preserve or the diamond mines in Kimberley or other sites of historic meaning to South Africa.

Only double guns are used, either side-by-sides or over/under 20 and 12 gauge. Shells are provided.

South Africa, seven days, including lodging on the train and all meals: about $16,000 per person for ten shooters, $18,600 for eight or fewer. Companions: about $4,000. Nonshooters: about $6,300.

South Africa/Botswana, nine days, including all of above: about $16,200. Companions and nonshooters same as above.

Wingshooting School

To learn the art, technique, and etiquette of wingshooting, take a day or two at one of the three Orvis Wingshooting Schools at Sandanona, in Millbrook, New York; at Mays Pond, near Tallahassee, Florida; or in Manchester, Vermont.

Sporting Clays

You can shoot sporting clays, which is like wingshooting without birds. It differs from trap and skeet shooting in that the trajectories of the clays mimic birds flushed from the underbrush. Some hunter-trainees find sporting clays a sport in its own right, and never get into actual birds.

You will also learn basic shotgun safety and what constitutes a properly fitted gun. You will be trained in developing your focus on a moving target, as well as how to shoot "going-away, crossing shots, low incomers, singles and doubles."

At Sandanona, in Millbrook, New York, Orvis, in business since 1856, maintains a nineteenth-century hunting lodge, with extensive rustic hunting grounds. It's a good place to learn the disciplines, rights, duties, and pleasures of a wingshooter. One day: $450. Orvis will help you find lodging at special rates.

CHAPTER 14

FLIGHTS OF FANTASY

In the century since Orville and Wilbur Wright wobbled off the field above the dunes at the Outer Banks in North Carolina in the first real flight in this country, planes have been stretched into sleek tubes that reach inconceivable altitudes and speeds. Most people use them like buses to get from one point to another; only astronauts and military pilots get to play in the sky.

But a few companies around the country are willing to share their fleet of nostalgia planes, most of them left over from world wars, in which you pull shut the clear cockpit roof, adjust your goggles, and do loop-the-loops to your heart's content. Some planes are still used by the military but were left behind on the aeronautical drawing board. Licensed and unlicensed pilots, and those with no flying experience but a lot of natural moxie, can engage in dogfights and act out whatever battles they pretend they are a part of, while spinning upside down and flying sideways in whatever aerobatics they and the aircraft are able to perform.

Warbirds, planes used reliably in some famous battles in World War II, are so popular they have fan clubs scattered around the world, with members who remember them or wish they had known the original, and who collect paintings of them, hold meetings, and where possible, actually fly them.

Warbirds: A B-25 and a T-6 roar through the sky. Climb into the cockpit from the wing, pull down your goggles, close the canopy, and fly one of these and other planes that date from World War II. *(Kathryn (KT) Budde-Jones/Warbird Adventures)*

FLYING WARBIRDS

Stallion 51 Corporation   3951 Merlin Drive, Kissimmee, Florida 34741. 407-846-4400 (tel); 407-846-0414 (fax). E-mail: mustang@stallion51.com; Web site: www.stallion51.com

Of all World War II propeller combat planes, the P-51 Mustang was among the most loved; and this company is the premier P-51 flight operations center. At Stallion 51, you can fly their dual-cockpit, dual-control, Rolls-Royce Merlin engine–powered TF-51 Mustang, known as Crazy Horse, and take it into high-performance aerobatics, if you know how.

This 2½- to 3-hour program requires no or little previous flying experience. After a preflight briefing, in which you get to know more about the plane, and the pilots you will be with get a feeling of the best customized flight experience for you, you climb into the cockpit in the seat behind a pilot and take the controls. Usually the pilot takes off and lands the plane, while you do as many fancy maneuvers as you are comfortable doing.

After a debrief, you get the video made from two in-flight cameras, a portrait of the airplane, and a flight profile certificate. Two and a half to three hours, with thirty minutes of flying time: $1,950; with sixty minutes of flying time: $2,750.

Stallion 51 also offers checkout training programs for P-51 Mustang owners; and training for pilots in unusual attitude.

Barnstorming Adventures, Ltd., California. Two hours south of LAX, forty minutes north of San Diego, near the McClellan-Palomar Airport. 800-759-5667 (toll free). Web site: www.eagle. he.net

You don't need previous experience to don a flight suit and parachute, pull on a helmet and goggles, and run with the pilot for the plane as soon as the klaxon sounds. Jump in and pull the cockpit cover closed as the plane taxis and sputters down the runway before takeoff. In the air, the baby is yours.

On their Wings of Gold flight, for example, spend an hour in the air in a North American T-6 Texan, a sturdy craft used to train World War II pilots. They were so good, in fact, Brits called them Harvard Mks and used them with modifications to train RAF pilots.

In your time aloft, you can do as much or as little flying as you want, including, loops, wingovers, and half Cuban eights. Sixty minutes: about $400.

Warbird Adventures, Inc.　Kissimmee Municipal Airport, 233 North Hoagland Boulevard, Kissimmee, Florida 34741. 800-386-1593 (toll free); 407-870-7366 (tel); 407-870-2295 (fax). E-mail: fly@warbirdadventures.com; Web site: www.warbirdadventures.com

Everything you need to know about flying a North American T-6/SNJ Texan/Harvard you will get before you climb on the wing and crawl into the cockpit. Once there, you can do as much or as little fancy flying as you want, in fifteen-minute flights ($150); thirty-minute flights ($250); or sixty-minute flights, with positive G experiences ($450).

Warbird Restoration School

Flying Tigers Warbird Restoration Museum   231 Hoagland Boulevard, Kissimmee, Florida, 34741. 407-933-1942 (tel). E-mail: programs@warbirdmuseum.com; Web site: www. warbirdmuseum.com

If you have one—any warbird—this is the place to come to learn how to restore it to flying condition. Also, take a look at the museum's collection of significant aircraft from a 1928 Fairchild KR-21 to a MiG 21 MF.

Five-day school: about $1,000. That translates into fifty hours of hands-on training that culminates with a free flight in a B-25 Mitchell Bomber, vintage World War II.

Fightertown Aviation, Inc.   3604 Airport Drive, Denison, Texas 75020. 903-786-2666 (tel); 903-786-3458 (fax). E-mail: service@ FTA-FBO.com; Web site: www.fightertownavigation.com

For licensed pilots only, Fightertown offers use of their TS11 Iskra or L29 Delfin warbirds in a full-profile training flight. Sixty minutes: $750.

THE HISTORY OF AVIATION

Fantasy of Flight   Polk City, Florida. Between Orlando and Tampa, off I-4 at Exit 21. 863-984-3500 (tel). Web site: www. fantasyofflight.com

Robert Redford became *The Great Waldo Pepper* operating out of this hangar, and "Sheena, Queen of the Jungle," the TV series, was filmed here, with imported wild animals. Aside from these diversions, a tour of the hangar will take you back to old wars. See a B-25 Mitchell take off with Doolittle Raiders and watch the aerial demonstration. Engage in World War II Pacific Theatre missions at their flight simulator. Visit the restoration museum, and some fabulous planes, from a Navy Panther jet to a German JU-52. Daily admission: adults: about $25; children: $14.

AIR COMBAT PLANES

This is the closest you will come to being an air attack fighter short of joining the Air Force or the Navy and going to school for many years. Depending on your imagination and your raw nerve, you can fantasize any battle situation and perform any crazy aerobatic trick you think of. Just stay in the air until it's time to land.

Varga VG-21

Barnstorming Adventures, Ltd.,   California. Two hours south of LAX, forty minutes north of San Diego, near the McClellan-Palomar Airport. 800-759-5667 (toll free). Web site: www. eagle.he.net

Barnstorming's combat planes are Varga VG-21s with tricycle gear, built from the period after World War II until the mid-1980s, and used by the military. They are smooth and easy-to-handle propeller planes, with tandem seats and a clear cockpit cover from which to spot the enemy. When you do, you have one thumb on the joystick button ready to shoot out the tracers and "bullets." Their pilots are active-duty Marine Corps and Navy pilots.

On their Top Dog Flight for Two, you don't need a pilot's license, just an enemy. You are in one aircraft, your enemy is in another. For the enemy, Barnstorming suggests bringing your "honey, sibling, neighbor, boss, or parent." About $480.

Top Dog Single is a flight in which Barnstorming supplies the enemy, which, given the pro stance of their pilots, might be an aerobatic challenge to remember. No pilot's licence required. About $300.

Extra 300L

Fighter Combat International. *In the United States:* Williams Gateway Airport, 5803 South Sossaman Road, Suite 102, Mesa, Arizona 85212. 866-FLY-HARD [359-4273] (toll free); 480-279-1881 (tel); 480-279-1882 (fax). E-mail: usa@fightercombat.com; Web site: www.fightercombat.com. *In Canada:* Niagara District Airport, Highway 55, RR#4, Niagara on the Lake, Ontario L02 1J0. 888-FLY-HARD [359-4273] (toll free); 905-684-5440 (tel); 904-684-3054 (fax). E-mail: canada@fightercombat.com; Web site:www.fightercombat.com

Fighter Combat uses German-built Extra 300L crafts, known for their superb maneuverability in the wildest of aerobatics. And in their Air Combat Mission, you, next to your instructor, have the choice of doing basic, everyday tactical maneuvers, or letting the craft loose in maneuvers that take over the sky.

The Centrifuge or the Corkscrew, performed while you are simultaneously pulling the trigger on enemy aircraft, will leave you a changed person, ready for just about anything. Extras use a laser weapons system (safe for the eyes) which, with smoke generators and combat sounds, closely mimics the real thing. You need no prior piloting experience.

Four and a half hours of Air Combat starts with ground briefing, during which your instructor and his team discuss combat tactical deployment, air combat skills, and cockpit safety. Then you pull on your flight suit, get strapped in, and take off with your pilot in control. Once in the air, it's your plane. Flying in formation with the competitor at more than 250 miles per hour, you begin with the ritual of weapons-system run-through and some warm-up maneuvers.

From there on, it's one-on-one, with "gunfire" spitting out of your plane, smoke billowing out of the other plane for a full hour. Back on the ground, after the high when you realize what you've just done, it's debrief time and a look at the cockpit video, taken from four views. You also get awards and plaques, photographs, and a certificate of achievement.

Four and a half hours: about $950. The video is extra: about $40.

Marchetti

Air Combat USA   National Headquarters, P.O. Box 2726, Fullerton, California 92837; or 230 North Dale Place, Fullerton, California 92833. 800-522-7590 (toll free); 714-522-7590 (tel); 714-522-7592 (fax). Web site: www.aircombatusa.com

Since 1989, Air Combat USA has been in the business of bringing air combat tactics and maneuvers to the nonflying public as well as to pilots who want to fly with other pilots and keep their hand in the business. They use the Italian-built SIAI Marchetti SF-260, a light attack fighter still is service in air forces around the world. No prior experience is required.

Everything builds from its Basic Phase I Air Combat Maneuvers. After a briefing, pull yourself into the Marchetti and learn Tactical Fighter Maneuvers-1. Six dogfights with the enemy (about $900 for one hour of flight, two hours of ground time) will convince you that you are ready to move on to Intermediate, then Advanced Air Combat Maneuvers, Phases 2 through 4. In these, you will learn defensive and high-G-load tactics. (A "G" is your body weight; the Marchetti can "pull 10 Gs," which means it can pull 10 times your body weight. When this happens, instructors say, tighten your stomach as hard as you can and bring blood to your brain.) Each phase is about $800.

From there, move into the Fighter Lead-In program (about $1,600). In this you will fly two separate missions, using everything you have learned, including vertical and oblique turns and flying in formation, plus dog fight tricks. But the main thing is that you will have earned the Commission as Major in the Air Combat USA Fighter Squadron. This gives special flying privileges, including entrance into the Frequent Fighter program, and a chance to move up to Lieutenant Colonel. (Along the way, you will pick up name tags with wings, a leather flight jacket, a nomex flight suit, and videos to amaze family and friends.)

Air Combat USA takes its Marchettis and air combat programs on the road to sixteen sites around the country. Check their Web site for times and locations.

MiGs

Incredible Adventures   6604 Midnight Pass Road, Sarasota, Florida 34242. 800-644-7382 (toll free); 941-346-2603 (tel); 941-346-2488 (fax). E-mail: info@incredible-adventures.com; Web site: www.incredible-adventures.com

This company runs MiG programs out of Moscow and Cape Town, South Africa. At the Zhukovsky Air Base outside of Moscow, you need to go through a security clearance and a preflight medical test. You will also be fitted for a flight suit, a G-suit, and a helmet. After spending time in the ejection-seat simulator, you will find out if you are ready or not to discuss the details of what you would like to do in your flight with a test pilot, who will design your custom flight.

Whatever you decide, you will be flying a MiG and you will go through the sound barrier to the edge of space and back. Fast.

You do not need a pilot's license, but you must be in reasonably good enough health to sustain the wear and tear of a MiG flight.

The Right Stuff tour gives you five nights at a first-class Moscow hotel and six days of tours around Moscow with three days of flight in an L-39 and MiG-29. Includes everything except international airfare: about $16,000.

You can choose from several other flight packages, depending on your zeal for MiGs.

Out of Cape Town, South Africa, expect to fly British jets. Their Buccaneer Adventure is six days/five nights, with two days in flight in a Hawker Hunter, preceded by an introduction to the jets and a safety briefing. On the second day, you will fly an aerobatic sortie in the Hawker and a low-level mission over the Atlantic in a Buccaneer at 650 mph.

Six days, including everything except international airfare: about $16,000.

Space Adventures   4350 North Fairfax Drive, Suite 840, Arlington, Virginia 22203. 888-85-SPACE (toll free); 703-524-7176 (fax). E-mail: info@spaceadventures.com; Web site: www.spaceadventures.com

Choose from a variety of MiGs for a wild flight out of Zhukovsky Air Base in Russia. The Fishbed, a MiG-21, for example, originally built in the late 1950s after the Korean War as a short-range supersonic fighter, is forty-four feet long with a twenty-three-foot delta wingspan and ready to fly.

Spend two nights in Moscow and one day at the air base, where you will be prepped on the flight plan, undergo a medical test, and receive a leather flight jacket (yours to keep) before taking off into the blue yonder and the edge of space. You need to bring a medical release from your own physician stating you are in good enough health to fly a jet.

Three days, including lodging, transport within Russia, and VIP immigration and customs processing: about $5,700.

ANTIQUE PLANES

Florida

Casablanca Air, Naples, Florida. 941-430-1133 (tel). E-mail: fly@casablancaair.com; Web site: www.casablancaair.com

Biplanes were the workhorses of early flying, because they could do just about everything. In one of Casablanca Air's stylish biplanes, strap on your helmet, pull down your goggles, and take the controls on a trip from Marco Island to Pelican Bay. You are accompanied by a pilot, who will take you on wingovers, chandelles, and lazy eights. Called The Waldo Pepper, this thirty-minute open-cockpit adventure costs $140.

This company is not named Casablanca without reason. Their 1942 Beechcraft 18 evokes the middle of World War II and Ingrid Bergman and Humphrey Bogart. Completely restored to the time when few people flew, and those who did flew first-class, Beechcraft 18 has leather seats, mahogany trim, and a stewardess in period uniform, from a time when stewardesses were nurses, prepared to help out with blocked ears and vertigo.

Choose from two tours over the Everglades; thirty minutes: $300; or the sixty-minute sunset tour with champagne and hors d'oeuvres: $650.

New Zealand and Australia

Pionair Adventures, Ltd.   P.O. Box 333, Christchurch, New Zealand. 011 +64 3 343-3333 (tel); 011 +64 3 343-3035 (fax). E-mail: enquiries@pionair.com; Web site: www.pionair.com

With its fleet of several renovated 1930s and 1940s propeller passenger planes, Pionair offers private luxury tours that combine nostalgia and adventure that evoke the Golden Age of Travel.

Their twenty-eight-passenger, completely retrofitted (with safety requirements exceeded) Douglas DC-3s, once the staple of passenger travel, have all the things you expect in a first-class jet flight. The Great New Zealand Expedition flies you over the country made famous most recently by *Lord of the Rings*. Pionair will carry you coast to coast with stops for cities, people, and magnificent scenery.

Ten days, including everything, first-class hotel accommodations, and all meals (but not international airfare): about $5,800.

Pionair does many trips for American universities and upscale travel companies. Get a group together, set up a charter, tell them your interests, and they know where to go. Their Golf and Gourmet tour, for example, will allow you to access the best of both in hops across New Zealand.

CHAPTER 15

HISTORY

ODYSSEUS

Time was, the world beyond the neighborhood was filled with one-eyed cannibals and witches who turned men into pigs. Gods and goddesses played favorites, lost their tempers without warning, and caused a heap of grief whenever it pleased them. Even heroes were never sure whether they were on the good side or the bad side of the divine.

Enter Odysseus, the Greek hero who designed the Trojan Horse. After the Trojan War, he went on a long cruise—so long, in fact, that after ten years people began to ask, whatever happened to Odysseus? His son grew up, and his wife was swamped with suitors, ready to marry whenever she finished weaving her tapestry. Finally, gods and family friends decided it was time to dispatch Telemachus, Odysseus's son, to find him; and the goddess Athena signed on as an interested and beneficial deity.

When Odysseus straggled back home nineteen years after he had left, he told of his astonishing adventures with god-willed storms and large hungry monsters, killer women and helpful kings, and a very long stay with the seductive Calypso.

An uneventful sail in a boat like his from Troy to Sicily to Ithaca might have taken about six weeks. But you can do it all in two, and be rested, tanned, and well fed—and without a tent city of suitors and their servants to wade through when you return home.

"George." History is many things to many people, and sometimes truly a fantasy. Our first president, George Washington has been depicted in many places, including the dollar bill, from which this drawing is made. *(Sketch by Beckwith, 1970. From the author's collection)*

Classical Cruises   132 East 70th Street, New York, New York 10021. 800-252-7745 (toll free); 212 794-3200 (tel). Web site: www.classicalcruises.com

The ninety-two-passenger *Sun Bay II*, launched in 2002, is a beautiful, fully equipped ship ready to take on Homer's *Odyssey*. Accompanied by a scholar, you will start appropriately in Troy (Turkey) and sail around the Peloponnese and kind King Nestor's realm. Then in the open Mediterranean, sail west to Malta, the island of Calypso, the nymph whose leisurely charms captured Odysseus for seven years, until the god Hermes reminded her that Odysseus had a family and should get back to Ithaca.

Odysseus took to the sea again, and subsequently encountered a bitter storm from an offended Poseidon, god of the sea; the less-than-hospitable Laestrygonians (in Sicily), uncouth giants who threw boulders on his crew as they tried to go ashore; the one-eyed cannibal Cyclops (near Naples); and the Sirens. For this trial, Odysseus put wax in his crew's ears and had himself lashed to the mast so the Sirens' song could not distract them from their course (Sorrento).

Sail then through the Straits of Messina, at the tip of the boot of Italy (the shifting rocks of Scylla and Charybdis), on to Taormina, the Kingdom of Helios, where Odysseus slaughtered the sacred cattle and incurred the sun god's wrath. Finally, cross the Ionian Sea to Corfu, the island of the helpful maiden Nausicaa. Then on to Ithaca.

Two weeks: about $7,000 to $9,000, depending on berth.

THE VIKINGS

Yes, sometimes they wore horned hats and Madonna-like breast-plates and rowed everywhere, but the Vikings got things done. When they stormed into soon-to-be-Normandy, resident peasants welcomed them and adopted their language and habits; in fact, a hundred years later, Normans stormed into England.

About the same time, Vikings were interested in what was happening in the West. Building some of the best ships ever, planked and designed to ease with the swells of the sea, Vikings put up sails and traveled to Iceland. According to the Icelandic sagas, Eric the Red, wanted for murder at home, founded a colony there. Shortly after they settled, he killed a man in a brawl, and moved on to explore icy Greenland, misnamed to seduce his countrymen into settling farther west.

In time, his sons Leif and Thorstein ventured even farther west into Newfoundland in search of vines and arable land. At a tiny site called L'Anse aux Meadows are the remains of a small colony of Vikings, who lived a rudimentary life and battled unfriendly Indians. What were their dreams? That's harder to reconstruct from the artifacts. What does seem likely is that they did not stay there long. But whether they returned to Greenland or continued on south to New England is a continuing archaeological mystery.

Clipper Cruises   7711 Bonhomme Avenue, Saint Louis, Missouri 63105-1956. 800-325-0010 (toll free). Web site: www. clippercruise.com

Clipper Cruises, which specializes in small-ship cruising, will give you an up-close and personal look at natural and historical Greenland and Newfoundland, "wherever the spirit of adventure takes us." Guided by an onboard historian, In the Wake of the Ancient Vikings will allow you to explore in small zodiacs this difficult and usually frozen land. Visit Surtsey, the volcanic island formed in 1963 off Iceland; travel around the tip of Greenland and follow Eric's and Leif's expedition to the coast of Newfoundland and the site of L'Anse aux Meadows. Spend the final day in Saint John's, Newfoundland. Sixteen days: from about $6,500 to $11,000, depending on berth.

American Museum of Natural History   Discovery Tours, Central Park West at 79th Street, New York, New York 10024-5192. 800-462-8687 (toll free); 212-769-5700 (tel); 212-769-5755 (fax). E-mail: info@amnh.org; Web site: www.discoverytours.org

Voyage of the Vikings, a Discovery Tour of the American Museum of Natural History, follows in the footsteps of the Vikings east to Scotland. Cruising on the expedition vessel *Explorer*, the trip begins in Reykjavik with a discussion of Viking lifestyles. Then you circumnavigate Iceland, exploring remote cliffs and fjords, empty beaches and grasslands, geysers and mountains, and begin to understand the geography in which they lived.

From Iceland, sail to Viking archaeological sites on the Scottish Isles of Orkney, Faroe, and Shetland, before spending some time in twenty-first-century Edinburgh. The trip is accompanied by Viking scholars and geologists. Sixteen days: about $7,000 to $13,000, depending on berth.

The Renaissance

Renaissance Faires

Society for Creative Anachronism   P.O. Box 360789, Milpitas, California 95036-0789. E-mail: directors@sca.org; Web site: www. sca.org. Renaissance Faire Web site: www.renfaire.com

A combination of "historical reenactment and performance art," Renaissance Faires, held at multiple locations throughout the world, replicate the late Elizabethan and Renaissance eras as closely as possible. Coming together for a celebration, knights joust, peasants sell loaves of bread on flat wooden boards, maidens dance, jugglers juggle, and fools keep the action moving.

Members dress in contemporary costume and speak the contemporary language as closely as possible. Not only do they engage in contests such as archery and weapons throwing, but they strum lutes and sing and dance. Actors circulate among the gathered crowd (of twenty-first-century people) and create situations by beginning conversations with things like, "I say, good man, have you ere seen a more magnificent fish?" Actors learn how to gently engage and disengage from conversations like this, and assure that it's all in good fun.

If you have ever had a desire to immerse yourself completely in another era, Renaissance Faires are for you. There is probably a chapter not far from where you live, which you can join. You will be given another name (probably beginning with "Lord" or "Lady"). You can take workshops in culturally accurate dress and speech, the meaning of heraldry, and calligraphy. At Faires, you can sign on to take part in tourneys or sell crafts or food, act, or sing and dance to a merrie tune.

California leads the way as the oldest organized Faire, with the most in one state. Call 800-52-FAIRE [523-2473] for a California listing.

Captain Bligh and the H.M.S. *Bounty*

Society Expeditions   2001 Western Avenue, Suite 300, Seattle, Washington 98121. 800-548-8669 (toll free); 206-728-9400 (tel); 206-728-2301 (fax). Web site: www.societyexpeditions.com

British seaman William Bligh, Captain of the H.M.S. *Bounty*, sailed to the South Pacific with a mission to collect breadfruit to introduce into the West Indies. Not known for his temperate personality, Bligh became more and more infuriated as his crew, led by the impetuous Fletcher Christian, settled into a life of ease and pleasure during their six-month stay in Tahiti.

When they finally resumed their voyage, Bligh's men mutinied, put Bligh off the *Bounty* in a small boat with few provisions, and headed to Pitcairn Island, under Fletcher Christian, where they lived happily ever after. (Bligh ultimately arrived in Timor and continued in his search for breadfruit.)

Society Expeditions in its 354-foot expedition ship, *World Explorer*, takes you from Easter Island through the Pitcairns to the Marquesas and Bora Bora and Tahiti in the Society Islands. In Pitcairn, you meet some of the forty-eight residents, most of whom are descendants of the mutinous *Bounty* crew. Their archaic English derives from the English spoken by the sailors in 1790.

In the Wake of the Bounty is South Pacific exploring at its best. Along its course of 2,000+ miles, the ship stops at uninhabited islands to take tours with a naturalist, and provides time for lots of snorkeling and diving. The ship also has a library, pools, a physician, zodiacs, two glass-bottom boats, and snorkeling and diving equipment.

But the trip also gives a sense of the sultry lure of the islands and the price that beauty exacts. At Mangareva, in the Gambiers Islands, for example, visit a cathedral with a mother-of-pearl altar built under the ruthless rule of a priest gone mad. In Papeete, Society Islands, visit artist Paul Gauguin's old haunts, as well as his grave in the Marquesas, where he died of syphillis.

Fourteen days, including everything except international airfare: about $8,500.

LEWIS AND CLARK

In 1804, Meriwether Lewis and William Clark were sent out by President Thomas Jefferson, as anxious to find an easy route to the Pacific as to have specimens of rocks and animals to add to his geological and natural history collections. For Lewis and Clark, the trip was a question of navigating canoes and rivers and dealing with tribes of Native Americans, many of whom were very accommodating. Without Indian princess Sacagawea as a guide, the expedition might have failed.

Lindblad Expeditions   720 Fifth Avenue, New York, New York 10019. 800-397-3348 (toll free). E-mail: explore@expeditions.com; Web site: www.expeditions.com

In seven days, Lindblad Expeditions has put together an exploration that captures the excitement of this early American discovery. The route, parts of which are still devoid of settlement, follows the Columbia and Snake Rivers into Idaho and through Hell's Canyon, the deepest gorge in North America. Traveling by expedition ship out of Portland, you can explore the beaches, gorges, wildlife, and Indian petroglyphs off the ship, in zodiacs, jet boats, and kayaks. Historians and naturalists aboard identify wildlife and describe the historical scene not only of Lewis and Clark, but of 10,000 years before them.

Seven days: about $2,500 to $3,800, depending on berth.

Odyssey Tours   P.O. Box 1573, Lewiston, Idaho 83501. 208-791-8721 (tel); 208-798-5101 (fax). E-mail: bek@hibek.com; Web site: www.hibek.com

Odyssey runs several tours of the Lewis and Clark Trail, all accompanied by Dr. Clay Jenkinson, a Chatauqua theatrical performer, who will give you the inside story from Meriwether Lewis himself.

On Odyssey's Lewis and Clark Athalon trip, for example, start in Missoula, Montana, hike up to 3,000 feet in the Bitterroot Mountains, ride mountain bikes and horses as you explore the historic trail, and listen to stories from Captain Lewis (a.k.a. Dr. Jenkinson) around the campfire at night.

Hike down the mountain to the van and have a hot shower in a lodge before exploring Lewis and Clark's canoe camp. Kayak or canoe down the river, meet the Nez Perce in the area, and stay the final night in a hotel at the confluence of the Snake and Clearwater Rivers.

Eight days: about $2,000.

PIRATE JEAN LAFITTE

RiverBarge Excursions Line, Inc. 201 Opelousas Avenue, New Orleans, Louisiana 70114. 888-282-1945 (toll free); 504-365-0000 (fax). E-mail: rel@riverbarge.com; Web site: www. riverbarge.com

In the 1820s, south of New Orleans in Barataria Bay, pirate Jean Lafitte maintained a fleet of 1,000 privateers and 50 ships. Earlier, this French renegade helped defeat the British in the Battle of New Orleans, but he would have no part of President Jackson's offer of citizenship.

Instead, as a stateless pirate he worked the profitable Texas and Mexican coasts, where, rumor has it, he stashed his treasure, never found.

You can scope the territory on a luxury riverbarge, the *River Explorer*, which provides all the amenities as it intimately travels the whole coast from New Orleans to Mexico. Ashore, you meet the people, many of whom are descendants of Lafitte's men; and you experience the marshland and waterways and their wildlife that made habitat unpleasant in Lafitte's day. The food is a terrific mix of Cajun, TexMex, and Mexican.

Seven days, including everything except airfare: from about $2,250 to $2,550, depending on stateroom level.

ERNEST HEMINGWAY IN KEY WEST

This is about as close as you can get to Hemingway, short of calling up his spirit from the great beyond. It helps if you even remotely resemble him, because Hemingway Days, held around every July twenty-first (Hemingway's birthday) in Key West, Florida, sponsors a look-alike contest. Streets downtown are filled with large men sporting white beards and dressed in khaki safari outfits. But the funky fun doesn't end there.

From Sloppy Joe's, the writer's famous hangout, multiple Hemingways compete in the running of the bulls—mostly wood and on wheels—before the choosing of the Hemingway who will reign for a year. Pig roasts, a sailing regatta, parties, including a 1940s costume party, and a 5K road race mark the celebration, along with serious literature prizes and scholarships for local kids.

Hemingway finished *A Farewell to Arms* and wrote *To Have and Have Not, Death in the Afternoon, The Snows of Kilimanjaro,* and *The Green Hills of Africa* at a studio adjacent to his house (now a National Historic Landmark) in Key West. For ten years during the Depression (with a break for the Spanish Civil War), he lived there with wife number 2 (of 4), his cats (their descendants remain), and the ever-present option of deep-sea fishing off the coast. Key West accommodates Hemingway fans with the $250,000 Drambuie Key West Marlin Tournament, the fish he loved to play with, write about, and catch. For details, see www.hemingwaydays.com.

The Pier House Resort and Caribbean Spa [800-327-8340 (toll free), 305-296-4600 (tel); Web site: www.pierhouse.com], has put together a Live Like Hemingway package, available from July to Christmas. Spend three nights in the Hemingway Suite, which overlooks the ocean and has a large red claw-foot bathtub. The package includes one day of deep sea fishing in a private boat, admission for two to the Hemingway House, plus a box of Conchitas cigars and a Key West–style dinner served on your private balcony.

Three days: $3,500.

Or try the Eden House [1015 Fleming Street, Key West, Florida 33040; 800-533-KEYS [5397] (toll free); 305-296-6868 (tel); E-mail: mike@edenhouse.com; Web site: www.edenhouse.com], a hotel built about the time Hemingway was spinning out his stories a few blocks away. This relaxed and comfortable hotel grew from two Conch houses built in the late 1800s, and preserves historical Key West (in creative ways, like converting a 1950 gas station into a café) and providing spaces like the hammock area, where library rules apply (whispering only), and readers can stretch out and sway with the wind or curl up on porch swings with a Hemingway novel.

BATTLEFIELDS

World War I

National Geographic Expeditions P.O. Box 65265 Washington, D.C. 20035-5265. 888-866-8687 (toll free). Reserve online at: www.nationalgeographic.com/ngexpeditions.

Military historian John Votaw, an expert on World War I, will guide you to Paris and the battlefields of Verdun, the longest battle of the war. Visit battlesites and cemeteries in Saint Mihiel and Thiacourt, then travel to Varennes-en-Argonne and lay a wreath at the American cemetery at Romagne. Go through Champagne to Chateau de Thierry and climb the hill that commands the Marne River, and see the Bulldog Fountain, which was the later inspiration for the mascot of the U.S. Marines. The trip ends in Paris. Ten days, including everything, as well as international airfare from New York: about $4,000.

D-Day, Normandy

Holt Tours Limited The Plough, High Street, Eastry, Sandwich, Kent CT 13 0HF, United Kingdom. 011 +44 800-

731-1914 (toll free); 011 +44 (0) 1304 612248 (tel); 011 +44 (0) 1304 614930 (fax). E-mail: info@holts.co.uk; Web site: www. battletours.co.uk

The arrival of American troops at Normandy ended the reign of World War II Nazi terror in Europe. D-Day, called "the mightiest armada in history," was complex and bloody. Called Operation Overlord, it combined American, British, and Canadian troops in two air and five sea invasions.

The areas around the beaches at Normandy are strewn with cemeteries and memorials. Guided by two experts in war history, this Holt tour encourages reconstruction of one of the most important battles in history. Spend five days touring Gold, Juno, Sword, Utah, and Omaha beaches and the museums and memorials near Calais, Bayeux, and Caen.

Five days, including shared lodging, half-board, and wine with dinner: about £600 (about $950).

Vietnam

Myths and Mountains　976 Tee Court, Incline Village, Nevada 89451. 800-670-6984 (toll free); 775-832-5454 (tel); 775-832-4454 (fax). E-mail: travel@mythsandmountains.com; Web site: www. mythsandmountains.com

Your own personal guide on the Battlegrounds of the Vietnam War trip is a ten-year U.S. Army veteran who did service in Vietnam. Begin in Saigon and travel back in time and through the war and your own remembered experiences, ending at Hue. Create your own itinerary with the guide (the price depends on where you want to go and stay, as well as the length of the trip).

Myths and Mountains is a company skilled in accommodating the needs of the customer and designing trips that include a deeper understanding of the people.

Gettysburg

International Ghost Hunters Society　PMB 8377, P.O. Box 2428, Pensacola, Florida 32513. 712-251-9089 (tel). E-mail: magicdimensions@aol.com; Web site: www.ghostweb.com

All battlefields are full of ghosts, but none quite so amazingly as Gettysburg. Maybe it's the autumn mists that look like smoke, or the stillness that vibrates with old pain. The Civil War took an enormous toll on troops from the North as well as the South, most of whom were young men with unfulfilled loves and lives. Many companies include the Battlefield of Gettysburg in their tours; this one takes a different approach.

Drs. Dave Oester and Sharon Gill of the International Ghost Hunters Society have devised a method of otherworldly contact using EVP, or *electronic voice phenomena*, in which voices of the dead are embedded in magnetic tape. Special software allows the listener to evaluate it.

Each year, the society hosts an international three-day conference at Gettysburg. Classes and lectures are interspersed with hands-on detection.

Three days, conference only: $80. The cost of Holiday Inn lodging is extra.

DRACULA, THE MAN AND THE LEGEND

Yes, there was a historical Count Dracula, Prince Vlad Tepes, known to his friends as Vlad the Impaler, born 1431. The fictional Dracula was not created until 1897 by Irish novelist Bram Stoker.

The major difference between the historical and the fictional Dracula lies in the ways they expressed their tastes for blood: Vlad impaled people because it was his way to keep order; Dracula punctured people because he needed blood to stay alive.

Scholar Elizabeth Miller (www.ucs.mun.ca/~emiller/) believes Bram Stoker never knew about Count Dracula Vlad the Impaler when he wrote his book. Instead, Miller believes, Stoker gave the name *Dracula* to the hero of the vampire novel he was writing after he saw a reference in a book on Transylvania to the meaning of the word *Dracul*, which is dragon, synonymous with the devil. Stoker's original name for his evil hero was Count Wampyr. Add a novelist's vivid imagination, and the deathless Dracula comes into being, a devilish vampire. Only later did the historical and the fictional get confused.

Dracula, the Book

Stoker's book opens with an innocent young Englishman named Jonathan Harker riding a train (probably the Orient Express) to Transylvania on business, where he is to deliver a letter from his employer to Count Dracula.

Stoker stops in Budapest, spends the night, and remarks on the food, rich in red pepper, and makes notations to himself to get the recipe for his fiancée. Then he takes a carriage through the Borgo Pass in the Carpathian Mountains to Bran, where he is to be met by a carriage sent by Count Dracula.

Unfortunately, Jonathan Harker is traveling on the eve of Saint George's Day, which, at midnight, becomes "a time when all the evil things in the world will have full sway," according to local superstition. The night is filled with strange lights, and things get drearier and drearier as the carriage travels toward Bran.

At Dracula's castle, the creaky door opens to reveal a tall, old man with a white mustache, dressed entirely in black, with ice-cold hands and long fingernails cut to sharp points. Count Dracula welcomes Harker, and invites him to dine on roast chicken, cheese, salad, and an old Tokay, so mellow, Harker enjoys two glasses.

And therein begins the tale of horror. Dracula, a polite conversationalist at dinner, nevertheless declines to eat, waiting, little does Harker know, for a later feast on the contents of his guest's veins.

Twenty-first Century Dracula

The idea of human vampires selling a kind of pyramid scheme, where one vampire begets two others, who each beget two more, and so on, has inspired countless films, from silent, black-and-white, to brilliant color; some silly, some good, and some great. Something in Stoker's evil tale has made it into a classic. Academicians faithfully attend a World Dracula Congress, sponsored by the Transylvanian Society of Dracula, part of an international society that joins people all over the world in their fascination with Dracula (see: www.afn.org/~vampires/html).

At this writing, controversy rages in Romania over the creation of Draculand, a theme park around the fictional Dracula, complete with people in costume, a medieval restaurant, a Dracula golf course, and Dracula souvenirs from chess pieces to T-shirts. Although UNESCO has no problems with the idea, and Coca-Cola is keeping an eye on an exclusive soft drink contract, many Europeans, among them Prince Charles of Great Britain, a member of a Roumanian environmental group, resist the idea because a theme park, in Prince Charles's words, "would be out of sympathy with the area."

Within Romania, much reluctance to commit to the park stems from the fact that Dracula, the vampire, is not a recognized Romanian, whereas Prince Vlad, aka the Impaler, is remembered as a medieval conquering hero. Funding for the park is tenuous, despite the fact that the Ministry of Tourism is fully aware that the fictional Dracula is far more likely to attract tourists and their dollars than Prince Vlad.

Dracula, the Tours

But the recreation of the Dracula story doesn't need a theme park. Romania itself has managed to maintain not only dank and foreboding castles and medieval churches, but cold foggy rivers, roads empty of everyone but lonely horsemen, and graveyards with tombs.

It's the spirit that counts.

Campbell Travel Service   455 Liquidambar Way, Sunnyvale, California 94086. 408-739-9297 (tel). E-mail: dracu-lady@ ilovetotravel.com; Web site: www.ilovetotravel.com

Somehow in the United States, Halloween replaced Saint George's Eve (May 4–5), as the night of evil spirits and the time to celebrate Dracula. But October is the better time to see Romania in its cool, gray autumnal moods.

On this trip, fly into Budapest, Hungary, then take the train to Romania, evoking Jonathan Harker's trip. From the former capital city of Cluj, travel to Bistrita Village to stop at the Golden Crown (for lunch), the same inn where Jonathan spent his final night before meeting Count Dracula (read Chapter 1).

This tour weaves together the multiple threads of Romania—its history in medieval villages such as Sighisoara, where Prince Vlad was born; the beauty of its rural area, with winding roads and leaves that change color, and unusual painted wood churches; small bazaars where you can buy beautiful handicrafts; and somehow, joining it all together, the peculiar draw of Bram Stoker's *Dracula*.

"Dracula Lady" Mary Williamson has been running Halloween tours to Romania for the past seven or eight years with great fun and "lots of surprises along the way." Bring your own costume to wear to the Dracula Ball held October 31 in Bran Village in a former Transylvanian fortress (the Citadel). The area around the medieval city of Brasov (Vlad's impaling territory) on that night is alive with parties, dancing, games, and people in costume.

The tour returns to the United States from Bucharest, where you can spend the night at the gaming tables; formal dress required (you *could* wear your costume).

Ten days, including hotels, most meals, guides, and international airfare: about $2,000.

Transylvania, Inc.   1350 Arnold Drive, Suite 102-T, Martinez, California 94553-4190. 925-229-4810 (tel). E-mail: info@undiscoveredlands.com; Web site: www.undiscoveredlands.com

Bring your Halloween costume for this tour, too, to celebrate Dracula at the party in Brasov Castle, but be prepared to delve more deeply into the art and architecture of Romania, which, before Prince Vlad, was an outpost of the Roman Empire, and home of many gypsies.

Fly out of New York to Budapest, and drive through the famous Tokay wine-growing region of Hungary, stopping for a tasting. In Satu Mare, Romania, visit Karoly Castle, once the seat of one of Hungary's oldest noble families. That night, go to the symphony, followed by a Transylvanian dinner with entertainment by a gypsy band.

As your van drives through the Carpathians and Transylvanian countryside, stop for monasteries and tiny painted churches, country folk arts, dancers (dance with them), gypsy musicians, and excellent food.

Drive back through Hungary to spend a night in Buda, and have a Hungarian dinner with "haunting Hungarian folk music." Fly back from Budapest.

Eleven days, including hotels, meals, guides, and international airfare: about $3,400, double occupancy; $3,750, single.

CHAPTER 16

HORSES

After five days on a horse, a rider said, centaurs are not so hard to imagine. Whether you believe horses and humans share a unique intelligence or not, bonding with a good horse is an experience unlike any other. A horseback riding vacation puts you in touch with a whole world of power and beauty, as well as the sheer thrill of turning that power into speed as you canter through a field or fly across an empty beach.

HORSE RIDING VACATIONS

Wyoming

Equitours   P.O. Box 807, 10 Stainaker Street, Dubois, Wyoming 82513. 800-545-0019 (toll free); 307-455-3363 (tel); 307-455-2354 (fax). E-mail: equitours@wyoming.com; Web site: www.ridingtours.com

Equitours is the country's oldest and largest riding tour company, and their experience has led them to hire excellent guides and devise a scale against which you can measure your own riding skill. You may think you ride one way, but your horse will immediately know the difference, so it pays to start off on the same page if you will be spending some time together.

The skill levels are defined as follows:

E, or Beginner, is a rider who has taken rides on horses in parks and who is able to hang on when the horse moves.

D, or Novice, is a rider who can get on and off by himself, knows how to walk, post a trot, and do short canters.

C, or Intermediate, is a rider who is confident and can control the walk, post, and canter, but who simply doesn't ride very often.

B, or Strong Intermediate, is a regular rider who is comfortable spending six hours in the saddle.

A, or Advanced, is a rider with "an independent seat, soft hands, and is capable of handling a spirited horse in open country."

These rules apply to riders familiar with either the English or the Western saddle.

Equitours advises that you estimate on the conservative side and consider taking an instructional program if you are not sure.

The other requirement of horse vacations is the matter of weight. Yours, not the horse's. Most trips mentioned will give the weight limit; it is usually between 185 and 210 pounds.

Finally, consider special accident insurance on these trips, just in case. Wear a hard hat.

Although Equitours sponsors horse-riding tours around the world, they have not overlooked their own backyard. On a Wyoming Pack Trip, you will spend eight days exploring the Greater Yellowstone Ecosystem with a naturalist guide, ride all day at a slow pace, then set up a comfortable camp at night and relax with a glass of wine before dinner.

You will climb up along switchbacks into mountain lion country, then weave down into valleys along creeks and rivers and across long stretches of meadows with grazing elk and an occasional grizzly bear. You will spend about six hours a day in the saddle. Wyoming is one of the least-populated states, with a lot of natural beauty. If that doesn't solve all your problems, perhaps bonding with your Arabian will.

Eight days at Novice (D) Level, including all meals, lodge and camping equipment, and horse: about $1,550.

Northern California Coast

Ricochet Ridge Ranch   24201 North Highway 1, Fort Bragg, California 95437. 707-964-7669 (tel); 707-964-9669 (fax). E-mail: larishea@horsevacation.com; Web site: www.horse-vacation.com

Endurance-riding cup winner Lari Shea breeds Russian Orlov and Arabian horses at her ranch near Mendocino, on the northern coast of California. A week's ride through the Redwood Forest and along the rugged Pacific coast on the ranch's fine horses is a guaranteed fantasy of old California and the unleashed beauty of the place.

Spend days weaving paths through forests and along ridges, exploring abandoned ranches, a working cattle farm, and ancient game trails, with lots of beaches on which to canter; and nights staying at historic B&Bs or the lavish Mendocino Hotel, where Mendocino's famous musicians entertain the guests.

Seven days: lodging, meals, and horse: about $2,000.

Wales

Eastern Trekking Associates   P.O. Box 357, Thomson, Georgia 30824. 888-836-6152 (toll free); 706-541-2450 (tel). E-mail: rides@horsevacations.com; Web site: www.horsevacations.com

Shelly and Albert Morris have been facilitating riding vacations for people from around the world for many decades. Eastern Trekking is adamant about your honestly representing your riding skill level, and will terminate your tour (without refund) if the ride master believes you were not frank about your level of ability. Their rides are for Novice, Intermediate, and Experienced riders, and assume some previous experience of all riders.

Eastern Trekking trips are excellent for riders who like to increase speed and endurance with each new trip. In Wales, for example, choose a Black Mountain Trail horse trek according to your level of ability. Those comfortable with walking, trotting, and cantering, for example, can spend a week riding the empty moors and steep hills on a Welsh cob, trained especially for the terrain.

Staying at an eighteenth-century farmhouse each night, you ride between eight and eighteen miles a day, stop for lunch at village pubs. The countryside includes woodlands and valleys; guides will help you over any rough spots.

Seven days: about $1,400.

If you are a skilled rider ready for a real challenge, take on the Trans Wales Trail, ninety miles in five days over varied and challenging hills and dales, which means speed as well as endurance. Some steep hill paths are too narrow for the rider, who must dismount and lead his horse to the top.

A guide accompanies you at all times, but your enjoyment depends on your level of physical fitness. Stay at a different hotel each night; sometimes have picnic lunches. If you love horses and Wales, this trip is for you.

Seven days: about $1,600. (Your horse gets a ride home.)

Eastern Trekking requires medical insurance and preventive medication for malaria for all safaris. It might also be wise to get travel insurance for any weather cancellations, stolen luggage, etc., as well.

Irish Coast

Drumgooland Country House & Equestrian Center   Frank & Alice McLeigh, 29 Dunnanew Road, Seaforde, Downpatrick, County Down, BT30 8PL, Northern Ireland. 011 +44 (0) 28 4481 1956 (tel); 011 +44 (0) 28 4481 1956 (fax). E-mail: Frank.Mcleigh@ btinternet.com; Web site: www.activityholidaysireland.com

Visitors say it's the sweet horses that make a stay at Drumgooland special; others say it's the proximity to the Irish Sea and riding for miles at the shoreline, with the silhouette of the Mountains of Mourne on the horizon.

Frank and Alice McLeigh welcome riders to their 100-year-old country home near Seaforde, where their horses in the adjoining Equestrian Centre are ready to match your level of skill. You have a choice of three- or six-day trail-riding holidays, during which you return each night to Drumgooland House for dinner.

Three graceful riders glide in a fine gallop across an Irish beach with nothing to stop them. *(Courtesy of Equitours 2002)*

Trails wind past ancient Norman castle ruins and waterfalls, through a nature reserve, over the cobblestone streets of a village, and on an old smugglers' trail, to a long beach that stretches along the Irish Sea, where you can feel as free as your horse. An experienced guide accompanies you and will help if you need it. An excellent golf course is nearby, as are Saint Patrick's grave and a pub with traditional Irish music.

Three days, including lodging, food, horse, and instruction: about €650; six days: about €1,200 (Euros; about the same in U.S. dollars).

POLO

Ireland

Equestrian Vacations Cross Country International; P.O. Box 1170, Millbrook, New York 12545. 800-828-8768 (toll free);

845-635-3300 (fax). E-mail: info@xcintl.com; Web site: www. equestrianvacations.com

Karen Lancaster has been uniting courses, horses, and comfort into first-class riding vacations for several years. Equestrian Vacations produces a fabulous catalog, designed to encourage anyone's wildest equestrian dreams, from Colorado to the Aegean, from trail riding to falconry.

In County Limerick near the village of Adare, for example, you can spend a week learning to play polo, or polishing your skills. Coaches will guide you in an understanding of the rules, the use of the mallet and the ball, basic strokes, scoring, and other aspects of the game. The Limerick Polo Club will challenge you in frequent matches. You must be a competent rider.

In downtime you can slip into the pool at the Dunraven Arms Hotel in Adare or spend some time at the lively village pub.

Six nights, including lodging, food, and instruction: about $1,900.

DRESSAGE TRAINING

This graceful union of rider and horse moving together like the wind is an ancient art form, for which you need an excellent instructor and "schoolmasters," or trained horses, many of which were bred for it.

Equitours   P.O. Box 807, Dubois, Wyoming 82513. 800-545-0019 (toll free); 307-455-3363 (tel); 307-455-2354 (fax). E-mail: equitours@wyoming.com; Web site: www.ridingtours.com

Equitours has found two excellent dressage programs. In Portugal, you will have access to an instructor who studied with the great dressage master Nuno Oliveira; and you will be able to ride Lusitano stallions. Four hours a day of instruction are varied with trail rides and swimming. For more information, see: nancie.equitours @dteworld.net. All riding levels except beginner; weight limit: 180 pounds. Per night, including three hours of riding a day, lodging, and meals: $150.

In New Hampshire, work closely with an instructor; have two lessons a day, and observe training of the horses. For more information, see: biggi.equitours@dteworld.net. Five days, including two group lessons a day and one private lesson: about $800. Accommodations and meals are not included.

England

Equestrian Vacations   Cross Country Vacations, P.O. Box 1170, Millbrook, New York 12545. 800-828-8768 (toll free); 845-635-3300 (fax). E-mail: info@xcintl.com; Web site: www. equestrianvacations.com

One week in Yorkshire, England, with Dressage Champions Christopher Bartle and his sister Jane Bartle-Wilson (three of thirteen lessons are taught by one or the other) will show you how dressage is done. The rest of the week you will receive group or private lessons with advanced instructors, who will also give lectures and demonstrations on dressage theory and stable management.

Stay at a guesthouse and enjoy the other sports available at the Yorkshire Riding Center, such as tennis and biking. One week, including lodging and meals and instruction: about $2,000.

Georgia

Garland Farms, Dahlonega, Georgia. 706-864-6699 (tel). E-mail: garland@alltel.net; Web site: www.gfdressage.com

Bring your own horse or ride Garland Farms' horses. Either way, focus on your dressage skills, as you stay in a small cabin or a studio. Five nights, including eleven lessons, lodging, and all meals: about $1,000. A weekend, including five lessons, lodging, and food: about $425.

THE KENTUCKY DERBY

Few horse races in the world have the importance or the panache of the Kentucky Derby, the epitome of genteel Southern ritual, including mint juleps, sipped from cooled silver cups.

American Museum of Natural History   Discovery Tours, Central Park West at 79th Street, New York, New York 10024-5192. 800-462-8687 (toll free); 212-769-5700 (tel); 212-769-5755 (fax). E-mail: info@amnh.org; Web site: www.discoverytours.org

Accompanied by two horse experts, one an authority on the complex intertwined evolution of man and horse, and the other on thoroughbred horse racing, this tour provides a private, behind-the-scenes look at horse breeding at the Derby—including an invitation to the renowned Hermitage Farm, where winners are bred—and a visit to the International Museum of the Horse. Watch breeders test their racers at Keeneland Racetrack, see the pre-race parade of breeds at Kentucky Horse Park, then join in the excitement of the running of the Derby at Churchill Downs.

After three days in Lexington, Kentucky, board the *Delta Queen* and head down the Ohio River for four days, past beautiful plantations and interesting small towns. A Southern architectural historian will fill you in on the culture of Kentucky. Nights aboard dance to jazz, blues, and big-band music.

Seven days, including all lodging and meals: about $3,500 to $6,000, depending on berth.

HORSE ECO-VOLUNTEERING

Przewalski Horse Reintroduction, Mongolia

Samar Magic Tours Co. Ltd.   National Ecovolunteer Agency. Attn: Mr. Cristo Camilo Gavilla Gomez. 976-11-311051 (tel); 976-11-327503 (fax). E-mail: ecovolunteers@samarmagictours. com; Web site: www.samarmagictours.com. *In the United States:* leave voice mail or send a fax: 206-888-4286.

This unusual horse vacation will let you ride off into the Mongolian steppes each day searching for the small Przewalski horse, thought to be the ancestor of all domestic horses, and the only true wild horse left ("wild" horses in the American West are feral).

When you do spot one of these horses (and jot in your notebook when and where you saw it, what it looked like, what it was doing, and where it was headed), you will remember having seen its pictures on ancient cave walls: it is small, massive, and light-colored, with a black stripe along its spine, a dark brush of a mane, and short dark legs. A particularly famous picture of one is at Lascaux Caves, dating from about 30,000 years ago.

As recently as 1968 the last one was seen in Mongolia, and only 200 Przewalski horses were thought to exist in zoos scattered around the world. In conjunction with the Mongolian Association for Conservation of Nature and Environment, which set aside 60,000 acres of steppe as the Hustain Nuruu ("Birch Mountain") Reserve, the Dutch Reserves Przewalski Horse Foundation arranged to release into the wild Mongolian steppe several groups, or *harems*, of Przewalski horses that had been bred in captivity.

So far, the project seems to be working. The horses are at home in the rugged mountains and able to fend off wolves threatening to attack their young. The Dutch group keeps a detailed database on every individual Przewalski horse. Because its ultimate health depends on the biodiversity of the area, which is often subject to drought, the area must be constantly monitored.

The project, which relies on volunteers, has two main objectives: to track the horses in the wild, and to monitor the health of the Hustain Nuruu Reserve.

The requirements for this project are a love of horses and a sense of adventure. You will be met in Ulaanbaatar, about sixty-five miles away, then spend three weeks living in a *ger*, a six-meter round tent, using a primitive toilet, bucket showers, and eating meat-based meals cooked over a fire. Project directors ask that you be at least eighteen, speak English, be comfortable on horseback (and willing to learn to ride small Mongolian horses Mongolian-style), not mind camping, and be able "to appreciate (or at least be able to stand) the silence" of the vast land of the nomad.

Three weeks, including food, lodging, transfer to and from Ulaanbaatar, and the first night in a three-star hotel there: about $1,600.

Eco-Expeditions 192 Nickerson Street, #200, Seattle, Washington 98109. 800-628-8747 (toll free); 206-285-4000 (tel); 206-285-5037 (fax). E-mail: zoe@zeco.com; Web site: www. zeco.com

The Land of Chinggis Khaan is a total-immersion trip that introduces you to the nomadic culture of Mongolia. Stay in gers and experience events, such as athletes' demonstrations of wrestling and archery, that Genghis Khan himself enjoyed. After several days of crossing the Gobi Desert by four-wheel drive, you spend the last day of the tour at the Przewalski Project, before helicoptering back to Ulaanbaatar.

You have opportunities to ride the small Mongolian horse and camels as well. A paleontologist guides you through the huge sandstone gorges known as Flaming Cliffs, and the Valley of the Dragons, which contains the world's largest dinosaur graveyard. At dawn, climb the 1,000-foot-high Singing Sands that stretch for miles, rising up from the Gobi.

Wildlife is abundant and includes animals you have seen only in zoos—the yak, the Siberian boar, and the golden Mongolian wild ass—and birds you have never seen before. The guide is wildlife expert Jonathan Rossouw, who is also a physician.

The trip begins in Beijing. Seventeen days, including everything except international airfare to Beijing: about $9,990.

FALCONRY

Mongolia

Boojum Expeditions 14543 Kelly Canyon Road, Bozeman, Montana 59715. 800-287-0125 (toll free); 406-587-0125 (tel); 406-585-3474 (fax). E-mail: webinfo@boojum.com; Web site: www.boojum.com

Falconry is an art, practiced for centuries in Central Asia, in which the powerful hunting instincts of the eagle are trained to capture and retrieve small furry animals. Few birds have better eyesight or more clever hunting strategies; and people who live in cold climates need the furry pelts that they bring back.

There is no better place to learn falconry than Mongolia. You will ride out on horses with falcon hunters, sometimes at a clip, over hills and into the mountains. The Kazakh Eagle Hunters of Mongolia expedition will teach you how to hold and coax the eagle to go, as well as how to capture and train female eagles.

Live in a warm ger and eat hearty meals. Travel is also by jeep and on foot. The downside is that the temperature in winter is never above freezing; and the eagles jump for the nearest furry thing around, which could be your hat. The group size is limited to six; a prerequisite is an interview (by phone) with Boojum.

Eleven days, not including international airfare to Ulaanbaatar: about $2,200.

This company runs horse trips to Mongolia and several other countries as well, including the Yellowstone National Park in the United States.

CHAPTER 17

HOTELS WITH A CERTAIN EDGE

Fantasy lodging vacations give travelers a taste of how other people live. If you are blessed with interesting friends or family, you might requisition an island for the weekend or stake claim to a wing of the family chateau. Lacking that, enterprising hoteliers and unusual property owners take advantage of the need most people feel to experience other lifestyles. Here's a sampling:

LUXURY

British Virgin Islands

Necker Island   British Virgin Islands. E-mail: necker@virgin. co.uk; Web site: www.neckerisland.com. *Contacts: in the United States:* Janine Cifelli, Limited Edition by Virgin, c/o Resorts Management, Inc., 456 Glenbrook Road, Stamford, Connecticut 06906. 800-557-4255 (toll free). *In the United Kingdom or Europe:* Carolyn Wincer, Limited Edition by Virgin, 63 Buckingham Gate, London SW1E 6AT, United Kingdom. 011 +44 800-716-919 (toll free). *Or book through:* www.wheretostay.com; 800-557-4255.

   In the 1970s, Virgin Airways and music magnate Richard Branson bought Necker, a tiny island at the verge of the British Virgin

Home. *The World* of ResidenSea, a collection of condos and onboard services that comprise a small town, sails the world. Join them at a port and sail to the next port, to experience the luxury vagabond lifestyle. *(Courtesy of The World of ResidenSea)*

Island chain and the Atlantic Ocean, as a getaway for himself and his family. He oversaw the construction of the main house, built with stone walls to fend off ocean storms, had the roof made in Brazil and shipped prefab, and ordered specially handmade furniture from Bali. He also included a library, built a Hindu meditation hut, and created a bird sanctuary.

Add five beaches, a tennis court, aqua trampoline, and invite no more than twenty-six guests at any time to occupy the thirteen bedrooms, plus make it accessible only by helicopter or boat, and Necker Island becomes the preferred getaway of people fleeing the paparazzi. It's possible to rent the whole island.

The best part is the staff of thirty-one, who outnumber the guests. You have the option of eating in the dining room in the main house, if you stay there; or if you stay at one of the Balinese villas on the cliffside, tell the chef or have the butler relay to the chef what you would like for dinner, and when and where you would like to eat. The rest is up to you.

Prices per room per night range from $15,000 for one to seven people, on up to $29,000 for twenty to twenty-four people. The price includes all meals and drinks, and helicopter transport to the island.

This place is popular. Make your plans as much as a year in advance.

Scotland

The Carnegie Club   Skibo Castle, Dornoch, Sutherland IV25 3RQ, Scotland 011 +44 (0) 1862894600 (tel); 011 +44 (0) 1862894601 (fax). E-mail: info@carnegieclub.com; reservations@ carnegieclub.com; Web site: www.carnegieclub.com

Steel millionaire Andrew Carnegie found his Scottish roots in Skibo Castle, to which he retired in 1901 and made into an old boys' hunting lodge, where he and his friends also golfed, fished, and swam, before feasting on the fruits of the hunt. The Carnegie Club has since become a millionaires' club, developed by Peter de Savary, with membership by invitation only.

But interested parties can be granted the privilege of a one-time stay, of any affordable length, before deciding to join. As a non- or yet-to-be member, you can stay in one of forty-one bed suites, each a vast unit in the vast castle. You can do whatever you want during the day, even stay in your suite to try to get your mind around the splendor.

Included in the daily guest rate of about $900 (to start) are all food and drink, newspapers, fishing gear, clay target shooting, use of the swim and gym facilities, bird-watching gear, falconry, and all the golf you might like to play on Skibo's championship eighteen-hole course.

For a bit extra, you can join the pheasant hunt, fish for salmon, have a massage, or go horseback riding.

Whatever you do, come 7:30 P.M., you are expected for drinks downstairs. One half hour later, bagpipers announce dinner, mandatory with the stay. The banquet table is abundant, but you probably won't remember the *table d'hôte* because you are expected to demonstrate your skills at conversation. If you successfully navigate the hills and pitfalls of nuanced and often outrageous chitchat (e.g., the decibel level of elephant farts), who knows? Maybe you will be invited back. Madonna was married here.

The Fiji Islands

Fiji Escape Travel   Melissa McÇoy, President, 355 Hukilike Steet, #207, Kahului, Maui 96732. 888-353-3454 (toll free); 808-871-5986 (tel); 808-893-0138 (fax). *On the East Coast of the United States:* call Mark at 877-875-7399 (toll free).

Fiji is an archipelago in the Pacific Ocean, 15 degrees south of the equator, famous as the site of the mutiny of Captain Bligh's crew and the preferred islands of shipwrecked or deserting (or mutinous) sailors. No wonder: The weather is never too hot, always soothed by the trade winds, and the emerald waters teem with colorful fish. For this reason, tourism is Fiji's principal source of foreign currency.

Fiji Escape Travel can provide any of a variety of beachfront bures (cottages or huts) that will make you feel as close to Robinson Crusoe as you can. The Jean-Michel Cousteau resort, for example, with twenty-five open-air (no walls) bures on seventeen acres of a former coconut plantation, has access to some of the best diving, snorkeling, or glass-bottom boating anywhere.

Five nights, including round-trip airfare from LAX: between $2,100 and $2,800.

Or you can rent one of fourteen couples-only cottages on Turtle Island, site of the movie *Blue Lagoon*. Your cottage comes with a private beach.

Five nights, including round-trip airfare from LAX: about $4,300 to $5,300.

For a bit more, try the Wakaya Club, a collection of eight large and luxurious bures, preferred by celebrities such as Bill Gates and his wife, who honeymooned here. Lots of hidden beaches, an otherwise empty island, your personal chef, and all amenities are included.

One week, including private flight from the international airport: about $17,000. Seven nights, including airfare from LAX, at the Vale O', a small villa privately perched on a cliff overlooking the ocean: $30,000.

Miami

Shore Club   1901 Collins Avenue, Miami Beach, Florida 33139. 305-695-3100 (tel). Web site: www.shoreclubbeach.com

Miami has a tradition of big-name hotel architects, and this is no exception. New, with a twenty-one-story tower rising above two art deco hotels with marble lobbies and smooth straight pools that seem to spill into each other and reach to the sea, the 324-room Shore Club was designed by British architect David Chipperfield.

Aside from luxury in every corner, and so many details corrected (too-sharp seashells in the paving, too-dark shades of teak in the restaurant) that it was late in opening, the hotel has celebrity names and faces everywhere. Model Christy Turlington is the chief investor in the ayurvedic Sundari Spa; actor Robert De Niro is part owner of the hotel's sushi Nobu Restaurant.

It's on the beach, but you never have to get sandy. Poolside rooms are about $500 per night. The 6,000-square-foot, three-story penthouse is $15,000 a night.

Paris

Hotel Meurice   228, rue de Rivoli, 75001 Paris, France. 011 +33 (0) 1 44 58 10 09 (tel); 011 +33 (0) 1 44 58 10 19 (fax). E-mail: reservations@meuricehotel.com; Web site: www.meuricehotel.com

In the middle of Paris, across from the Tuilleries Gardens, this hotel, built in 1835 and restored a couple of years ago, is a paradigm of the grand tradition of magnificent hotels. Paris's oldest four-star hotel, the Meurice lacks the grandeur of the Crillon or the Ritz, the city's five-star celebrity magnets; but its impeccable "old-money" refinement has made it a favorite of an impressive list of royalty and world leaders. It was the second home of the Duke and Duchess of Windsor.

From the sweeping marble lobby to the salon and gallery, filled with fresh flowers and decorated with gold, white, and painted panels and Louis XV silk-covered furniture, the Meurice delivers value, class, and substance. Broad and quiet mirrored halls lead to 125 bedrooms and 20 suites, including two presidential suites, all recently redone.

The Meurice was built as a stopping place for traveling Brits in 1817, and you can have English tea or spend the afternoon settled into one of the sixty armchairs in the Jardin d'Hiver, under the glass Art Nouveau dome, surrounded by palm trees and other plants. The restaurant is five-star; the chef, Marc Marchand, blessed by the Michelin.

Each room has a different scheme. The Tuilleries apartment, 500 square meters, and the rooftop Belle Etoile Suite, a huge 2,500 square feet, each offer views of Paris that rival those from the Eiffel Tower. Both the Opera and the Louvre as well as the Faubourg shops are nearby.

This hotel is very popular with international leaders and artists. Salvadore Dali kept an apartment here. Book well in advance.

A single room with garden view is about €600 a night; a double room without a garden view is about €700. A suite with a Tuilleries view is €1,850 (Euros; about the same in U.S. dollars).

France, Italy, and Scotland

Abercrombie & Kent, Inc.   1520 Kensington Road, Oak Brook, Illinois 60523-2141. 800-757-5884 (toll free for brochures); 800-323-7308 (toll free); 630-954-2944 (tel); 630-954-3324 (fax).

E-mail: info@abercrombiekent.com; Web site: www. abercrombiekent.com

Abercrombie & Kent's Concierge Service is a program that brokers a number of luxury homes in France, Italy, and Scotland and provides informed local service that will take care of all the details of your vacation, from making reservations at restaurants, arranging for a car (or a helicopter or yacht), finding a secretary, and taking care of fees and equipment to play golf or go fishing. They also arrange a three-course candlelit dinner for your first night and lunch in your new quarters your first morning there.

One week: from $20,000 to $34,000.

New Zealand

New Zealand Hideaways is a fourteen-day trip in which Abercrombie & Kent arranges luxury lodging, rental cars, and planes as you cross this magnificent country. Their local contacts take care of details like reservations and tickets.

One week: about $9,000; plus air: about $950. International airfare is extra.

THE WORLD

The World of ResidenSea   Web site: www.residensea.com. *For rentals:* Corporate Office, Miami. 800-970-6601 (toll free); 305-779-3399 (tel); 305-269-1059 (fax). E-mail: guestservices@residensea.net. *For sales:* Miami: Philip P. Freedman and Johni Orr. 305-264-9090 (tel); 305-264-5090 (fax). E-mail: pfreedman@residensea.net. *New York:* Jacquelyn Sonenberg. 212-332-1660 (tel); 212-332-1663 (fax). E-mail: jsonenberg@earthlink.net. *Beverly Hills:* Lynette Dodds. 310-887-7090 (tel); 310-887-7087 (fax). E-mail: Lynetted@earthlink.net.

"Travel The World Without Leaving Home" is the slogan of The World, a luxury resort community that is a 644-foot cruise ship with 110 privately owned condos and 88 guest suites. The ship keeps its itinerary circling the globe, spending up to five days at each port. Do Cannes during the Film Festival, Rio at Carnavale, or Monte Carlo during the Grand Prix. Or simply relax, play golf or tennis, do water sports at their onboard marina, attend seminars, shop, go to the Clinique La Prairie spa, tell your private chef how many are expected for dinner, or pick up something at the Deli. Evenings, go to the theater, a concert, or movies; and never worry about air pollution.

The World properties, between 1,100 and 1,400 square feet, range from about $2.1 to $3 million, with yearly maintenance fees of between $65,000 to $116,000. Each is designed by a famous designer, working within the constraints of the ship: no fireplaces, and lamps that are bolted down. Among the current pioneer owners, the average age is about fifty, with (as one owner said) Type A personalities—the same energy it took to create the wealth and inspire the imagination to buy into The World. (Criminal background checks ensure against outlaws.) Many maintain land homes where they keep their pets. Grandchildren must remain landside, too.

If you would like to try it out, sail with them to designated ports on seven- to seventeen-day trips around the world (for example, London to Fort Lauderdale) for about $5,000 to $20,000.

Don't expect your average cruise; everyone remarks on the dignified quiet of the public spaces.

HISTORIC HOTELS

National Trust for Historic Preservation   1785 Massachusetts Avenue, NW, Washington, D.C. 20036. 202-588-6000 (tel); 202-588-6038 (fax). Web site: www.nationaltrust.org

Historic Hotels of America comprise their own fantasies. Many were built in the era when hotels were the end destination of long trips by train or slow cars, such as the Mount Washington Hotel at Bretton Woods in New Hampshire, where families drank in the cool mountain air for a week or two in August.

Other hotels were jewels set in cities to house traveling magnates, such as the Historic Strater Hotel in Durango, Colorado, where it's easy to imagine the owner of a pack of silver mines with loosened evening bow tie, enjoying a snifter of brandy and the attentions and charms of a famous actress draped like an odalisque across the bed. Today, the rooms have Jacuzzis, cable, and Internet access, but otherwise, the hotels might still be of the era.

City Breaks

The Historic Trust has not only compiled a book of the 185 Historic Hotels (at least fifty years old and eligible for the National Register of Historic Places), but devised a series of Driving Journeys and City Breaks that include them.

These unique tours are for the independent traveler who wants the details taken care of, and the rest left up to his or her own whims. For City Breaks, the Trust identifies what's worth seeing in four days in each of twenty cities in the United States; asks the traveler to select a theme or interest (for example, listening to blues in Saint Louis or Chicago; or tracing Lewis and Clark in Portland); gets tickets to museums, theaters, or whatever; books lodging; takes care of parking; and develops an itinerary that will satisfy the imagination of the traveler.

For more information on City Breaks, see www.historichotels. org, or call 877-782-2045.

Theme Suites

For hotels in other places with built-in fantasies, try a formerly ordinary hotel that has transformed its rooms into scenes from other epochs.

Salt Lake City, Utah

The Anniversary Inn   678 East South Temple, Salt Lake City, Utah 84102. 800-324-4152 (toll free); 801-363-4900 (tel). Web site: www.anniversaryinn.com

The Anniversary Inn is located at two sites in Salt Lake City—an

1889 Queen Anne mansion which has fourteen theme suites; and the Salt City Jail, a sturdy stone former brewery and later Prohibition speakeasy, now home to thirty luxury theme suites. Testaments to the muralists' and designers' art, the suites range from the golden Mysteries of Egypt (a gold ram's head next to the pallet bed), Sun Valley (a log cabin from the Old West), an Oval Office look-alike, a jungle safari with a leopard draped above the bed, and the Sultan's Palace (an elephant keeps watch). Prices per night: about $120 to $330.

Minnesota and Wisconsin

Fantasuite Hotels   800-666-7829 (toll free). Web site: www. fantasuite.com

You can sleep in Cinderella's white coach, a 1964 Lincoln Continental parked in the decor of a drive-in movie, an igloo, Sherwood Forest, the basket of a hot-air balloon, and other schemes and themes wrought with clever interior designs. The hitch is you have to be in Burnsville, Minnesota, or Dodgeville, Wisconsin, to enjoy. Honeymooners are welcome.

ECO-HOTELS

The best source for an international selection is www.eco-res.com.

Scottsdale, Arizona

The Boulders   34631 North Darlington Drive, Carefree, Arizona 85377. 877-999-3223 (toll free); 480-488-9009 (tel); 480-488-4118 (fax). Web site: www.wyndham.com

The Boulders is your average Wyndham Luxury Resort located near Scottsdale, except that for $40 you can pick up night-vision goggles for a guided trek after dark into the surrounding Sonoran Desert. You will see a lot. Cacti bloom at night, and wild cats and other creatures hunt at night. Who knows what else you might see?

If you prefer daylight for outdoor activities, check out their Yoga for Golfers program at the Golden Door Spa, and dazzle everybody with your new range of motion. Or walk the labyrinth or climb the 12-million-year-old sandstone boulders, into which the hotel is built. Call for rates.

CASTLES IN SCOTLAND

Scotts Castle Holidays   11, Barclay Terrace, Edinburgh, EH10 4HP, Scotland, United Kingdom. 011 +44 (0) 131 229 7111 (tel); 011 +44 (0) 131 229 1777 (fax). E-mail: sales@scottscastles.com; Web site: www.aboutscotland.com/scottscastle/holidays.html

Because most castles were built to last, and the families who inherited them have found them pricey to maintain, castle rentals are a hot item. Actress Ashley Judd got married in one in Scotland, which is where a lot of castles await your call.

Options abound. You can rent the whole thing for a conference, wedding, or incredible party; or stay in as many rooms as you need. You can rent with or without a staff; or as guests of the owner, who sees to it you receive breakfast as well as dinner. You can rent drafty ones with ghosts, and big ones in the middle of nowhere with locked rooms that you are not allowed to enter, like Heathcliff's doomed abode.

Castle Stuart, for example, built in 1625 near Inverness, not far from Culloden, was used as a refuge by the Earls of Moray and later by the Stuart family. Each recently refurbished room is decorated with its own tartan and furnished with a four-poster bed. The Great Hall is lined with flags and fitted with a fireplace large enough to roast an ox. The castle also has a drawing room, with piano and harp for after-dinner concerts, and a billiards room.

Couples with breakfast and dinner will pay about £300 ($450) per night. If you want the entire place for your sixteen guests, it is available for about £1,500 ($2,200) a night.

For more options, try www.castles.org.

CASTLES IN GERMANY

Castle auf Schoenburg　Family Huettl, D-55430 Oberwesel/
Rhine, Germany. 011 +49 (0) 6744 93930 (tel); 011 +49 (0) 6744
1613 (fax). E-mail: huettl@hotel-schoenburg.com; Web site: www.
hotel-schoenburg.com

Germany is strewn with castles, many of them built by Mad King
Ludwig in the throes of paranoia. But others were constructed by
knights in the Middle Ages, and in many structures at least part of
the original building remains.

The four-star Schoenburg has an amazing view of the Rhine
River cutting through the valley below, the better to serve the protective knights who oversaw the area from the battlements in the
great tower more than a thousand years ago. The Schoenburg staff
will arrange a wine-tasting tour of the nearby Riesling vineyards,
followed by a five-course Riesling candlelight dinner in the oak-
paneled castle dining room.

The tower has only two rooms. Each overlooks the Rhine and
has a four-poster bed: €185 per night (Euros; about the same in
U.S. dollars). Twenty-two other rooms are about €145.

Many enterprising hoteliers have redone castles that are excellent for family vacations. Try Sleeping Beauty Castle, for example,
which provides a free bike and even welcomes the family dog. Or
you can go full-medieval, and dine on a typical knight's feast. Try
www.Germany-castles.net.

FRENCH CHATEAUX

Chateaux & Hotels de France (www.chateauxhotels.com) handles
523 properties and offers special deals, such as Romantic Getaways
and Passion Packages. They suggest a Passion Break at the Chateau
de Berne, near Lorgues in Provence. Set in the midst of a vineyard,
with private gardens, a pool, and tennis, the chateau offers "absolute
tranquility." Thirteen rooms; two suites; the air redolent of grapes,
herbs, and lavender; and the beach not far away are included in this
Passion Break. Cost: €470 (Euros; about the same in U.S. dollars).

Or try a stay at Henri IV's former trysting place:

Chateau Saint-Paterne   Charles-Henry et Segolene de Valbray, 72610 Saint Paterne, France. 011 +33 (0) 2 33 27 54 71 (tel); 011 +33 (0) 2 33 29 16 71 (fax). E-mail: paterne@club-internet.fr; Web site: www.chateau-saintpaterne.com

The Chateau Saint-Paterne, now the private home of Charles-Henry and Segolene de Valbray, accepts visitors year-round. The chateau, completely restored with a tower, has a pool and a small park, and each room is done in a different decor, with four-poster beds.

Henri's favorite room, next to the tower, has a double bed in a cozy alcove. The ceiling is supported by the original sixteenth-century beams interspersed with the coats of arms of Henri and his favorite paramour. The bath is luxurious. Dinner is candlelit and family-style, with fresh herbs and vegetables in season from the kitchen garden.

Prices range from €105 to €125 (Euros; about the same in U.S. dollars) per night, depending on the season.

FRENCH BARGES

France Cruises, LLC.   3039 Seaboard Avenue, Palm City, Florida 34990. 866-498-3920 (toll free); 772-781-1433 (tel); 707-215-6811 (fax). E-mail: FranceCruises@adelphia.net; Web site: www.FranceCruises.com

Barges offer the ultimate small-boat cruise, going places other boats cannot, and being able to tie off at small towns to allow you to run to the market and buy fresh cheeses, fruits, and breads. France Cruises operates several barges on some of the many canal and river routes that network France.

On the comfortable *L'Etoile* and *L'Etoile II*, for example, cruise through Burgundy during wine harvest, stopping at Beaune for a wine tasting at the Marche aux Vins. Cruise through locks at Fontaines and stop to visit Romanesque churches, a medieval village, and chateaux.

Seven days, six people chartering *L'Etoile*, half-board (breakfast and lunch and recommendations for restaurants for dinner): $13,000.

TUSCANY FLATS AND FARMHOUSES

There are so many properties for seasonal rent in Tuscany, where do all the Tuscans go? Numerous companies are happy to help you find the perfect farmhouse, nestled among cypresses and vineyards, in which to stay while you revel in deliriously good food and magnificent art. The farmhouses are for the most part long removed from any trace of chickens; some are remodeled from the ancient stones of the original structures, which define the exterior but contain a completely modern interior. Most are spare and cool, overlooking the vistas of the lovely Tuscany hills; many have beautifully tiled emerald swimming pools.

Aside from farmhouses, the choices are vast, from flats in Florence to houses on the beach.

Here is a sampling:

The Parker Company   Seaport Landing, 152 the Lynnway, Lynn, Massachusetts 01902. 800-280-2811 (toll free); 781-596-8282 (tel); 781-596-3125 (fax). E-mail: Italy@theparkercompany. com; Web site: www.theparkercompany.com

Ten years in the business of providing travel and rental stays in Italy, with a knockout catalog featuring rental properties throughout the country, The Parker Company is committed to helping people individually, and preferably, on the phone. Providing personal contact and sharing their intimate knowledge of the properties they handle, the company believes, are the only way to make sure you have a good vacation.

The choices in Tuscany range from converted convents to apartments in ancient walled cities. Amid vineyards and medieval towns in central Tuscany, halfway between Siena and Florence, is the private hamlet of Santa Maria in Chianti, a community of five thirteenth-century stone town houses and four apartments in an eighteenth-century church rectory.

Each town house sleeps between two and four guests, has a fireplace, modern kitchen and bath, and is well furnished, including TV and telephone. The complex has a pool, laundromat, and owners happy to offer weekly tours of the Chianti vineyards.

Price per week: between $750 and $1,300.

The Parker Company also offers one-day Actividayz, day trips arranged from wherever you are in Italy.

Studio Brandini   Via Masaccio, 167, 50132 Firenze, Italy. 011 +39 055-578012 /-500225 (tel); 011 +39 055-580973 (fax). Web site: www.studiobrandini.it

Studio Brandini has been in business since 1978 and has a large multilingual staff anxious to help. Their Web site is easy to navigate, with each property listed by size and location and also rated with stars.

A popular way to do museums in Florence is to rent a private flat, where you can toss off your shoes at the end of the day and whip up your own pasta if you can't move a muscle to go out. What better way to get to know what it's like to really live in Florence?

A clean, tiled, four-star studio, for example, with a tiny kitchen and a super bath on the fourth floor of an elevator building in central Florence, freshly redecorated and with an astounding view of the Duomo from the queen-size bed, is €1,190 a week, with a €200 deposit (Euros; about the same in U.S. dollars).

Homebase Abroad, Ltd.   29 Mary's Lane, Scituate, Massachusetts 02066. 781-545-5112 (tel); 781-545-1808 (fax). E-mail: info@homebaseabroad.com; Web site: www. homebaseabroad.com

Homebase Abroad deals only in private, owner-occupied homes, and the agents travel often to Italy to check and recheck the status of the properties they handle. They offer a variety of homes, many on Italy's dreamy and timeless lakes.

A three-bedroom house in Positano, for example, has a staircase that goes directly to a sandy beach. The spacious house sleeps six and welcomes children. It is also close to town for restaurants, markets, and shops.

One week, June to September: $5,500.

ICEHOTEL, SWEDEN

Icehotel AB, 981 91 Jukkasjärvi, Sweden. 011 +46 (0) 980 66 800 (tel); 011 +46 (0) 980 66 890 (fax). E-mail: info@icehotel.com; Web site: www.icehotel.com

A hundred and twenty miles north of the Arctic Circle, in the land of the midnight sun in summer and the northern lights in winter, in an ancient market village inhabited only by the Sami Laplanders and their tiny reindeer, a group of international sculptors and artists aided by a Swedish tourism company conceived of a hotel built out of snow and ice carved out of the River Torne. That was in 1989.

In 2000–2001, the Icehotel had 14,000 overnight guests. Celebrities from around the world, including Swedish royalty, Euro supermodels, and rock stars come for the Absolut Bar, an ice palace with thirty-foot ceilings, pillars of ice, ice chandeliers lit by fiberoptics, and drinks served in ice glasses.

The Icehotel, which melts every summer back into the River Torne and "becomes a water hotel," is reconstructed every October to be ready for the crowds in December. Now, in addition to an ice church (with an ice cross) where it's possible to get married, an ice model of the Globe Theater (with *Hamlet* presented in Sami), access to dog sledding, as well as science tours with the Swedish Institute of Space Physics to help launch a weather balloon or study the amazing display of aurora borealis, the less hardy can stay in a choice of about thirty rooms, heated and built of wood, some fitted with skylights so you can fall asleep watching the dancing lights.

But the diehard aficionado of the North, the true snowy explorer, can stay in an ice room, sleeping on a smooth ice bed in a designed-for-the-Arctic thermal sleeping bag under reindeer skins. The indoor temperature hovers around 20 degrees F; outside, it is colder than the moon. The Icehotel units are carved with majestic arches, and decorated with fine ice sculpture. Honeymooners can sleep in a sculpted Viking ship. No windows distract; no bathroom tempts, either, but there is a W.C.

In the morning attendants bring hot lingonberry juice (it's like cranberry juice) before you slip off to the sauna and bring your core temperature back to normal. The truly hardy can visit the little sauna house next to a pool carved in the river ice, and take a stimulating dip in the icy Torne. Then breakfast on eggs and sausage and hot coffee.

In the summer, when the Icehotel is a memory, you can stay in a more normal summer hotel, and celebrate Midsummer's Eve with a maypole dance. That and much more.

A room in the Icehotel: between 2,000 and 2,500 SEK (Swedish kroner) (between about $225 and $270) per night. The Deluxe Suite (with elaborate sculpture): 5,600 SEK (about $590) per night. A subsequent night in a cabin or wood hotel is less.

CHAPTER 18

LONG TRIPS

Before you throw in the towel on whatever problems are clouding your life, consider the sage advice of everyone from your grandfather to your therapist: Put time and distance on the problems.

No better way to do that than to take the Long Trip, the one in which you farm out pets, plants, and plans; pack the bags; lock the door; and take off to exotic lands for a long time.

TAKE A CRUISE

Circumnavigate Africa

Classical Cruises   132 East 70th Street, New York, New York 10021. 800-252-7745 (toll free); 212-794-3200 (tel). Web site: www.classicalcruises.com

Fly to Seville, then board the *Sun Bay I*, a brand new ship (commissioned June 2001) built in the Cassens Shipyard, Germany. It berths ninety-two guests and has all the amenities for a trip that will take you around all of Africa in seventy days.

(Opposite): The "Treasury" at Petra, Jordan (a king's tomb, carved out of the sandstone), faces the end of a natural chasm, 1,200 meters long and a 100 meters steep, which kept the city secret. As early as 400 B.C.E., Petra was the capital city of Nabataean traders, who made the long desert trip from the East to the Mediterranean, carrying treasures. *(Roger Archibald)*

From Spain, you cross to Morocco, then sail down the Atlantic coast to South Africa. At each port of call, you can make excursions to visit interesting places, people, or museums. In East London, South Africa, fly to Victoria Falls for an overnight. Then rejoin the ship and sail on to Zanzibar, Kenya, Djibouti, Egypt (with an overnight to Luxor and Cairo), then the Mediterranean, Crete, Malta, and back to Spain.

Onboard experts in Africa will lecture and answer any questions you might have. They are an impressive list, with former Ambassador to Mali David Rawson, for example, and naturalist and author Peter Mathiessen, who has written extensively about Africa, including the fictional *At Play in the Fields of the Lord*, which was made into a movie.

Seventy days, including international airfare: from about $43,000 to $60,000.

Island-Hop in the Middle of the Atlantic

Lindblad Expeditions   720 Fifth Avenue, New York, New York 10019. 800-397-3348 (toll free); 212-765-7740 (tel); 212-265-3770 (fax). E-mail: explore@expeditions.com; Web site: www.expeditions.com

They're all out there, those islands that only *Jeopardy* can locate: Gough, South Georgia, Tristan da Cunha. On this thirty-seven-day trip, join Lindblad Expeditions in the sturdy ship *Endeavor* for a cruise over the Mid-Atlantic Ridge.

Start in Miami, fly to Santiago, Chile, then to Port Stanley in the Falkland Islands, off the Argentina coast. Britain and Argentina clashed over political differences in the Falklands War in 1982. But way before that, it was where ragged and weary sailors stopped after rounding Cape Horn. Penguins live there, it is so far south.

From there, go to South Georgia Island, where Sir Ernest Shackleton found help at the Stromness Whale Station after being stranded without a ship in Antarctica. His resting place is here, as are glacial peaks that resemble the Alps. More penguins live here.

From here sail north to Gough Island, probably a sight for sore eyes in 1731 for the captain of the British ship after whom it is named. Then to Tristan da Cunha and Nightingale Islands, both of them mariner refuges and places for migrating birds. The Atlantic Ocean here is wide open.

Sail north to Saint Helena, where Napoleon met his end after exile; then to Ascension, and north to Cape Verdes and the Canary Islands.

All Lindblad voyages have onboard experts in natural history, history, oceanography, and travel.

Thirty-seven days, including international airfare from Miami and to Madrid from the Canaries: about $8,000 to $11,000, depending on berth.

Cross Africa from Top to Bottom

Truck Africa, Ltd.   Wissett Place, Norwich Road, Halesworth, Suffolk IP19 8HY, United Kingdom. 011 +44 (0) 1509 88-1509 (tel); +44 (0) 1986 87-4114 (voice and fax). E-mail: Sales@ truckafrica.com; Web site: www.truckafrica.com

In the bush, Africa and Land Rovers go together. But on The Last Great Overlanding Challenge, twenty weeks, or five months, of day-to-day adventure, you go by truck, and you will have a learning experience that will forever embed Africa in your psyche.

This company has been trucking from the United Kingdom to Cape Town, South Africa, since 1972. Their trucks are chosen for durability and modified for traveling on sand, which marks the common condition during Section I (five months), the first part of the trip from Marrakesh, Morocco, to Mount Kilimanjaro in Tanzania.

Cross the Sahara and the Atlas Mountains to Mauretania and Mali, a full-Sahara experience during which you can witness African ritual dances near Timbucktu, take a piroque trip on the River Niger in the Sahel, and shop at markets where you can buy food as well as exotic trinkets. At each point, guides will direct you to the most interesting places.

Safety in Africa, often in political turmoil, is possible if you know the area, and Truck Africa's guides do. Nights are spent camping in campgrounds, if possible, or in the bush, if not. Two-person tents, occasional showers, and what Africa hands know as miles and miles of bloody Africa (MMBA) will be the drill. But you will connect with things like stilt dancing in Ivory Coast, slave forts in Ghana, the Yankari Game Reserve in Nigeria, the Pics de Rhoumseki in Cameroun, Jebel Mara in Sudan, Blue Nile Falls in Ethiopia, mountain gorillas in Uganda, the Source of the Nile in Uganda, Rift Valley Lakes in Kenya, Olduvai Gorge in Tanzania, plus do whitewater rafting, see all kinds of wildlife for pictures, and swim under waterfalls. If you want, and can, climb Mount Kilimanjaro. Guides will be along to help.

And that's just the first part.

Section II continues for eight weeks more from Tanzania down to South Africa, a much more tourist-friendly area.

Flexibility is the number one requirement on this trip; the itinerary can change suddenly if necessary. Bring a mosquito net, sleeping bag and mattress pad, and comfortable footwear and clothes to layer to cover extremes in temperatures. Visas and health and accident insurance are a must, as are all the inoculations and vaccinations your doctor can give you. Bring a medical kit, maps (the Michelin 953, 954, and 955), a camera, and an open mind.

From London to Marrakesh to Tanzania, twenty weeks: about £2,400 ($3,800), plus a shared "kitty" for food: about £600 ($950). For both sections, including Tanzania to South Africa: 28 weeks: about £3,000 total ($4,800).

Travel the Ancient Silk Road

Mir Corporation   Off the Beaten Path Small Group Tours, 85 South Washington Street, Suite 210, Seattle, Washington 98104. 800-424-7289 (toll free); 206-624-7289 (tel); 206-624-7360 (fax). E-mail: info@mircorp.com; Web site: www.mircorp.com

No one knows the earliest date of the passage that marks the Silk Road; traders might have been going strong, carrying goods in the Bronze Age, about 3500 B.C.E. But with the Renaissance in Europe, kingly wealth demanded Oriental spices and bolts of silk; Venetian traders could barely wait for the slow shipments to arrive.

Mir Corporation's Ancient Caravan Route, Xian to Khiva, travels through China, Kyrgyzstan, and Uzbekistan, and back in time to a fabled and romantic era, known to Marco Polo.

Traveling by the most efficient means available, from camels to planes, this company that specializes in Russia, China, and Mongolia offers a small group tour that begins in Beijing, goes to Xian (with the buried clay army), once the farthest-east point of the Silk Road, where goods were loaded onto camels and transported to the Middle East.

From Xian travel to the next Silk Road stop, Dunhuang, at the end of the China Wall, where the amazing centuries-old Mogao Caves preserve some of the finest Buddhist frescoes anywhere.

Then cross most of the vast continent of China, where small tribes live almost as they did when the trade route flourished. Stop at the desert oasis Turpan, where aquifers water fields to grow melons and grapes. From there, go to Kashgar, separated from Russia by mountains, where Marco Polo was welcomed by the Chinese emperor Kublai Khan. Today it is still a large market town.

Cross the 12,000-foot Turogart Pass into Kyrgyzstan, a small country composed mostly of mountains and bazaars. Bishkek, the capital city, has broad avenues and beautiful places to hike near Lake Issy-Kul; and its watchtower overlooks the Silk Road. Drive through the Fergana Valley, once lined with trading villages famed for silk weavings and ceramics, to Osh, a market town where you can buy traditional felt hats.

Crossing overland to the largest city in this region, Tashkent, you are in the very heart of the Silk Road. In Uzbekistan are the "Golden Road" cities of Samarkand, home of Tamerlane (or Timor the Lame), the fourteenth-century conquerer of Central Asia;

Bukhara, with magnificent blue mosaics; and Khiva, full of mosques set against the mountains, and bazaars and markets, fueled by the same energy as in the 1300s. Tamerlane made Samarkand into the Rome of Asia. Known as the Blue City, for its blue glass mosaics, it had palaces and libraries, gardens, and broad avenues. This is truly remote and exotic.

Mir Corporation arranges visits with hospitable local families. On the final night, fly back to Tashkent for dinner with an Uzbek family.

Twenty-six days: with six to nine passengers: about $4,800 per person; with ten passengers: about $4,400. International airfare is not included.

Three other companies offering Silk Road trips are listed below:

TCS Expeditions   2025 First Avenue, Suite 500, Seattle, Washington 98121-2176. 800-727-7477 (toll free); 206-727-7300 (tel); 206-727-7309 (fax). E-mail: travel@tcs-expeditions.com; Web site: www.tcs-expeditions.com

Take the vintage China Orient Express from Beijing and stop at the main Silk Road market villages. From Urumichi, fly to Chengdu to visit the Giant Panda Breeding and Research Center. Fourteen days: from about $8,000 to $11,000, double occupancy.

Mountain Travel Sobek   6420 Fairmount Avenue, El Cerrito, California 95430-9962. 800-687-6235 (toll free); 510-527-8100 (tel); 510-525-7710. E-mail: info@mtsobek.com; Web site: www. mtsobek.com

You have a choice of hiking the Trail of Genghis Khan, a circular route in central Mongolia that begins in Ulaanbaatar, with horses carrying your gear, accompanied by an assisting van (thirteen days, including camping and hotels: about $3,000); or doing the whole route from Xian to Kashgar and back by plane, camel, and car (seventeen days: between about $3,100 and $3,500, per person depending on group size, plus $1,120 internal airfare).

USA Adventure Center   1311 63rd Street, Suite 200, Emeryville, California 94608. 800-227-8747 (toll free); 510-654-1879 (tel); 510-654-4200 (fax). E-mail:ex@adventurecenter.com; Web site: www.adventurecenter.com

By bus and train, do the Silk Road from Xian to Urumqi, then fly to Kashgar in time for the huge Sunday market. From there, continue along the old caravan trail south on the Karakorum Highway, through the fabled Shangri-La (where no one ever ages) to Islamabad, Pakistan.

Twenty-three days: $2,500 to $2,600.

Circle the Globe by Private Jet

Intrav   7711 Bonhomme Avenue, Saint Louis, Missouri 63105-1961. 800-456-8100 (toll free); 314-727-0908 (fax). Web site: www.intrav.com

In a private Boeing 747 luxury jet (leather seats, first-class service on land and in the air) with this first-class company, you circumnavigate the southern globe, starting in Maui, Hawaii, with a helicopter trip over Molokai's cliffs.

Then jet across the Pacific Ocean to Cairns, Australia. Here you take a gondola ride through the rainforest and a cruise over the Great Barrier Reef in a boat with an underwater observatory.

From there, fly to Ho Chi Minh City in Vietnam; Singapore (and a night visit to the world's first night wildlife park); and the island of Mauritius. You spend two days at each of these places, before flying to South Africa and the Sabi Sand Game Reserve. Here you meet up with trackers and guides and go on safari for three days.

From South Africa, fly across the Atlantic to Rio for three days, with a private excursion to Iguacu Falls. Spend one day in Palm Beach before flying home.

Twenty-four days, including everything, from $250,000 travel insurance to first-class hotel accommodations (such as the Four Seasons Hotel in Maui and Raffles in Singapore): about $50,000.

CHAPTER 19

MOTORCYCLE TOURS

Motorcycle touring took off in the 1980s when Harley-Davidson invented an engine that didn't require a degree in mechanics to repair, and when Zen meditation became a respected means of relaxation. Put the two together, add an appreciation of the sleek metal beauty of a motorcycle and the need to control a half-ton of speeding steel without doors and a roof, and grown men and women with corner offices took to the road on "bikes." *Freedom* was the word they used whenever anyone asked why.

To enable riders even more by minimizing the details of motorcycle trips, several companies offer tours that provide mechanical support, maps with gas stations as well as the best restaurants and points of beauty, and reservations at comfortable places to spend the night. All you have to bring is your helmet.

MOTORCYCLING IN THE UNITED STATES

The Carolinas

Carolina Motorcycle Tours   280 Haynes Road, Summerfield, North Carolina 27358. 336-643-1367 (tel); 336-643-0636 (fax). E-mail: sonny@carolinamotorcycletours.com; Web site: www. carolinamotorcycletours.com

A trusty bike, the open road, and thou. A biking pair snap their silhouette on a tour in Arizona. Motorcycle touring gives a freedom that other forms of transportation lack. You have speed, the wind against your helmet, and with a touring group, the benefits of help, if you need it. *(Photo by Ray Mathews, courtesy of Chrome Caballeros Tours)*

This small company organizes bike tours of the Carolinas, from the Outer Banks to the Blue Ridge Mountains. Put your baggage on the support van and leave the driving to yourself—you can bring your own bike or rent a touring bike there.

Their Great Smoky Mountain Fall Foliage Tour allows you to ride safe back roads through spectacular mountain scenery. The company arranges tickets to the Vanderbilt Biltmore Estate in Ashville, North Carolina, and a train tour on the Great Smoky Mountain Railroad.

Four days over a weekend, including lodging, two breakfasts, two dinners, and tickets: about $750 for two.

Arizona

Chrome Caballeros Tours   1280 North Vulture Mine Road, Wickenburg, Arizona 85390. 877-684-5799 (toll free); 928-684-5799 (tel); 928-684-0486 (fax). E-mail: ChromeCabDW@w3az. net; Web site: www.chromecaballeros.com

This luxury motorcycle camping tour company provides stateside safaris on bikes in the wilderness of the American Southwest. Bring your own bike or rent one out of Phoenix.

Ride all day at your own pace, arrive at tent grounds marked on your map, and find your commodious tent outfitted with clean linens and towels, your baggage on the rack, and snacks on the bedside table. Enjoy the equivalent of sundowners with the rest of the group while the cook bakes bread and grills the baby back ribs for dinner. Spend the evening using the telescope, since there is nothing between you and the outer reaches of the universe.

Their Lost in Arizona Tour, for example, takes you to the most remote and the most familiar parts of Arizona, from the Mogollon Rim to the Hubbell Trading Post and Canyon de Chelly, with a spin down the Coronado Trail, a 95-mile stretch with 525 curves. You will cover about 1,250 miles; a minimum of six people is required.

Five days, including luxury tents, meals, and backup: one person: about $750; two people: about $1,400.

Ride America Motorcycle Tours   888-781-7433 (toll free). E-mail: info@rideamerica.com; Web site: www.rideamerica.com

This Texas-based company specializes in tours for HOGs (Harley Owners Groups). If you've never ridden a Harley, this is a chance to rent one for seven days, if you take advantage of their Texas, Southwest, Florida, or Carolinas tours. A riding escort accompanies you to troubleshoot and carry your bags.

Their Carolinas Tour maps out a route along the clear coast from Myrtle Beach to Nag's Head and around Cape Hatteras, with a stop at the Wright Brothers Museum. Then, over seven days, the tour goes through back roads and small towns in southern and eastern North and South Carolina, riding about 200 miles a day or less. Stop for a full day of golf, and spend a day in the gracious city of Charleston.

Seven days, including Harley rental (all models), riding escort, lodging (Hilton or equivalent), and liability insurance: about $2,200, with shared hotel room; $2,500, for private room; passenger on back: about $650. Meals are not included.

MOTORCYCLING ELSEWHERE

The Alps

Beach's Motorcycle Adventures, Ltd. 2763 West River Road, Grand Island, New York 14072. 716-773-4960 (tel); 716-773-5227 (fax). E-mail (Operations): judycooper@adelphia.net; Web site: www.beachs-mca.com

If you like mountain touring on bikes, try this company's summertime-only Alpine Adventure, two weeks of nothing but clear air, switchbacks, and stretches of green fields, with time out for shopping and spas, and walking tours of some interesting places. Beach's has been offering the Alpine tour since 1972. They also organize motorcycle tours to Norway and New Zealand.

In the Alps, you ride on their BMW R1150s or F650 tour bikes, developed for Alpine use, and guaranteed comfortable for both rider and passenger over long distances.

The trip begins in Munich and crosses southern Switzerland toward Italy, doing all the major mountain passes. In Italy, you bike around and among the astounding Dolomites, which just rise out of nothing. Then cruise back through Austria, with a stop at the old Roman spa town of Villach, and Salzburg, home of Mozart, before heading back to Munich.

Fourteen days, including lodging at luxury hotels, meals, and bikes: rider: about $4,200; passenger: about $3,300.

Bhutan

Himalayan Roadrunners Motorcycle Tours and Expeditions
In the United States: Box 1402, Waitsfield, Vermont 05673. 888-RIDE HIGH [743-3444] (toll free); 908-236-8970 (tel); 908-236-8972 (fax). E-mail: roadrunr@ridehigh.com; Web site: www.ridehigh.com. *In the United Kingdom:* Charles House, Hamstreet, Ashford, Kent TN26 2JH. 011 +44 (0) 1233-733-001 (tel/fax).

A love of old British motorcycles and an affinity for the Himalayas brought this pair of travelers, Rob Callander and Ed Shuttleworth, to share some of their more than twenty years' experience with other riders. On their Bhutan: Ride the Dragon trip, you will ride a Royal Enfield Bullet 500cc motorcycle, outfitted with crash bars, and provided with saddlebags. For this trip, you must be an experienced rider and reasonably fit.

The trip starts in Kathmandu, Nepal, where you spend a couple of days in a Land Rover four-by-four looking for Bengal tigers in the Royal Chitwan National Park. On Day 3, take a shakedown ride to get the feel for the bike; then on Day 4, head out toward the Kosi Tappu Wildlife Reserve, rarely visited, and one of the world's best.

Ride the border with India, past tea plantations, to Darjeeling, with a stay at a hotel once used by maharajahs. Proper dinner dress is required. You have a chance next day to visit the Mountaineering Institute built in memory of the famous Sherpa guide Tenzing Norgay Sherpa. The ride in the afternoon will take you through what was once the tiny kingdom of Sikkim.

The peaks of the Himalayas are everywhere now, and the mountain roads grow narrow as you enter Bhutan and its capital city, Thimphu. Two days' ride will take you to a hotel that was once the Bhutanese Royal Residence, from which you can spend a day exploring the Paro Valley beneath the sacred, 24,000-foot peak of Jomolhari.

On the final day, you fly back to Kathmandu.

Fourteen days, including motorcycle, most meals, gasoline, support vehicle, map, first-class hotels or resorts, map, and T-shirt: rider: about $4,000; passenger: about $2,800.

Learn how to Ride a Motorcycle

If you don't know and would like to learn how to ride motorcycles, try:

Eduvacations   1431 21st Street, NW, Washington, D.C. 20036. 202-857-8384 (tel); 202-463-8091 (fax). E-mail: eduvacate@ aol.com; Web site: www.eduvacations.com

Begin on the street in Washington, D.C., or Pittsburgh, Pennsylvania. The intensive, one-on-one, hands-on riding and safety course takes two days. From here, work up to the two-day intensive, rider-accompanied, three-students-per-instructor course, on twisty roads in the Blue Ridge, the Smoky Mountains, or the Switzerland of Ohio. Lawrence Grodsky, columnist for *Rider Magazine*, instructs, with in-helmet communication and on-bike videotaping.

Two days, including training, lodging, and some meals: $650 to $1,000. Two days of on-the-street training: $800.

CHAPTER 20

MUSIC AND DANCE

CHAMBER MUSIC

For the love of music, chamber musicians practice for hours to be able to experience the deep pleasure of playing in a group. Some groups meet religiously; others form spontaneously.

Now for performers as well as for devoted listeners, total-immersion chamber music trips allow you to live, breathe, and sleep chamber music, with the added plus of being able to join the musicians' rehearsal sessions as a player.

Vivienne Pittendrigh   Chamber Music Holidays and Festivals. E-mail: info@chambermusicholidays.co.uk; Web site: www. btinternet.com/~chambermusicholidays/0000/home.html

Vivienne Pittendrigh started organizing trips for fellow chamber players twenty years ago. Now she manages regular trips to important festivals and concerts in places such as Corfu, Florence, Vienna, Esterhaza, Budapest, and Sydney, where art, architecture, museums, gardens, and other civilized expressions are available for musicians and music lovers when they are not playing or listening.

In Corfu in September, for example, stay at a luxury hotel with twenty-five acres of manicured gardens overlooking the emerald sea. Each morning in the outdoor theater, two Czech string quartets present *Divertimenti in Corfu* concerts, playing Schubert, Haydn, Mozart, Smetana, and Dvorak. During rehearsals, music stands and cello rental are available, as is coaching by the musicians.

A couple dance a smoldering tango in the street in Caminito, a section of Buenos Aires. *(Courtesy of www.tctango.com)*

Afternoons and evenings, explore the sea on a private chartered boat, take tours into town, swim, play golf—or practice.

Seven days, including half-board, all concerts, music library, coaching, and excursions: £660 (about $1,000); fourteen days: £1,180 (about $1,700). Arriving fares (by air or sea) are extra.

The Amateur Chamber Music Players   1123 Broadway, Room 304, New York, New York 10010. 212-645-7424 (tel); 212-741-2678 (fax). E-mail: webmaster@acmp.net; Web site: www.acmp.net

If you are a chamber player who would like to network with others, especially while you travel, for a membership fee of about $20, you can be listed in or just get a copy of the *Amateur Chamber Music Players Directory*, an international list of chamber singers and instrumentalists.

MUSIC TOURS

Schubert, in Austria

Habsburg Heritage Cultural Tours   158 Rosendale Road, London SE21 8LG, United Kingdom. 011 +44 (0) 20 8761 0444 (tel); 011 +44 (0) 20 8766 6151 (fax). E-mail: info@habsburg. co.uk; Web site: www.habsburg.co.uk

At a 1648 hotel, refurbished with pool, tennis courts, sauna, and steam room, stay above Lake Constance in western Austria in the Schwarzenbergerwald. Here in 1817 Franz Schubert presented his *Lieder*, lyrical songs accompanied by a piano, for friends and interested strangers, and they were so popular they became known as the *Schubertiade*.

For five afternoons in small concert halls in Bezau and Schwartzenberg, listen to sopranos, tenors, baritones, and basses sing Schubert's haunting songs. Mornings you can hike in the forest (where nightingales live), then relax in the sauna.

Six days, including lodging, ten concerts, excursions, and airfare from Heathrow: about £1,400 (about $2,100).

OPERA TOURS

Italy

Morgan Tours   879 Shefford Road, Suite 100, Ottawa, Ontario
K1J 8H9, Canada. 800-667-4268 (toll free); 613-721-9875 (fax).
E-mail: travel@morgantours.com; Web site: www.morgantours.com

The Northern Italy Viva Verdi tour celebrates not only Verdi's
genius but the genius of the places in which he worked and traveled.

Begin in Venice to capture the rhythm of fast boats and sundials
that measure only the "happy hours." Then travel to Ravenna for
the Festival, one of the greatest events in Europe. Look forward to
evening performances, after touring the city with its famous church
mosaics built to commemorate the Emperor Constantine's conver-
sion to Christianity.

Then on to the marble Roman amphitheater at Verona for no
less than four operas on successive nights: Verdi's *Aida* and *Nabucco*,
Puccini's *Turandot*, and Bizet's *Carmen*. Each day you take excursions to nearby places such as Padua; Lake Garda and the Bardolino
area (with wine tasting at the Chianti Wine Estate); as well as tours
of Verona, of castles and churches and the sites where Romeo and
Juliet played out their tragedy.

Enroute back to Milan, pass through Verdi's birthplace, Le Ron-
cole, home of his youth at Busseto, and Sant'Agata, the estate where
he retired.

Twelve days, including hotels, breakfast, some meals, ground
transportation, four operas, two Ravenna performances, and one
concert in Venice: about $5,500.

Austria and Italy

Martin Randall Travel, Ltd.   10, Barley Mow Passage,
Chiswick, London W4 4GF, United Kingdom 011 +44 (0) 20
8742 3355 (tel); 011 +44 (0) 20 8742 7766 (fax). E-mail: info@
martinrandall.co.uk; Web site: www.martinrandall.com

This trip conveys the kind of delight that fueled Mozart. Summer Opera in Europe begins in Salzburg, Mozart's city, with Mozartian places: his birthplace, his home and museum, the cathedral where he was an organist, with at least two operas in evening performances as part of the Salzburg Festival. Exactly which ones depend on the year you choose to go; in previous years, they have been *The Marriage of Figaro*, *Falstaff*, and *Jenufa*.

From here, you go to the Opera Festival in Bregenz for an outdoor performance of Puccini's *La Bohème* on a stage built on Lake Constance; then drive through Switzerland to Italy and the Torre del Lago in Tuscany, Puccini's home. Enjoy two more opera performances there.

Drive across the Appenines to Verona for Verdi's *Aida* and *Nabucco*, and Bizet's *Carmen*, performed outdoors in the Roman amphitheater.

Fifteen days, including airfare from London, eight operas, hotels, breakfast, some meals, and ground transport: about £3,200 (about $4,800).

CRUISES

Jazz

Jazz Cruise   200 South Hanley, Saint Louis, Missouri 63105. 800-762-6737 (toll free); 314-862-7777 (tel); 314-862-5148 (fax). E-mail: info@thejazzcruise.com; Web site: www.thejazzcruise.com

Each year, a different ship, different Caribbean or Florida ports, but aboard, nothing but jazz and performers like Dick Morgan Trip plus One; the Count Basie Orchestra, directed by Grover Mitchell; blues players Red Holloway Quartet; pianist Bill Charlap; bassist Keter Betts; Bill Mays Duo with Martin Wind; and many others.

Choose one or two weeks and sail around the Caribbean or to Mexico. Lodging ashore, meals, and concerts: Please call for pricing.

Rock

The Rock Boat www.therockboat.com

Each year around Labor Day, performers such as Sister Hazel and Edwin McCain charter a whole Carnival Cruise ship and tour the Caribbean for four days. As one fan said, "Imagine being trapped on a ship with your favorite bands!"

As you cruise from Tampa around Key West to Nassau, the Bahamas, you listen to the best of rock, which, because everybody's there where it counts, can be entirely spontaneous. Dexter Freebish, Cowboy Mouth, the Pat McGee Band, and Chuck Carrier from Marathon are some of the performers.

Check the Web site for details on the costs and to make reservations online.

Bluegrass

Rafting and Banjos

Adrift Adventures, Jensen, Utah. 800-824-0150 (toll free). E-mail: info@adrift.com; Web site: www.adrift.com

Raft a little, strum a little. On this trip you can combine a love for riding rapids with a love for bluegrass. Bluegrass, Banjos, and Boats takes you for five days along the Yampa River in Colorado or for four days on the Lodore River in Utah. Depending on the season, rapids run from Class III to IV, which means buckle your seatbelt, but no big deal.

The best part is that there is only you, Nature, and the acoustic banjo band. On quiet stretches, you can stop along the river and play, or lash the rafts together and have a floating concert. At night when you stop to camp, you dance and sing to your heart's delight around the fire, keeping the bighorn sheep awake.

Five days on the Yampa River, including guide, camp, and meals on the river: about $760. Four days on the Lodore River, including guide, camp, and meals on the river: about $700.

Dance Workshops

Tango in Argentina

Buenos Aires is the home of tango, the dance of love. Tangoists perform in the street, ever perfecting their dips and sharp turns, their straight backs and firm jaws, evoking an erotic heat as they move like jungle cats across the sidewalk.

Bridge to the Tango   Dance Traveler, Inc. 888-DTANGO7 [382-6467] (toll free). E-mail: dtango7@aol.com; Web site: www. bridgetothetango.com

This company has succeeded in finding not only the *milongas*, the backstreet social dance clubs of Buenos Aires, but the *milongueros*, the older dancers who set the tango tone in the 1940s and 1950s.

Now, in tango tours to Buenos Aires, they introduce you to the older dancers so you can learn from their special fire; and arrange for you to have younger professional dancers who are bilingual as your instructors. Daily group lessons allow you to immerse yourself in ten days of tango.

The first thing you do is shop for tango shoes when you arrive, and from there, it is total tango in the city that never sleeps. Interspersing lessons with sightseeing tours of some special places, such as Evita Peron's resting place or the Café Tortoni for hot chocolate, you spend the evenings with a tango instructor escort of the opposite sex doing the milongas.

Nine nights, including airfare from New York or Miami, four-star hotel room, breakfast, daily classes, seven milongas, and ground transport: about $3,500.

Alojargentina   011 +54 11 4966 1388 (tel). Email: info@ alojargentina.com; Web site: www.alojargentina.com

Alojargentina, a company that provides lodging and car rentals throughout Argentina, will arrange either of two twenty-one-day package tango study tours for you.

On one package, you stay with a host family in a single room, with breakfast daily. You will have time on your own to sightsee in Buenos Aires, before you seriously settle into tango lessons each day, taught by a professional.

Twenty-one days, including city tour, one tango show and dinner, lodging, and sixteen tango lessons: about $580.

On the second option, you stay in a furnished apartment downtown. Twenty-one days, including all of the above: about $800.

TC Tango   Maipu 726 Piso 3 Oficina B (C1006 ACJ), Buenos Aires, Argentina. 011 +54 11 4328-5376/77 (tel); 011 +54 11 4322-3942 (fax). E-mail: info@tctango.com.ar; Web site: www. tctango.com

TC Tango is a Buenos Aires–based tour operator run by five Argentinian tour professionals. They specialize in customizing tours that range from the tango districts of Buenos Aires to adventure trips throughout Argentina. Contact them to arrange a tour of the milongas.

Salsa in Havana, Cuba

Bridge to the Tango   Dance Traveler, Inc. 888-DTANGO7 [382-6467] (toll free). E-mail: dtango7@aol.com; Web site: www. bridgetothetango.com

Bridge to the Tango is a U.S. Treasury–licensed company authorized to take American tourists to Cuba (which is the way tourism from the United States works at this writing).

Their Salsa in Havana, Cuba trip will give you a choice of classes in salsa, tango, Afro-Cuban dance, and salsa Rueda de Casino (a salsa circle dance) in a specially rented dance hall. You can also study Cuban music and culture.

In addition to daily lessons and practice time, you will be introduced to the older generation of Cuban dancers and will hear lectures from authorities on Cuban salsa culture.

Evenings, practice what you have learned at Havana's clubs. You will have a lot of opportunity to explore some of Havana's fascinating museums.

Nine nights, including round-trip airfare from Montreal or Cancun (the only way U.S. citizens can enter Cuba), special visa/tourist pass, four-star hotel (a UNESCO "treasure") with breakfast, and daily lessons: about $2,600. Two nine-day trips are run in January. For both programs: $4,900. Book early because of the extra work involving visas.

Flamenco in Spain

From complex Moorish, Jewish, and Gypsy roots, the dance of flamenco "talks" with the feet, in rapid heel-toe tapping, to which the partner responds. A dance of seduction (in which Carmen of opera fame excelled), flamenco is an exciting dance to watch and to perform. Andalusia, Spain, the area near the mountains of Gibralta, where roses grow (one behind the ear is meant to attract; one held in the teeth is meant to be taken), is where it is entrenched.

EduVacations   1431 21st Street NW, Washington, D.C. 20036. 202-857-8384 (tel); 202-463-8091 (fax). E-mail: eduvacate@ aol.com; Web site: www.eduvacations.com

This company provides in-country language training with stays with host families, and access to lots of local cultural involvement. EduVacations will customize a package stay for you. You have the choice of staying for one or two weeks (or more) alone, with a partner or spouse, or with your entire family.

You can stay with a host family, in student residences, in an apartment shared with a native, in an apartment of your own, or in a hotel. Total immersion experiences—language, art, music, and excursions—leave you with a lot to take home.

The best part is that in Spain you can study flamenco as much as you want, while you study the language. In Madrid, for example, stay with a host family for two weeks for about $1,350 per person (call for prices for more than one); and study flamenco for eight hours a day for two weeks for an extra $260.

Zydeco in West Virginia

Cajun/Creole dance is unique to this country. It developed when French settlers were evicted by British settlers from Acadia in Nova Scotia. They went south to Louisiana, where they became Cajuns (a corruption of *Acadien*). Over time, Creole, a mixture of African, French, and Spanish culture, married Cajun culture in music and dance and produced Zydeco.

Augusta Heritage Workshops   Gordon Blackley, Publicity Director, Davis and Elkins College, Elkins, West Virginia 26241. 304-637-1350 (tel); 304-637-1317 (fax). E-mail: augusta@ augustaheritage.com; Web site: www.augustaheritage.com

This thirty-year-old workshop takes over the campus of Davis and Elkins College in the summer with one-week workshops on traditional American dance and music. Working four to six hours a day, with performances in the evening either planned or spontaneous, you can learn Zydeco dance. Or spend the week with swing (the Savoy Lindy, East and West Coast swing), blues dance, Cape Breton step dancing, or Appalachian flat-foot dancing.

In April, gather with teachers and instrument makers and study the dulcimer; in October, meet the master artists of the fiddle. You can study gospel piano here, too. Lodging is on campus or in hotels.

Week-long class: $350.

CHAPTER 21

RV CARAVANS

The advantage of the recreational vehicle (RV) is that your transport is also your primary homestead. You can conquer the world without ever leaving the safety of your own home, and do it on the back roads, with the panorama of the night sky to protect you at dinner.

More and more people are open to the idea that true exploration comes only after you sell the "stick" home (the one on a street with a number on the door), downsize to the important possessions, then get out the maps. The drawback is that, as a traveler, most of the people you meet are strangers.

Now several companies are making it possible to travel in caravans. You buy the tour, get in the caravan line, and take comfort in knowing there is (1) a guide (the "wagonmaster") at the beginning of the line to tell you where to go and lead you to the best places to get gas, and (2) a backup person (the "tailgunner") at the end to help if anyone breaks down. At dinner, you have a lot of friends with whom to discuss the day's events and anticipate what's coming.

And you don't have to own the RV; these companies make it easy to rent one for you.

Fantasy RV Tours   103 West Tomichi Avenue, Suite C, Gunnison, Colorado 81230. 800-952-8496 (toll free); 970-642-4573 (fax). Web site: www.fantasyrvtours.com

RV caravanning, long popular in Europe, is perfect for exploring the United States. Here caravanners barbecue dinner on the Oregon Grape and Grain wine- and beer-tasting trip of RV Caravan Tours. *(Photo by Teri Fahrendorf/RV Caravan Tours)*

Fantasy RV Tours will put your RV on a train along with you or park it in a secure, guarded parking lot while you ride the train to marvel at the spectacularly grand Copper Canyon. That's just part of several trips they offer to Mexico. On the Tennessee and Mississippi Rivers, they park your RV on a barge, while you ride the double-decker touring boat through the locks on the Intra-Canal Waterway. In Canada, they arrange for you to see the Calgary Stampede. In Alaska, they arrange the best fishing places.

Their tours include excellent guides, first-class accommodations, all camp fees, briefings, maps, tips, currency exchange, plus travel and emergency medical assistance insurance. They handle the border crossing from Mexico, too.

Taking an RV on an African safari is probably one of the best ways not only to see wildlife, but to experience Africa. Their thirty-five-day Wildlife RV Safari flies from Atlanta to Cape Town, South Africa, spends three nights there, then picks up the RVs and some groceries and heads up in the caravan as far as Kruger National Park. An optional trip will take you to Victoria Falls in Zimbabwe.

Thirty-five days, including round-trip from Atlanta, some meals, and all fees: about $7,000.

RV Caravan Tours   P.O. Box 10931, Eugene, Oregon 97440. 866-324-8084 (toll free); 541-686-3038 (tel); 541-284-6232 (fax). E-mail: info@rvcaravantours.com; Web site: www. rvcaravantours.com

RV Caravan Tours specialize in regional "loop" tours that take one or two weeks. Returning to the spot where you started enables people who fly in from other parts of the United States or other countries to rent an RV and return it without a drop fee.

The guides know the region well, take you to places not on other tours, and are able to secure the best campsites as well as tickets to attractions as part of the tour. If you want to go hiking, they will provide the maps you need, plus the shuttle to the trailhead. The caravans are kept to four RVs; and if one wants to opt out and drive off to another area for a day, that's okay.

Their Grape and Grain Tour celebrates Oregon's spectacular wines and brews, as well as sake. During the Oregon Brewers' Festival, the tour visits Oregon's microbreweries, takes a walking and tasting tour of a vineyard, and explores the mysteries of making sake at the only 100 percent American–owned sakery. The guide is a brewmaster himself.

Seven days, including all fees, breakfasts and some meals, plus tours, and guides: about $1,000.

For more options, and to connect and network, see www.rv-info. net/rvcaravans.html.

CHAPTER 22

SAFARIS

Technically, *safari* is an Arabic word meaning "journey," which found its way into Swahili in East Africa. In the era of Theodore Roosevelt and Ernest Hemingway, it meant a journey in Africa with porters carrying the camp, and guns with which to shoot wild animals, which would then be skinned and transported on trains to the ships that carried them back to the United States to be stuffed and hung on the study wall.

Safari captures an era of rugged individualism and machismo, composed of leather, Scotch whiskey, and a sense of privilege which charged the safari takers with the obligation to return and lead countries or write great books.

That was then.

You can still capture that fantasy, but without guns, and with the totally different mind-set of a photographer or a naturalist. Tour companies, many of them second- and third-generation African-born, know how to create the ambiance of being on safari, with all of its fantasy of tent camps and lodges with mahogany furniture and voluminous mosquito nets above the bed, with hot coffee in the camp before setting off on a morning walk or "game run" in the bush. The bush belongs to the animals, but the camp is yours. "Sundowners," drinks after the afternoon exploration, when the stars begin to come out and the fire is lit, are a part of a very civilized tradition.

All muscled intention, a young lion positions herself on a vantage point before racing after prey in Amboseli National Park, Kenya. *(Stephanie Ocko)*

AFRICA

Tourism is flourishing as never before in East Africa, from Kenya south to Cape Town in South Africa. This is home to the Big Five: lions, elephants, hippos, rhinos, and giraffes. Sometimes this list is configured to include leopards, cheetahs, and cape buffalo. But these are only the beginning: The wildebeest, which migrate back and forth from the Serengeti Plain in Tanzania to around the Maasai Mara Reserve in southwest Kenya, travel in herds of a million, accompanied by tens of thousands of zebras looking for greener pastures and water in the winter, and places to have their young in the summer.

Crocodiles inhabit the rivers; and numerous species of graceful antelope leap and graze across the savannahs. Ostriches walk the walk across the desert. Plus, there are wild dogs, small cats, snakes, and very large insects. "Someone asked me if Africa had a lot of insects," said a tour manager, "and I said no, we don't have many, but the ones we have make up for it in size."

Paleontologists believe that Africa is the original home of all human beings, and that our earliest ancestors, no one knows how many million years ago, evolved here and migrated in different waves at different times north to the rest of the world. This might explain the ease, despite the exotic and savage nature of the wild, that most visitors experience in Africa.

Kenya

Micato Safaris   15 West 26th Street, New York, New York 10010. 800-642-2861 (toll free); 212-545-7111 (tel); 212-545-8297. E-mail: info@micato.com; Web site: www.micatosafaris.com

This thirty-five-year-old company knows their areas—Kenya and Tanzania—and how to deliver a comfortable and informed safari.

Each safari opens with a lecture the first night by Masai elder Rakita Ole Nkere, who explains the customs, ceremonies, rituals, and rites of passage of the Masai, the indigenous people. On a city tour of Nairobi, you visit the house where Karen Blixen (a.k.a. Isak Dinesen) lived, and have tea at a former colonial tea plantation.

A personal concierge attends to your needs at the hotel in Nairobi, and will help you shop for proper gear for the bush. Once you are in the bush, each safari is accompanied by safari directors and driver-guides, who take you to the likeliest areas for game viewing.

Their Hemingway Wing Safari is a classic trip, minus the hunting, that Hemingway would have enjoyed. You fly most legs of the trip in a private plane to maximize your time in the bush. From Amboseli and two days of game near Nairobi, you fly to the foothills of Mount Kenya to stay at a Treetops resort, The Aberdares, which overlooks a salt lick and a waterhole.

Then drive north a short distance to the Samburu/Shaba Game Reserve for its rarely seen game; then travel south for a stay at the classic Mount Kenya Safari Club, straight out of British East Africa, with riding stables, golf, tennis, and trout streams.

From there fly over the Rift Valley early in the morning for an amazing view back in time, to the Masai Mara, one of the best game-viewing places in Africa. Here for three days, you will also visit a Masai village and enjoy their hospitality, before joining your group for farewell cocktails at sunset on the Escarpment. Just like Hemingway.

Fourteen days, including everything but international airfare: about $4,500.

A portion of each trip's proceeds goes to America Share, a foundation begun by Micato to support needy East African children, many in orphanages. If you would like to donate kids' stuff (everything from school tools to blankets), Micato will send you a duffle bag, which you can fill and bring to be collected on arrival in Nairobi.

Tanzania

Thomson Safaris   14 Mount Auburn Street, Watertown, Massachusetts 02472. 800-235-0289 (toll free); 617-923-0426. E-mail: info@thomsonsafaris.com; Web site: www.thomsonsafaris.com

Thomson specializes in Tanzania, with native-born Tanzanian guides, customized Land Rovers, and a good knowledge of the nine game parks, home to abundant game. The Selous Game Reserve, in fact, has the largest concentration of game on earth.

Their Serengeti and Selous Safari, for example, begins in Serengeti National Park, staying at one of Thomson's Classic Camps (a comfortable walk-in tent with furniture and a private toilet). Next day, move on to the Ngorogoro Crater, the ten-mile wide caldera from a million-year-old collapsed volcano. You actually descend the 1,500 feet into the crater, which is a watering hole and grazing spot to huge numbers of mammals. Stay in a lodge overlooking the crater.

From there, the trip flies to the remote Ruaha National Park, in the interior; then to the Selous Game Reserve, where you spend two days living in a safari camp (a permanent tented camp, like a lodge with canvas walls) and exploring by car, by boat, and on foot.

Fourteen days, including airfare from the U.S. East Coast: about $7,400.

Mount Kilimanjaro

Mountain Travel Sobek   6420 Fairmount Avenue, El Cerrito, California 95430-9962. 800-687-6235 (toll free); 510-527-8100 (tel); 510-525-7710. E-mail: info@mtsobek.com; Web site: www. mtsobek.com

Mountain Travel Sobek runs several trips to East Africa, and a couple to Kilimanjaro, the 19,340-foot snowy peak ("as wide as the world," said Hemingway) that dominates the surrounding savannah in Tanzania. The climb is not a technical climb, but it goes straight up. The altitude is seriously high, and the ascent is steep.

Their eighteen-day Kilimanjaro & Beyond tour begins in Nairobi then spends two days in nearby Amboseli National Park, famed for its elephants. For the next three days, you begin your assault on Kilimanjaro, by hiking from the rainforest up through different ecosystems to camp at 15,000 feet. Here, mysteriously, are bones of savannah animals: an elephant, an antelope, and a leopard. When Hemingway climbed Kilimanjaro in the 1930s, the leopard was a frozen carcass. No one knows why these animals ventured up.

After 15,000 feet, the ascent to the peak is steeper yet. Almost at the top, you can peer into the center of the volcano's crater and marvel at the remnants of the glaciers. From the peak, at dawn you might be able to see some of the savannah below; but Kilimanjaro is famous for her veils, and a cloud or mist layer might obscure the view.

From Kilimanjaro, drive north to Tsavo East National Park, with its unique maneless lion population, then spend five days hiking with guides along the river in wild bush country (the guides are armed). For the final three days, drive east to Malindi on the Indian Ocean and relax on the beach at a deluxe resort.

Eighteen days: about $5,000, plus $700 for park fees.

Botswana

Eco-Expeditions   192 Nickerson Street, #200, Seattle, Washington 98109. 800-628-8747 (toll free); 206-285-4000 (tel); 206-285-5037 (fax). E-mail: zoe@zeco.com; Web site: www. zeco.com

Landlocked Botswana, shot through the middle with the delta of the Okavango River, is also home to the Bush People and the Kalahari Desert. Wild game is everywhere, especially concentrated in five camps, all of which are visited in Eco-Expedition's Ultimate Botswana, linked by privately chartered bush planes.

At Xigera in the Delta, spend three days exploring and living in a luxury tented camp. From there travel to Chitabe Camp, on one of the islands in the delta. Here you can explore by night with spotlights and on foot.

Spend four days at Mombo, one of the best tented camps in Botswana, where you will see abundant zebras and buffaloes and their predators—lions, cheetahs, and leopards—and have a good chance to watch the dramatic interaction among them. The next three days are at the Linyanti Wildlife Reserve at Dumatau Camp. Then fly to the Kalahari Desert on the edge of the largest salt pan in the world. Drive your own ATV across this place, then hop in the open four-by-four with Bushmen guides to do some serious game tracking. Stay at the famous Jack's Camp.

The final two days are spent at the Royal Livingstone Hotel, in the grand African tradition, located next to Victoria Falls, over which you will helicopter.

Twenty-one days, not including international airfare: about $14,000. Lex Hes, a native-born South African, is the guide.

Siemer & Hand Travel   750 Battery Street, Suite 300, San Francisco, California 94111. 800-451-4321 (toll free); 415-788-4000 (tel); 415-788-4133 (fax). E-mail: travel@ siemerhand.com; Web site: www.siemerhand.com

Wings Over Botswana is a fourteen-day trip that is guided by an ornithologist and visits some of the richest places in the world for bird-watching. Beginning in Johannesburg, with rare birds near the hotel, fly to the Mashatu Game Reserve, stay in a tent camp, and see everything from greater blue-eared glossy starlings to ostriches to Kori bustards.

At the Chobe National Park and the Moremi Game Reserve, you

will have seven days in which to see some of the 300 species of large and small, daylight and nocturnal birds that live there. See all the other game as well.

Fourteen days, not including international airfare: about $5,500.

LOWLAND GORILLAS IN GABON

In the mountain lowlands in Central Africa and in Gabon are reserves of gorillas, endangered in the wild, which tourists watch and photograph respectfully from about twenty feet.

Bushtracks Expeditions   P.O. Box 4163, Menlo Park, California 94026. 800-995-8689 (toll free); 650-326-8689 (tel); 650-463-0925 (fax). E-mail: info@bushtracks.com; Web site: www.bushtracks.com

Africa's Great Congo Basin is a rare look at an amazing and all-but-forgotten area, from northern Gabon inland to the Pygmies' rainforest, with a final two days spent at the scarcely ever visited island of Principe, off the coast of Gabon.

Fly into Libreville, then travel to the Dzanga-Sangha Special Reserve in the Central African Republic, smack in the middle of the continent. Here Pygmy guides will tell you about their home, how they track and hunt the small forest elephants. If you are lucky, they will take you to spots where they believe the itinerant gorillas will be, and point out clues that indicate an animal's presence. Home is at a simple lodge on the Sangha River, which you can explore by pirogue, an African dugout.

From there go to the Odzala Game Reserve in the Republic of Congo/Brazzville. Then fly out to Principe, for some ocean snorkeling and bird-watching among the remnants of ancient volcanoes. Stay at a five-star luxury marine lodge.

Bushtracks provides deluxe trips in its Cessna planes and Land Rovers, and pays careful attention to detail.

Twelve days, not including international airfare: about $10,000. This is for a group of six. If you have a smaller group, please call Bushtracks to arrange a custom trip.

USA Adventure Center   1311 63rd Street, Suite 200, Emeryville, California 94608. 800-227-8747 (toll free); 510-654-1879 (tel); 510-654-4200 (fax). E-mail: ex@adventurecenter.com; Web site: www.adventurecenter.com

This international company, with a home office in the United Kingdom (Explore Worldwide Ltd.), travels the world in small groups with expert guides, often in conjunction with organizations that help the host country or area.

Lowland Gorilla Search, run in conjunction with ECOFAC, an NGO that works to preserve Central African forest systems, is a trip for those looking for rainforest immersion. Six nights are spent at the Lope Wildlife Reserve in the middle of Gabon, from which you will have an opportunity to track with a local guide some of the 5,000 gorillas that live in the area. Walking through dense rainforest, you will listen for the sounds that identify gorillas: the snapping of branches, low grunts, occasional scrappy howls. Each family group consists of about five to ten members.

The trip begins in Libreville, then travels by train through the dense rainforest to the Lope Reserve and Lodge, on the Ogooue River, which you can explore by boat. On land, by foot and four-wheel drives, explore various terrains, including the savannah and the wildlife: primates, forest elephants, duikers, and lots of birds. From Lope Lodge, pirogue down the Offoue River to the Mikongo Primate Research Centre, where you will begin your search for gorillas in the bush.

Eight days, not including international airfare: about $2,050, plus $200 country fee.

MOUNTAIN GORILLAS IN UGANDA

Rainbow Tours   Canon Collins House, 64 Essex Road, London N1 8LR, United Kingdom. 011 +44 (0) 20 7226 1004 (tel); 011 +44 (0) 20 7226 2621 (fax). E-mail: info@rainbowtours.co.uk; Web site: www.rainbowtours.co.uk

Uganda is primate country, with the largest number of species located throughout its multiple ecosystems. You will see wildlife here that you don't see in other parts of East Africa, such as bush pigs, red forest buffalo, and giant forest hogs, plus 200 species of butterflies. It is also a country subject to political problems, from which, fortunately, it is bravely recovering.

Southern Uganda is part of an area once known as the Switzerland of Africa, for its mountains, deep lakes, and fresh and clear air. Many tea growers settled here, and a lot of colonial Africans used to come on vacation, building good roads and grand hotels, many of which remain.

The trip begins in Entebbe, then drives southwest to the Queen Elizabeth National Park. Here for two days, you can search for chimpanzees in the Kyambura Gorge, snap pictures of bathing hippos on a cruise on the Kazinga Channel, and take early morning and late afternoon game drives to scope some of the wildlife unique to Uganda.

Next day, drive through the highlands and spend the night on an island in Lake Bunyoni, then on to Bwindi Impenetrable National Park, home of the mountain gorilla. Of the 600 mountain gorillas thought to exist, about 300 live here. With expert tracking guides, spend three days on treks through the forest, looking for them. You might also see or hear black and white colobus monkeys. Nights are spent in a chalet overlooking the rainforest.

Back in Entebbe, visit the Chimpanzee Sanctuary in Ngamba Island.

Eight days, including lodging, in-country transportation, and meals: £1,800 to £1,950 (about $2,700 to $3,000).

Note: The Ugandan government issues no more than twenty permits a day to see gorillas in the wild, at a price of about $250. Book early. Also, expect fairly challenging jungle walks in search of the gorillas. Lodging is deluxe. This company will customize the safari for you, if you wish.

CHEETAHS IN NAMIBIA

Earthwatch Institute International   3 Clocktower Place, Suite
100, P.O. Box 75, Maynard, Massachusetts 01754. 800-776-0188
(toll free); 978-461-0081 (tel); 978-461-2332 (fax). E-mail: info@
earthwatch.org; Web site: www.earthwatch.org

This is a totally twenty-first-century kind of safari, on which you
help a naturalist save cheetahs from extinction in Namibia. As the
farmer population has grown in north central Namibia in the last
twenty years, the cheetah population has declined. Deprived of their
wide-range territory, cheetahs attack farm animals, and farmers
legally shoot them. In addition to their range problem, they are also
prey for lions.

Sorting out how humans and cheetahs can survive happily
together is the job of Laurie Marker, who was nominated by *Time*
magazine as one of its "Heroes of the Planet." Laurie formed the
Cheetah Conservation Fund in 1990 in an effort to save cheetahs.
Their numbers have gone from the hundreds of thousands throughout Africa to the tens of thousands in only a few countries.

You can help by lending your talents for two weeks, counting and
tracking cheetahs; analyzing what, when, and where they eat; and by
caring for captive cheetahs. If you have a conversational gift, you
can visit local schools and groups in the area and spread the word
on cheetahs and why they matter.

Lodging is in a simple bungalow on a 15,000-hectare working
farm, Eland's Joy, which is headquarters for the Cheetah Conservation Fund. Share the cooking. Experience what living in Africa is
really like.

Two weeks: about $3,000.

DESIGN YOUR OWN SAFARI

The following companies will set you up with your own private
safari, with as much or as little help as you need. The concept is
this: You want to travel at your own pace and stay at a certain kind

of place, say a lodge, rather than a tented camp; or you want to stay in a luxury tented camp or in your own tents. You don't know whether you will need a guide or not, or what the best guidebooks or maps are.

The solution is to contact a knowledgeable company, many of which own their own properties at or near game reserves, and all of which can provide guides, drivers, information, reservations, and even food and drink, if you want.

The Pride of Safaris   P.O. Box 24696, Nairobi, Kenya. 011 +254 2 884258/884259/882124 (tels); 884445 (fax). E-mail: thepride@iconnect.co.ke; Web site: www.theprideofsafaris.com

The Pride of Safaris offers luxury private tented camps with everything provided, including wine and beer, laundry service, and a "cordon bush" cook. Standard equipment at the camps also includes bottled water, paper tissue, umbrellas, and flashlights. Their guides are specialists in birds, animals, geology, geography, and biology, and will bring you to the best place for your special interest, whether it's witnessing lions at a kill or seeing the Southern Cross.

They provide four-wheel-drive Toyota Land Cruisers with roof hatches and VHF radios, as well as bush planes.

Denis Finch Hatton, the dashing Edwardian lover of Isak Dinesen (see *Out of Africa*), was also an African guide. His camp—with ten-foot vaulted ceilings, the finest bed linens, crystal glassware, and the best wines—set a tradition for safari, and is one that you can request if you like.

Safari Drive Limited   Wessex House, 127 High Street, Hungerford, Berkshire RG17 ODL, United Kingdom. 011 +44 (0) 1488 681611 (tel). E-mail: Safari_Drive@compuserve.com; Web site: www.safaridrive.com. Contact: Charlotte Chilcott.

Safari Drive encourages in-depth exploration of Africa, and offers to arrange tours with the guides appropriate to your special interests, from elephants to thorn trees. Their camps are luxury tented camps; and you have the choice of a driver or a self-drive Land Rover (they provide detailed maps and books). They will also arrange special extras such as horseback trips, on-foot safaris, trips assisted by or riding camels, and balloon rides. Their territory comprises all southern African countries, including the Indian Ocean islands.

A self-drive Safari Land Rover, equipped with complete camping gear, some tins of food, 100 liters of gasoline, and emergency backup service: from £145 to £175 a day, depending on the country (about $220 to $265); guide fee: £75 (about $112).

Geographic Expeditions   2627 Lombard Street, San Francisco, California 94123. 415-922-0448 (tel); 415-346-5535 (fax). E-mail: info@geoex.com; Web site: www.geoex.com

GeoExpeditions works in conjunction with Royal African Safaris and its first-class staff to bring you the best in private mobile tented safaris, with guides and complete equipment. Call to arrange your custom tour.

Abercrombie & Kent, Inc.   1520 Kensington Road, Oak Brook, Illinois 60523-2141. 800-757-5884 (toll free for brochures); 800-323-7308 (toll free); 630-954-2944 (tel); 630-954-3324 (fax). E-mail: info@abercrombiekent.com; Web site: www. abercrombiekent.com

A&K owns several luxury properties in Kenya, Tanzania, and Botswana. They will arrange your independent travel at an exclusive campsite, lodge, or tented camp at whatever level of luxury you prefer. A&K will also accommodate sidetrips to Zanzibar and Uganda.

NON-AFRICAN SAFARIS

Tigers in India

Brits in India under Queen Victoria set the standard for the luxury safari, on which they took all the comforts of home (adjusted for the climate). Their prime game a hundred years ago was the tiger. Today tigers are at risk from poachers, who kill them to sell parts of their bodies for use in Chinese traditional medicines. Many groups have formed to protect tigers from extinction.

Betchart Expeditions   17050 Montebello Road, Cupertino, California 95014-5435. 800-252-1910 (toll free); 408-252-4910 (tel); 408-252-1444 (fax). E-mail: BetchartExJohn@earthlink.net; Web site: www.betchartexpeditions.com

The India Wildlife Safari incorporates some of the most beautiful examples of built India (the Taj Mahal, Agra Fort, and the Khajuraho Temples) with the magnificent untamed, an elegant combination. Accompanied by naturalist James Jiler, the tour begins in Delhi, then drives to Ranthambore National Park, Rajasthan's first Project Tiger Reserve, where you will see Bengal tigers, and a host of other animals unique to India, such as the gaur, the small-eared elephant, and the one-horned rhinoceros.

From there, visit Keoladeo Ghana National Park, home to some of India's more than 1,000 species of birds, including the Sarus crane that whoopingly greets the dawn. Then spend three days at Bandhavgarh National Park, where you hunt for tigers from the back of an elephant. You will also have a chance to explore on foot in the morning, looking for tracks of tigers, sloth bears, and leopards.

Sixteen days, including first-class accommodation and sleeper train: about $3,500. Airfare from New York: about $1,200. In-country flight: about $200.

Mountain Travel Sobek   6420 Fairmount Avenue, El Cerrito, California 95430-9962. 800-687-6235 (toll free); 510-527-8100 (tel); 510-525-7710 (fax). E-mail: info@mtsobek.com; Web site: www.mtsobek.com

This trip centers on tigers and poachers in India and Nepal.

After a couple of days in Delhi, fly and drive to the Bandhavgarh National Park, a protected tiger space. Here for three days, you hunt for a glimpse of them from a jeep and riding an elephant.

Back in Delhi, fly to Kathmandu and then to Nepalgunj and the Royal Bardia National Park on the Karnali River. This has long been the route of smugglers. Here, staying four days at the Tiger Tops Karnali Lodge and Tented Camp in a beautiful forest, you can learn more about tigers and their problems from Dr. Charles McDougal, Smithsonian Associate for the Nepal Tiger Monitoring Project. Fly home from Kathmandu.

Seventeen days, including lodging, meals, and land travel: about $4,000. Round-trip from Delhi to Kathmandu: about $375. Mountain Travel Sobek donates profits from this trip to the Fund for the Tiger, a California charity that works to save the tiger.

Panda Bears in China

Posh Journeys   530 East Patriot Boulevard, #172, Reno, Nevada 89511. 775-852-5105 (tel/fax). E-mail: contact@poshjourneys. com; Web site: www.poshjourneys.com

Called the recluse of the forest, giant panda bears are hard to see in the wild. Forty pandas live in the China Conservation and Research Center for the Giant Panda, located in the remote mountains in Wolong in Szechuan Province. Here for a day you can volunteer your time with the caretakers as they feed and tend the highly endangered and cuddly panda bear. At the end of the day, you will receive a certificate to commemorate the priceless time spent feeding and playing with pandas.

This tour incorporates the very best of China, in addition to the two days you spend with the pandas. In fifteen days you visit the nontouristy places of Beijing, Xian, and Shanghai, with first-class hotels and the best food.

Sixteen days, including airfare from San Francisco: about $4,000.

Myths and Mountains   976 Tee Court, Incline, Nevada 89451. 800-670-MYTHS (toll free); 775-832-5454 (tel); 775-832-4454 (fax). E-mail: travel@mythsandmountains.com; Web site: www. mythsandmountains.com

This interesting trip visits one of the few areas in China where pandas still live in the wild, thought to number about 1,000. Start in Chengdu with a visit to the Giant Panda Breeding Center, where pandas are bred by artificial insemination. Szechuan is also the home of opera (visit the Opera School) and great food, such as mushroom hotpot and honey wine.

At the Wanglang Panda Reserve, spend four nights and days with Reserve naturalists, who introduce you to the habitat of the panda bear, the bamboo forest, where pandas eat almost thirty pounds of leaves a day. Naturalists will accompany you on bird-watching jaunts and vegetable- and mushroom-collecting trips. Evenings are spent in the Reserve Center listening to presentations by Reserve personnel on their work to save pandas.

On your way back to Chengdu, stay with the Baima tribal people, of whom only about 4,000 exist in China. They are hospitable hosts to strangers, and will take you to their sacred hill and tree. This, plus the pandas, will give you invaluable insights into China, especially if you wrap it all up with a therapeutic foot massage in Pingwu.

Fifteen days, including everything except international airfare: from about $2,700 per person (for a group of ten to fifteen people) to about $4,100 (for two people).

ORANGUTAN IN BORNEO

Their long arms, red fur, staring brown eyes, and intelligence caused local inhabitants to believe orangutans were human. The so-called Person of the Forest, the orangutan was the first ape classified by biologists venturing into the dense tropical rainforests of Sumatra and Borneo.

Seeing them in the wild is a challenge. For one thing, there aren't many of them: Females give birth once every eight or nine years, and hold on to their babies until they are about four years old. Males are the original drifters, avoiding even other male orangs. They spend most of the day searching for food over a wide area (unfortunately sometimes near the harvested parts of the rainforest), and bed down in a different tree fifty feet up each night. All of this makes them very difficult to spot. But Borneo is home to so-called biculturual orangs, those that have been reintroduced to the wild; it is also home to twelve other primate species, including proboscis monkeys and lemurs, and provides an exotic rainforest safari.

Orangutan Foundation International   822 South Wellesley Avenue, Los Angeles, California 90049. 800-ORANGUTAN [672-6488] (toll free); 310-207-1655 (tel); 310-207-1556 (fax). E-mail: ofi@orangutan.org; Web site: www.orangutan.org

The Orangutan Foundation International, an organization dedicated to preserving the habitat of the orangutan, offers a five-day tour to the Tanjung Puting National Park, home to some of the dwindling number of apes scattered throughout Borneo. Logging, fires, and poaching have diminished the wide area orangs need to look for food.

Across the river from the Tanjung Puting Rehabilitation Center is the famous Camp Leakey, established by the colorful Dr. Birute Galdikas in 1971 to reintroduce captive orangs back to the wild.

A 200-meter boardwalk that traverses the swamps in the rainforest is great for wildlife viewing and for encountering so-called bicultural orangs and their young, as they return to Camp Leakey in the late afternoon from the rainforest. No guests stay overnight here, but you can visit and trek into the jungle to look for orangs in the study area.

Five days, including jungle lodge, meals, and guide: $850. Additional days: $125 per day. International airfare is not included.

Eco-Expeditions   192 Nickerson Street, #200, Seattle, Washington 98109. 800-628-8747 (toll free); 206-285-4000 (tel); 206-285-5037 (fax). E-mail: zoe@zeco.com; Web site: www.zeco.com

This trip begins in Kuching, Sarawak, with a night at the Hilton. Then you head out to visit the Iban tribe, where you will explore the area in a longboat and stay in a long house, the traditional architecture of the Iban.

From there you visit some of Borneo's amazing caves—and their bats—before going to Kinabalu National Park and its canopy walkway, elevated 100 feet above the rainforest. From here you will see gibbons, giant squirrels, maroon langurs, as well as some amazing birds.

In the Danum Valley Conservation Area, the orangutan area, visit another treetop canopy walkway. At night a guide will take you on a spotlight tour around your lodge. In Sekau at the Lower Kinabatangan River, watch crab-eating macaques plummet into the river swiftly to avoid the crocodiles. Finally, at the Sepilok Rehabilitation Center, where orangs have been reintroduced to the wild, you can see them return faithfully each afternoon for milk and bananas. Jonathan Rossow, a physician and naturalist, and former lawyer and naturalist Holly Faithfull are the guides.

Sixteen days, including lodging, meals, and in-country transportation: about $7,300.

POLAR BEARS IN CANADA

International Expeditions, Inc. One Environs Park, Helena, Alabama 35080. 800-633-4734 (toll free); 205-428-1700 (tel); 205-428-1714 (fax). E-mail: nature@ietravel.com; Web site: www.internationalexpeditions.com

If you can stay awake for twenty-four hours straight, join the Polar Bear Tundra Safari on either of two tours in October, and stay at the Tundra Buggy Lodge, at Gordon Point, near Churchill, Manitoba's most northern point. You will never see so many polar bears in one place anywhere else.

There, in the Land of the Midnight Sun, polar bears gather to wait for the ice to freeze, so they can return north to hunt seals. You will be able not only to photograph them, but to talk about them with experts in informal talks in the evening. Polar bears spend the summer eating small mammals and berries, then wait for the ice to form so they can return to Hudson Bay.

The tour begins in Winnipeg, then flies to Churchill, where you look for polar bears in a tundra buggy, before moving to Gordon Point, where the ice forms first, and polar bears gather.

Eight days, including round-trip air from Winnipeg, lodging, meals, and viewing from the buggy: about $4,200.

GRIZZLY BEARS

Knight Inlet Grizzly Bear Adventure Tours   c/o Knight Inlet Lodge, 8841 Driftwood Road, Black Creek, British Columbia V9J 1A8, Canada. 250-337-1953 (tel); 250-337-1914 (fax). E-mail: grizzly@island.net; Web site: www.grizzlytours.com

Grizzlies, or brown bears, as they are called on the Alaskan coast, wake up from their winter slumber in the spring and travel to riverbanks to drink and eat spring shoots. In the fall, when the salmon begin to run, grizzlies congregate as close to the jumping salmon as they can get, and fill their bellies before they go into hibernation.

Knight Inlet Lodge runs two- to eight-day tours from June to October. Each tour begins at the Campbell River float dock, where you catch a float plane to go to the lodge. There you can settle in, between treks to viewing sites, which, in the spring, are from a boat, and in the summer and fall, from viewing platforms along the river. In the spring or shoulder season, from early May to late June, mothers tend their cubs when they are not mating.

Professional guides know a lot about the grizzlies; expect to see ten to fifteen at one time.

Two nights, including float plane, lodging, meals (except the first night at Campbell River), boat rides, bird viewing, and wildlife tracking to make plaster casts of animal tracks (some of them grizzly): $715 (low season) to $860 (high season). Eight nights: $3,015 (low season) to $3,425 (high season).

GRIZZLY BEARS IN ALASKA

Katmai Coastal Bear Tours   P.O. Box 1503, Homer, Alaska 99603. 800-532-8338 (toll free); 907-235-7251 (fax). E-mail: ast@ xyz.net; Web site: www.katmaibears.com

This safari is a photographer's dream. On a sturdy ship, the seventy-three-foot M/V *Waters*, you travel with wildlife biologists; ecologists; a nature photographer, Buck Wilde; and Dr. Lynn Rogers, called "the Diane Fossey of Black Bears," who has done numerous TV specials for the Discovery Channel and National Geographic Explorer.

Coastal Bears of Katmai National Park begins with a sixty-minute seaplane ride to the Shelikof Strait, a bay where the *Waters* is anchored, 150 miles from the nearest road. Grizzlies are there in abundance in the wilderness; and eighteen-foot boats will transport photographers to the shore.

Katmai is also home to hundreds of migrating birds, including puffins, oyster catchers, and eagles; as well as stellar sea lions, seals, foxes, otters, and whales. The tour includes three meals a day from the gourmet chef, a maximum of eight guests, and nothing to distract.

June to September; book early; the shoulder seasons are just as fruitful for viewing as midsummer. The company recommends trip cancellation insurance because of weather.

Four days: $3,250.

CHAPTER 23

SAILING

Sailors know that sailing is a metaphor for life. To keep the vessel shipshape, you have to be in fairly good shape yourself. To make it move, you have to orchestrate the weather, wind, sea conditions, and other members of the crew. Crises constantly test your smarts and your mettle; the crew consoles each other when things go wrong, celebrates with champagne when they go right. At times, you can't wait to get home. When you get home, you can't wait to go again.

RACE AROUND THE WORLD

Clipper Ventures PLC, Shamrock Quay, William Street, Northam, Southampton SO14 5QL, United Kingdom. 011 +44 (0) 023 8023 7088 (tel); 011 +44 (0) 023 8023 7081 (fax). E-mail: info@clipper-ventures.com; Web sites: www.clipper-ventures.com

Clipper Ventures races eight yachts around the world, more than 35,000 nautical miles in about ten months. The race, run every two years, is highly competitive, because the ships—Clipper 60s, sixty-foot ocean-racing yachts—are identical, and the captains are professionals. The crew? The crew is you.

You need no prior experience on a sailboat. Minimum age: eighteen; there is no maximum age. Since 1995, more than 1,000 people from all walks of life and most every profession have sailed on these

Tight and trim, these sailboats vie for the best wind as they tack out from a harbor to resume their ocean race. *(Roger Archibald)*

races. Each yacht is sponsored by a different international city (e.g., Glasgow, Hong Kong, New York).

Before the race, you spend two weeks in training both on and off the water, in and around the United Kingdom, before you sail to open water off Portugal to try some competitive racing and racing in light winds and heavy weather. In the month before the race, you will learn everything from sail repair to electronics to first aid, and will become an important member of the sailing team. "Chess with push-ups," is Clipper's description of racing training.

Once under way, the race is done in six legs (for example, Liverpool to Cuba; Cuba to Hawaii; Hawaii to Hong Kong), with port stops during which all the competitors can relax together. But at sea, the trim cutter rig is set to glean the most from the wind day and night, and the ride can be very exciting.

This is more than a race, writes Sir Robin Knox-Johnston, the Chairman of Clipper Ventures; it's about leaving "the rat race" and living with the rest of the crew in tight quarters, an experience that creates lifelong friendships. It also, says Knox-Johnston, gives time to "realize that life can offer much more if you are prepared to reach out and try it."

The entire trip from Liverpool to Liverpool: £26,500 (about $39,000). It is possible to join the ship at a later leg, provided you are trained. Each leg: £7,000 (about $10,500).

SAIL A SQUARE-RIGGER AROUND THE WORLD

Barque Picton Castle Voyages   1 Woodbine Lane, Amherst, New Hampshire 03031. 603-424-0219 (tel); 603-424-1849 (fax). E-mail: info@picton-castle.com; Web site: www.picton-castle.com. Coordinator: David Robinson.

Everything you bring aboard the *Picton Castle* when you step on deck, intending to spend a year sailing around the world, has to fit in your bunk. The *Picton Castle*, a 179-foot wood square-rigged barque, built in 1928 and completely refitted in the 1990s, carries twenty-three passengers, who pay for the privilege of going to sea. Called "amateur hands," passengers must put in several hours of work a day to keep the ship on course and on a happy keel. They work side by side with the professional crew of seventeen and the captain, Don Moreland.

Let your imagination roam as you visit the Galapagos, Pitcairn Island, Fiji, Vanuatu, around Cape Horn to Cape Town, Saint Helena, and Bermuda. See whales, sunrises, sunsets, exotic birds, and strange fish. Visit ports and meet people around the world. Learn to hoist sails, lower sails, secure sails, and understand the wind. Cook on the superefficient 1893 stove. On the midnight watch, see stars no one would believe and sea creatures you can't believe you're seeing.

You need to be at least eighteen; there is no upper age limit. Your physician must declare that you are fit enough to do moderately strenuous work, but you do not need to come with sailing experience. At the end of the trip you will be able to qualify to take the Able-Bodied Seaman Certificate exam.

The whole trip from Lunenburg, Nova Scotia, around the world, and back to Lunenburg—one year and two weeks: $32,000. However, you can catch up with them at other ports if you don't want to do the entire voyage, and pay about $750 to $800 a week.

Sail a Tall Ship

The Bay of Islands, New Zealand

Adventure Center   1311 63rd Street, Suite 200, Emeryville, California 94608. 800-227-8747 (toll free); 510-654-1879 (tel); 510-654-4200 (fax). E-mail: ex@adventurecenter.com; Web site: www.adventurecenter.com

The 106-foot square-rigged brigantine, *Søren Larsen*, was built in 1949 in Denmark. Like many tall ships, it fell into disuse and became almost forgotten until the 1970s, when film companies provided the revenue to have it retrofitted to its glorious mahogany paneling and gleaming brass fittings. After several global circumnavigations, the *Søren Larsen* today takes paying crews sailing the Bay of Islands in New Zealand. It is a beautiful experience.

For about $100 a day, you can haul on the lines that set some of the 6,500 square feet of sail. You learn how to secure the lines and tie knots. You keep watch for part of every twenty-four-hour period, and scale the mast to set the topsails, if you like. Comfortable berths have fresh hot water showers and electric lights.

Adventure Center provides two options: Ocean Sailing Voyages, which take you into open water from destination to destination; and Island Cruising Voyages, which visit remote places and little ports in the South Pacific.

Six days: cruising the Bay Islands, New Zealand: about $650; eleven days: cruising from Vanuatu to New Caledonia: about $1,550. Price includes berth and all meals.

East Coast, United States

HMS Bounty, P.O. Box 141, Oakdale, New York. 631-588-7900
(tel); 631-471-4609 (fax). E-mail: mramsey@tallshipbounty.org;
Web site: www.tallshipbounty.org

Tallships and the movie industry often find each other at the
right time. The H.M.S. *Rose*, for example, a three-masted full-rigged
replica of a Revolutionary War British frigate that took hundreds of
sail trainees, families, corporate teams, and teens on week-long trips,
succumbed to the charms of 20th Century Fox and moved to California to make a series of Patrick O'Brien films.

The H.M.S. *Bounty*, on the other hand, was built specially to star
in the MGM 1962 film *Mutiny on the Bounty*. After being abandoned
by Hollywood, it languished at the dock, until it was rescued by a
group who restored it to its original polish, and now take overnight
paying sail trainees around ports along the New England and New
York coasts. In the winter, it cruises south toward Cuba.

About $150 to $200 a day provides a comfortable berth and
meals, in return for your hands on deck to keep her under sail.

THE SEA CLOUD:
A LUXURY YACHT

The *Sea Cloud* was an expensive toy when it was built in 1931, even
by wealthy pre–World War II European standards. Conceived by
financier E. F. Hutton and his wife, cereal heiress Marjorie Meriwether Post, it was the ultimate in luxury yachts, a 356-foot, four-
masted square-rigged barque, commissioned *Hussar V.* It was by far
the favorite place to be invited for a weekend or a week for European and American society, including the Duke and Duchess of
Windsor. Today, its original fireplaces keep away the chill in the
spacious staterooms; bathrooms are marble; and some of the original antiques are among the stately furniture.

After the Huttons' divorce, she got the yacht and renamed it *Sea
Cloud*. Here, with her daughter, actress Dina Merrill, Marjorie

Meriwether Post spent half the year cruising. In 1935 she married ambassador to the U.S.S.R. Joseph Davies, and the yacht served as a diplomatic plus until World War II rearranged alliances, and *Sea Cloud* was put to work tracking U-boats in the North Atlantic. Retrofitted in 1979 to most of its original dazzle, *Sea Cloud* has thirty-four spectacular cabins ready to book.

The Caribbean

National Geographic Expeditions   P.O. Box 65265, Washington, D.C. 20035-5265. 888-866-8687 (toll free). Reserve online at: www.nationalgeographic.com/ngexpeditions

To cruise from Antigua to Grenada, the National Geographic Expeditions' Under Sail in the Caribbean is accompanied by marine biologist Sylvia Earle. Part of each day is spent snorkeling in the warm clear waters. In addition to marine activities, the trip includes a visit to the last Carib village in the Caribbean, on Domenica. You'll have lots of opportunities to hike and explore the Windward and Leeward islands, then dress for dinner with the captain, as did those from another era.

Nine days: from about $5,000 to $10,000, depending on berth.

The Greek Islands and Turkish Coast

Abercrombie & Kent, Inc.   1520 Kensington Road, Oak Brook, Illinois 60523-2141. 800-757-5884 (toll free for brochures); 800-323-7308 (toll free); 630-954-2944 (tel); 630-954-3324 (fax). E-mail: info@abercrombiekent.com; Web site: www.abercrombiekent.com

Abercrombie & Kent's sixteen-day Athens-to-Istanbul trip includes a seven-night *Sea Cloud* cruise from Piraeus to Izmir. Combine lodging and meals on *Sea Cloud* with stops at Santorini, Bodrum and its Underwater Archaeology Museum, Patmos and its Monastery of Saint John, and Ephesus in Turkey.

Sixteen days: about $7,000 to $17,000, depending on berth.

SAIL A GULET

The Turquoise Coast, Turkey

Wilderness Travel   1102 Ninth Street, Berkeley, California 94710. 800-368-2790 (toll free); 510-558-2488 (tel); 510-558-2489 (fax). E-mail: info@wildernesstravel.com; Web site: www. wildernesstravel.com

This twelve-passenger two-masted luxury yacht, known as a gulet, is home for ten days as you sail the beautiful inlets and stretches where the cliffs fall into the sea of the Turkish coast.

Each day, you hike ashore to view Lydian Greek and Roman amphitheaters, temples, towns, and the city of Ephesus. You have lunch with a family in a rural village. You snorkel over sunken ancient buildings and fallen columns, visit the birthplace of Saint Nicholas, and shop for kilims. Onboard, the crew catch the fish the cook will prepare for dinner. Tanned, with one foot in this world, the other in the ancient world, you return to Istanbul.

Each cabin has a private bath. The trip is accompanied by an expert in Turkish archaeology and history.

Sixteen days, including hotel, meals, and the gulet: from about $3,200 to $3,800, depending on the size of the group. International airfare to Istanbul is not included.

A CRUISING YACHT IN THE SEYCHELLES

Zegrahm Expeditions   192 Nickerson Street, #200, Seattle, Washington 98109. 800-628-8747 (toll free); 206-285-4000 (tel); 206-285-5037 (fax). E-mail: zoe@zeco.com; Web site: www. zeco.com

Le Ponant, built in France in 1991, is a three-masted, 290-foot expedition sailing vessel, with an enormous 16,000 square feet of sail. Swift and comfortable, *Le Ponant* matches fifty-six passengers with a crew of thirty.

Maybe because they are remote from most of the Western world, maybe because not many people live there, the Seychelles have been called Paradise, Eden, and the end of the world.

Sailing the Seychelles in the magnificent blue-green Indian Ocean is a spectacular natural history experience. Species that occur nowhere else on earth are here in abundance. On this trip, start in Mahe, the largest island, then sail to the most interesting of the Seychelles, which you can reach further by zodiac. Dive, snorkel, hike, or walk in a new land full of black parrots and blue pigeons, thousand-year-old palm trees, and the largest nuts on the planet, which weigh about thirty pounds. There are forests of baobab trees, and an island with 150,000 giant Indian Ocean tortoises.

If you are a bird-watcher, your list will be more complete. If you like lemurs, they live here in all colors and sizes, and number in the thousands. Onboard are naturalists, marine specialists, historians, and ornithologists.

Seventeen days (flying from Paris to Mahe), including all services on *Le Ponant*, lectures and briefings, excursions ashore, meals, and wine: about $9,800, double occupancy; about $15,780, single occupancy. International airfare is not included.

CHAPTER 24

SHARK DIVES

The great white shark, a.k.a. *Jaws* and the "Eating Machine," grows to twenty-one feet in length to qualify as the largest predatory animal in the ocean, and our favorite monster. On the coasts, according to our modern legends, sharks terrorize beachgoers, chew on surfers, and attack small boats with a vengeance.

Why can't we learn to love sharks the way we love whales?

Start with a shark cage, the reinforced steel two- or four-person platform that is lowered a few feet beneath the surface to spy on sharks. Aside from being an adrenalin and testosterone stimulant, seeing sharks from a cage can lead to a deeper understanding of them.

Once you see sharks in a group eating, says Captain Lawrence Groth, a veteran commercial diver who runs trips to shark feeding grounds, you realize how gentle and slow they can be. "You'll come away from that experience with an almost reverent understanding of the wild ocean and the white shark's place in it."

Sharks remain, despite their infamous stardom, a mystery. Recent studies from Stanford University found that sharks range huge distances over the whole ocean, rather than preying on populated beaches in the summer; and they prefer water temperatures in the fifties (F). At least four of the study's tagged subjects lingered for several months in the middle of the Pacific Ocean (no one knows why), far from the coast and swimmers and surfers.

A great white shark in the flesh scopes the photographer in the seal feeding grounds in the Gulf of the Farallones National Marine Sanctuary, west of San Francisco. *(Photo by Scot Anderson, NMS/NOAA)*

Few people have grown sentimental about sharks on shark dives, but it's a great way to get good pictures of sharks in the wild; and no shark has ever attacked a cage either.

FARALLONES ISLANDS, CALIFORNIA

About thirty miles off the coast of San Francisco, west of the Golden Gate Bridge, is a small archipelago where huge elephant seals live. Since elephant seals are the principal diet of great whites, visits to these islands in the fall raise your chances considerably of being able to photograph a subsurface shark fest.

Note: The cages use surface air, so they aren't considered a dive. Therefore, technically, you don't need scuba certification. Nevertheless, if you lack a card, you have two options: one, go in the cage with an instructor, who will decide whether or not you can handle it; two, stay on deck and watch from there.

Absolute Adventures   415-235-9410 (tel). E-mail: staff@ absoluteadv.com; Web site: www.sharkdiver.com

Trips to the Farallones on Captain Lawrence Groth's thirty-two-foot fishing vessel, *Patriot*, leave at 6 A.M. and return at 7 P.M. Maximum: six passengers. Each dive lasts twenty to forty minutes, and is about four feet below the surface. The shark cages carry two or four passengers, and each has a good viewing portal.

Onboard, there are a shower and an enclosed rest room, and a fresh-water trough for rinsing off camera gear. Bring only your wetsuit, gloves, booties, hood, and mask. One full day, including gourmet lunch: between $900 and $1,000. Special discounts for groups, law enforcement, firefighters, and active military personnel.

Isla Guadalupe, Mexico

Incredible Adventures   6604 Midnight Pass Road, Sarasota, Florida 34242. 800-644-7382 (toll free); 941-346-2603 (tel); 941-346-2488 (fax). E-mail: info@incredible-adventures.com; Web site: www.incredible-adventures.com

In conjunction with Absolute Adventures and Golden Gate Expeditions, Incredible Adventures has teamed up with Captain Lawrence Groth to pilot the *Searcher*, a ninety-six-foot dive and fishing vessel with fifteen cabins, four rest rooms, and two showers for a five-day live aboard shark-diving expedition.

The pristine Isla Guadalupe is home to great whites and mako sharks, all hefty and hungry, feeding in the tropical and clear (to 100 feet) water. Success in seeing great whites on an expedition here is in the 98 percent range.

The plus on this trip is that shark researchers ride for free. Tagging sharks is best done when sharks are engaged in feeding and not aware that a scientist is attaching an electronic tag. The boat captain also stops to fish along the way for such things as yellowfin tuna and mahi mahi.

Five days aboard (leaving from San Diego and anchoring off the Isla), including three days with multiple cage dives, meals, and lodging aboard: $2,250 to $2,400 (varies with the date).

SOUTH AFRICA

Wildwings   577-579 Fishponds Road, Bristol BS16 3AF, United Kingdom. 011 +44 (0) 117 9658 333 (tel); 011 +44 (0) 117 9375 681 (fax). E-mail: wildinfo@wildwings.co.uk; Web site: www. wildwings.co.uk

In conjunction with shark expert Scot Anderson, Wildwings offers a ten-day trip to Seal Island in False Bay, off Cape Town. An estimated 64,000 Cape Fur seals loll about here, occasionally being scooped up by cruising great whites.

Weather permitting, you spend as much time as possible on False Bay, helping scientists do research, including tagging, identifying, and hydro-acoustic recording; as well as cage diving and photographing. The *National Geographic* did a television story on sharks here in 1999.

Note: You must be a certified scuba diver (PADI open-water certificate, for example) to enter the cage. Nondivers stay on deck.

Ten days, including round-trip airfare from London, lodging, cage dives, air tanks, weight belts, lectures, and ground transport: about $3,550.

Incredible Adventures   6604 Midnight Pass Road, Sarasota, Florida 34242. 800-644-7382 (toll free); 941-346-2603 (tel); 941-346-2488 (fax). Web site: www.incredible-adventures.com

A legend in False Bay says that there lives a shark nicknamed Submarine, more than twenty feet long and with the personality of the star of *Jaws*. Local people tell stories about it around the fire.

On a twenty-six-foot catamaran, Incredible Adventures in partnership with African Shark Eco Charters, runs one-day trips thirty miles out of Cape Town to False Bay. Using GPS and communication with land, the crew are able to identify where sharks have gathered. The four-person cage, attached to the boat, has an emergency air supply.

Note: You must be a certified scuba diver (PADI open-water certificate, for example) to enter the cage. Nondivers stay on deck.

African Shark Eco is linked with several research organizations for which you can help tag and identify individual sharks. The trip is weather dependent.

One day, including lunch: $250.

CHAPTER 25

SPACE: READY FOR LIFTOFF

Thanks to films, video games, and simulations, space travel seems easy and familiar.

Wearing a helmet and a bulky silver suit, astronaut/pilots crawl into the capsule, click a few buttons, give a thumbs-up, then brace for the thrust into space and the G-pull, which does horrific things to the flesh on the face. When that's over, it's time to take off the bulky suit, marvel at Earth from above, look at the stars, and uncoil in an aerial somersault to float to another part of the spaceship.

Once at the space station/moon/Mars, or a new planet, it's time to get to work and carry out procedures.

SPACE TOURISM

Well, while we have been watching all of this, space tourism advocates have been trying to come up with easy ways to put a dozen or so tourists on a space bus, send them on a breathtaking tour more than sixty miles up for about an hour, bring them back safely, and give them astronaut wings, all for around $100,000 (see www. space.com). Projected for sometime after 2005, suborbital space travel will use reusable launch vehicles (RLV).

Zero G. Flying without gravity allows you to jump, twist, and spin in space. These lucky people are aboard the Russian Space Agency's IL-76 MDK "flying laboratory." *(Courtesy of Incredible Adventures, Inc.)*

Until the bus comes along, Space Adventures, in conjunction with Xerus Corp., has developed a two-person suborbital rocketship, which will deliver about a hour of fantastic extraterrestrial travel, probably in late 2005 or 2006. Closer to development is Cosmopolis XXI, a sleek ship designed to carry three space travelers by 2005.

HOTELS IN SPACE

Recent public opinion polls indicate that between 60 and 85 percent of those questioned said that they would go into space in a heartbeat if they could, and furthermore, would be willing to pay three months' salary to do it, and to stay there for a week to a couple of months.

Stay where? This is where the real visionaries come in. It's one thing to take people on a suborbital tour around Earth, another to shoot them to the International Space Station (ISS). Dennis Tito and Mark Shuttleworth, millionaires with time enough to spend training as junior astronauts, joined in with the ISS crew to help out. Shuttleworth actually performed several independent scientific experiments.

But tourists? NASA pales at the word. However, the space program could use a booster dollar. Aiming at the day when space "tourism" will be an okay thing, several companies are at the drawing board. Mir Corporation in Amsterdam (www.mir-corp.com) is experimenting with three-passenger Mini-Station 1, designed to host guests up to twenty days. SpaceHab (www.spacehab.com) is working on a detachable module that will serve as a bed and breakfast for tourists at the ISS; and Las Vegas hotel owner Robert Bigelow (www.bigelowaerospace.com) is manufacturing "inflatable habitat modules," structures that will increase living space at the ISS, and ideally reflect the sleek design of the space hotel in *2001: A Space Odyssey*. No one has a definite date in mind.

UNTIL THEN . . .

Get ready. You can train for every step of the way into space, and in the process, participate in some pretty fantastic space experiences. Some require a lot of venture capital, but most do not. Plus, you do it all in Russia, because NASA and the United States have yet officially to approve space travel and tourism.

Space Adventures   4350 North Fairfax Drive, Suite 840, Arlington, Virginia 22203. 888-85-SPACE [857-7223] (toll free); 703-524-7176 (fax). E-mail: info@spaceadventures.com; Web site: www.spaceadventures.com

This company, begun by astronaut Buzz Aldrin, works in conjunction with many shuttle astronauts and other former astronauts, who give VIP backroom tours of Kennedy Space Center launches, private trips to witness the takeoff ceremonies of the paid space guests to the International Space Station (like Dennis Tito and Mark Shuttleworth), and often accompany MiG flights and guest astronaut training in Russia. Their presence is comforting, as well as informative.

Wildwings, a British travel company, is one of many agents who work in conjunction with Space Adventures around the world. See www.wildwings.co.uk.

The following details are from Space Adventures trips:

Astronaut Training

At this writing, all training is done at the Yuri Gagarin Cosmonaut Training Center in Star City, Russia, with flights from Zhurkovsky Air Base, about an hour out of Moscow.

Weightlessness or Zero G

G is for gravity, the universal gravitational constant that reflects the pull of the earth. On earth we experience 1G, which is our body weight. Anyone who has ever ridden a roller coaster has probably experienced 2Gs, gliding over the top and plummeting to the bottom, feeling as if you weigh twice as much.

Zero G means you experience life as a butterfly. This trip will take you up in a Russian Ilyushin-76. It rises in a steep (45-degree) pitch to the edge of space, glides over the edge, then reenters Earth's atmosphere. At the top, the plane performs parabola maneuvers, during which you will experience thirty seconds of zero G, which is what residents on the ISS experience all the time. You can float, fly, and take pictures. At pull-out, the flight will press 2Gs on you, but you will lie safely on the padded floor of the plane.

Do this eight or ten times, and you will have a sense of how very different being in space is.

Space Adventures advises a light breakfast and motion sickness medication, just in case. This flight has not been called the Vomit Comet for nothing.

The flight is safe, however, and veterans of ten or more parabolas say it is out of this world.

Three days, including Moscow hotel, NOMEX flight suit, flight certificate, video, and photo of you and the crew: $5,400.

Neutral Buoyancy and the Centrifuge

In the Hydrolab, where all Russian cosmonauts have trained, you can learn what it is like to walk and work in space. Wearing an Orlan-M space suit, you are hoisted (with audio communication devices) into the pool, which is twelve meters deep, and told to perform certain tasks. It is strenuous, technically challenging work, and you need an international diving certificate to qualify.

The world's largest centrifuge is at the Yuri Gagarin Center, capable of generating a pull of 10Gs. Train here from zero G to as many Gs as you can stand (with a guide close by). The centrifuge most closely simulates an orbital launch and reentry, when the pull of Gs is greatest.

For these experiences, Space Adventures will put you up for two nights in Moscow and provide all transport in Russia, along with VIP customs treatment, a NOMEX suit (to keep), and an on-site medical exam. Bring a medical release from your personal physician stating that you are in good health.

Three days, Neutral Buoyancy: about $7,000. Centrifuge is a one-day add-on: about $1,800.

Soyuz Simulator

The *Soyuz* spacecraft carried many cosmonauts to Mir, the Russian space station. Now it is used as a training craft for anyone going into space. Safely using a simulator, you can learn how to fly it from launch to touchdown, so liftoff will be a breeze if you go to the ISS.

Space Adventures facilitates your use of the *Soyuz*, and provides two nights in Moscow, the NOMEX flight suit, and all transport in Russia for about $8,500.

Suborbital Flights

You cannot go yet, but space is filling fast, so sign up now.

The whole progam includes four days of preparation and training, during which you will experience zero gravity and in-flight gravity pulls. Study safety procedures on the reusable launch vehicle (RLV), and gain an understanding of its systems, the program, and the flight operations.

Then on the fifth day, you don the NOMEX suit, step into the RLV (designed for tourists, not astronauts), and go through the countdown. Rocket engines will boost you up to about sixty miles (the average commercial flight is about six miles up). Travel twice the speed of sound in the comfort of your seat.

The rockets stop; in the quiet, you and your fellow passengers, weightless for about five minutes, will be able to see the blue earth below, black space beyond. Video cameras inside and outside the cabin record the trip; and you can snap pictures.

(In 2040 or 2050, if all goes well, you might be able to check in at a floating space hotel above the earth and spend a day or two.)

At the end of thirty to sixty minutes, the rockets fire up, point back to the earth, and you return. High-fives and champagne will greet you.

Total cost is about $100,000. You can make a deposit of $10,000 now and subsequent payments of $12,000 a year for three years before your flight. The balance is due six months before the flight. For the price you get not only a ride in space, but lodging at the local hotel, flight-training suit, the in-flight video, photos of the team, astronaut wings, badge, medal, and plaque. And lifetime membership in the Space Adventurers Club.

You need to be at least eighteen years old, and have to complete a lengthy medical screening questionnaire.

Orbital Flight Qualification Preparation

This is preparation for the real thing: getting ready to go to the International Space Station (ISS).

For this you need lots of money and good health. Be prepared to undergo an intensive medical examination in Russia that includes "complete blood tests, heart tests, neurological tests, dental tests, auditory tests, and comprehensive body scans." You need to learn Russian and be able to do all the training devices in Star City.

In the *Soyuz* simulator, you must dock with the ISS. Prove that you are comfortable at zero gravity on a chartered flight, and fly at Mach 2.5 to 80,000 feet in a MiG 25, the world's fastest operations aircraft. Whether you like that or not, next, you do aerobatics in a MiG 29.

Sit in the continuous as well as the discontinuous Coriolis spinning chair; then experience 5,000 meters altitude in the hypobaric altitude chamber.

Pass the Neutral Buoyancy Test (diving certification required); and be able to withstand 5 or 6Gs in the centrifuge, which mimics the force exerted on the return to earth.

Mark Shuttleworth described the return as an adrenalin high. But it was a challenge, he said in an interview on the NBC *Today* show. "It was certainly more comfortable to adapt to space than it was to adapt back to being on earth. Your legs know what they should do, but they just seem unable to get it all right in the right sequence."

The fourteen-day Flight Qualification Program, including everything (excitement, fatigue, five-star hotel, great food, guides, an American escort, and a lot of fun): $200,000. At the end, the committee will let you know if you passed.

Orbital Flight

If you are chosen, you will need eight months in which to complete the difficult and demanding training—plus meet the price tag of $20,000,000, for which you may spend a week at the ISS.

Not everyone was meant to fly into space, says Space Adventures. Those who do, realize their wildest dreams, and probably secure a tiny place in history.

Space travel is not yet a walk in the park.

Incredible Adventures, Inc.   6604 Midnight Pass Road, Sarasota, Florida 34242. 800-644-7382 (toll free). E-mail: info@ incredible-adventures.com; Web site: www.incredibleadventures.com

Incredible Adventures offers similar programs in Russia. Please see their Web site.

SPACE CENTERS ON EARTH

If you're not sure you are ready to commit to a physical space fantasy, try watching the beauty of a rocket liftoff.

Kennedy Space Center Visitor Center Complex
State Road 405, six miles inside Kennedy Space Center, 45 minutes east of Orlando. 321-449-4444 (tel for information). Web site: www.KennedySpaceCenter.com

Kennedy Space Center is the site of the launch pad from which the shuttle lifts off to the International Space Station. You can be a witness to the amazing event of a launch from a waterfront viewing site a few miles away. Billows of smoke signal the firing rockets, then, as the earth trembles, the flaming oranges and reds shoot out from beneath the lifting rocket, before the arching stream of white smoke plumes into space.

Launch transportation tickets are $36.50 for adults, $26.50 for children ages three to eleven. This includes admission to the Visitor Complex. On your visit you can opt to Dine With an Astronaut. This is a special program that is preceded by an introductory video of life onboard the shuttle, followed by a question-and-answer period with an astronaut, and lunch. Dessert, the Chocolate Liftoff, is worth a mention: it is a milk chocolate space shuttle with whipped cream, berries, and melba sauce. Prices start at about $30.00 for adults; and $20.00 for children ages three to eleven.

Space Center Houston, the Official Visitor Center of NASA's Johnson Space Center. 1601 NASA Road 1, Houston, Texas 77058. 281-244-2100 (tel). E-mail: schinfo@spacecenter.org. Web site: www.spacecenter.org

"Houston, do you read me? Come in, Houston."
Crackle crackle.
"This is Houston. We read you, Apollo."

The space communications center of NASA's Johnson Space Center provides the contact with the earth that men and women in space depend upon. A visit to the museum of NASA and the Manned Space Flight Program won't get you online with the shuttle, but you can experience every aspect of the history of NASA in realistic exhibits. Admission: about $16.00 for adults; $12.00 for children ages four to eleven.

PREPARE TO VISIT MARS

The Mars Society   P.O. Box 273, Indian Hills, Colorado 80454. 303-980-9947 (tel). E-mail: MarsSocinfo@aol.com; Web site: www.marssociety.org

To go to Mars has been a fantasy for a long time. Early telescope gazers wondered: Are the straight lines that network its surface a series of canals? Who or what created the unusual architecture of its mountains? Are there Martians?

In this century, information streaming in from orbiting cameras and probes suggests that the mysterious red planet might once have been wet, and some of that water might be trapped beneath the surface, harboring ancient life forms. Chemical probes of the atmosphere paint a fairly hostile picture. The "architecture"? It's in the eye of the beholder.

If we ever do manage to send a team of humans to Mars, will we be prepared?

A team of geologists, astrobiologists, engineers, and other scientists are laying the groundwork for travel to Mars in four Mars Analog Research Stations, placed at spots around the earth with geological environments similar to those on Mars. The team, living in isolation as if they were on Mars, tests robotic rovers and new space suits, as well as collecting data on parts of Earth that have not been well documented.

Researchers at the stations—located on Devon Island, Alaska; Utah; Australia; and Iceland—study living in extreme environments on Earth. Fossils in the Australian outback, for example, are thought to be the oldest on Earth, and might resemble fossils on Mars. Iceland's volcanic landscape provides Mars-like challenges, as do the ice-bound Arctic and hot-by-day, cold-by-night, remote and rocky Utah desert.

The Mars Society Projects take volunteers with various professions and skills, but they must be physically fit and psychologically ready to live for a few weeks as a team under extreme conditions. Generous donors are invited as well. Check their Web site.

CHAPTER 26

THE SPY TRADE

The woman pushes a baby stroller through the mall, stopping to look in windows, returning the smiles of those who look at her baby. She pauses to adjust the baby's bottle, then throws a tissue into a trash receptacle and walks on.

A few feet away from the receptacle, a man wearing shorts and a ball cap sits on a bench, eating a hamburger. Within moments, he gets up, wraps the hamburger in its paper, and throws it in the trash. At the same time, he retrieves the crumpled tissue containing a microchip that the young mother has just deposited.

They are both spies, engaged in a dead drop.

SPY TOURS

Washington, D.C.

Spy Drive, Washington, D.C. 866-SPYDRIVE [779-3748] (toll free). Web site: www.spydrive.com

"There are more foreign spies in Washington than in any other city in the world," said Ray Mislock, former chief of the FBI Field Office in Washington.

Scenarios like the one described above are just a taste of some of the juicy spy dramas that go on behind the stately and not-so-stately facades of public and private Washington buildings.

Spying is all about information: who has it, how to get it, how to use it, how to guard it. In this poster from 1943, the U.S. Office of War Information warns against "careless talk" during World War II, when it was believed Nazi spies could be anywhere, listening. (*Northwestern University Library,* www.library.northwestern.edu/govpub/collections/wwII-posters/)

Former CIA, FBI, DOD, and KGB officers and agents who specialize in counterintelligence will lead you on a once-a-month, two-and-a-half to three-hour motorcoach tour of Washington and its environs. With their guidance, you will be able to spot a signal site, a mark on a wall that indicates a dead drop, for example; identify a car being tailed by another; or see a surveillance team working a street. This, plus all the places where spies did or did not accomplish their missions, and the stories they generated, will give you insights into "the secret side of Washington."

You must reserve in advance, either online at SpyDrive.com or though Ticketmaster [800-551-7328 (toll free)]. Tours are given one Saturday a month, usually the first. The tour leaves at 9:15 A.M., but you won't know the rendezvous spot until you see your ticket.

Cost: $55 per person.

The Centre for Counterintelligence and Security Studies
Web site: spytrek.com.

The mission of the Centre for Counterintellgence, located in Alexandria, Virginia, is to provide quality education to corporations and the general public on counterintelligence, counterterrorism, and security. To this end, a staff of retired and former officers in American and former Soviet intelligence services give seminars on intelligence activities and practices on everything from the history of counterintelligence to technical surveillance techniques to declassified details of the Ames and Hanssen spy cases.

To generate knowledge about counterintelligence, the Centre also offers the Spy Drive (above) and a Spy Cruise (below), a week-long cruise that combines lectures and seminars with all the relaxing elements of a normal cruise (with some idiosyncratic fun thrown in).

Spy Cruise   E-mail: info@spycruise.com; Web site: spytrek.com. *For travel questions:* please contact All Aboard Travel at 800-741-1770.

In the days before transatlantic cruises were replaced by jet travel, travelers between the United States and Europe spent four or five days at sea. The long cruise to Europe was popular with honey-mooners, and during the Cold War, with spies. There was no better place to reinforce a newly turned agent.

In 1963, two FBI agents boarded the *Queen Elizabeth II*. Traveling alone on the same cruise was Dmitri Polyakov, a new agent who was returning to Moscow. For four days the three met to discuss and organize Polyakov's needs and the methods he would use to gain and transmit information once he was reseated in the Soviet Union.

You can join a group of former KGB, FBI, CIA, and other agents as they once again sail the *QEII*, one of her last translatlantic voyages ever, and recapture the days when venerable cruise ships and spies were comfortably at home together.

The theme for the London trip is British Traitors and Espionage, and lectures, seminars, and informal talks will cover British spies from the beginning of World War II, including the Cambridge Five, ULTRA and Bletchley Park, and the role of women spies.

Accompanying the cruise are intelligence author Christopher Andrew (*Her Majesty's Secret Service* and *KGB: The Inside Story*, among many others) and author Nigel West, historian of MI5 and MI6, and the Venona project, among other topics.

Who else is aboard? Spy buffs, some of them former members of the intelligence community; others, avid readers of spy novels. Can you tell the difference?

Six days at sea: from about $1,650 to $5,600 (depending on berth). Six additional days in London: about $900, includes hotel and guided tours of spy-related sites, such as Bletchley Park, Churchill's War Cabinet Room, and a special reception at West-minster, courtesy of Nigel West, who in another life was Rupert Allason, Member of Parliament. You'll also take a spin or two on the London Eye Ferris Wheel (remember *The Third Man*).

Europe

National Geographic Expeditions   P.O. Box 65265, Washington, D.C. 20035-5265. 888-866-8687 (toll free). Online reservations: www.nationalgeographic.com/ngexpeditions.

Espionage and the Spy Capitals of the World will take you through a reenactment of the Cold War with spy expert Thomas B. Allen, who wrote the book on spies (*Spy Book: The Encyclopedia of Espionage*) and is a consultant for the International Spy Museum in Washington.

Spend the first three days in Washington, visiting famous spy sites, then fly to Berlin. There you will be able to evoke the atmosphere surrounding the years of the Berlin Wall, before you fly to Moscow. After visiting the Kremlin and the Hall of Federal Service of Security of Russia Museum, spend the next two days touring the city and having lunch with former Cold War KGB agents.

Eleven days, including everything as well as international return airfare from Washington: about $5,600.

SPY MUSEUM

International Spy Museum 800 F Street, NW, Washington, D.C. 20004. 866-SPY-MUSEUM [779-6873] (toll free); 202-EYE SPY U [393-7798] (tel). Web site: www.spymuseum.org

All is not what it seems.

The first public espionage museum in the world, the International Spy Museum has brought together some famous and not-so-famous remnants of spying missions from the Cold War and before. Some people you never thought were agents have their pictures here.

On display are some incredible disguises and ordinary clothing altered to include tiny cameras and recorders. James Bond's beefed-up Aston Martin from the movie *Goldfinger* is on display, replete with retractable machine guns, rotating screws that emanate from the wheel covers to puncture tires of pursuing vehicles, and electronically changeable license plates.

Exhibits explain codes and the people who devised some of them, including the Navajo speakers who baffled the enemy; code breakers and some of the machines that helped them decode, such as the Enigma, which Germans used for encoding during World War II; plus some technological wonders made for the Cold War: exploding lipstick tubes, coins with microdots loaded with information; and lots of other cloak-and-dagger stuff.

Drop in at the Spy Café, wearing dark glasses and a trench coat (and false heels on your shoes).

For all things pertaining to James Bond, see: www.ianfleming.org.

COVERT OPERATIONS

Incredible Adventures, Inc.   6604 Midnight Pass Road, Sarasota, Florida 34242. 800-644-7382 (toll free). E-mail: info@ incredible-adventures.com; Web site: www.incredible-adventures.com

Here's the scenario: An ultrasecret paramilitary unit has selected you to be part of a team doing something incredibly dangerous in a very unfriendly country. But you need to brush up on your skills.

Enter a small band of former Green Berets and contract mercenaries who will put it to you straight.

Covert Ops, at a camp located somewhere near Tucson, Arizona, gives you three days of everything you have ever seen in a spy movie. And you get to do it all.

Do the car chase, for starters. Called "counter-terrorist evasive driving skills," this course will teach you how to do fancy turns-on-a-dime, as well as how to run the terrorists' car off the road and to ram through barricades.

Get out of an ambush next, by jumping into a fast attack vehicle (it looks like a car with much of the exterior removed), and tear across the desert.

Dump the attacking bad guy with your secret black belt skills, by learning how to disarm and pin him in less than ten seconds.

Learn how to fire a pistol on the range, how to take over a room, and how to fire at multiple targets at once.

Complete your mission on the final day with a hostage rescue operation, using all the skills you've been taught (and paintball). "Action is faster then reaction," said an instructor.

Three days, including lodging, meals, and all the stuff you use: about $3,800.

You can also opt for a two-day Covert Ops, which includes lodging, meals, and all the stuff, but does not use the fast attack vehicle, live fire, or teach you contact driving (ramming): about $2,000.

URBAN OPS—COMBAT MISSION 101

Urban Operations, military interaction in city situations, becomes important in terrorist events. In the film *Black Hawk Down*, Army Rangers, using flawed intelligence, aimed to extract a Somalian leader from the second floor of a downtown Mogadishu office building. It entailed jumping out of a helicopter, rappelling down the side of a building, taking over the entire floor by securing every office, then escorting the captives out of the building.

At a 734-acre "town" in North Little Rock, Arkansas, you can spend three days practicing on twenty-one structures, learning how to scale buildings from the exterior, rappel down, and "fast rope" out of a helicopter (shimmy down, then jump). You will also learn how to shoot a pistol and an assault rifle; how to engage in a close-quarter battle (includes room clearing and taking down a stronghold); how to fight in a close-quarter battle during a rescue mission, using simunitions, like paintball, but with real weapons; and how to "insert" yourself into a city.

You have props: a schoolbus and a regular bus, a DC-9, and two helicopters. Some Ops take place at night, but you get to sleep in your own bed at a local motel after days spent in a fantasy takeover of a town.

Three days, including instruction, two lunches, and one MRE (Meal Ready to Eat, a package containing a sample from each food group, used by the military only when necessary): about $3,500. Lodging is extra.

SPECOPS—ANTITERRORISM SEMINARS

A weekend seminar in Personal Safety will give you skills and awareness that will allow you to protect yourself and your family at home and in your car. You will cover everything from food, water, and first aid to the effects of weapons of mass destruction and chemical, biological, and nuclear attacks.

Incredible Adventures gives this course specialized for security personnel and media; and will customize it to include self-defense tactics and shooting-range instruction. Call 800-644-7382 for more information.

Two days: about $1,500. One day: about $800.

Antikidnapping Courses

You're driving alone at night in the rain, still fifty miles from the nearest city and hotel. The lights in your rearview have been there for the last thirty miles, and you have a bad feeling about them. Suddenly, on a lonely stretch, the unknown car pulls up alongside you. You feel the bump of steel on steel. You slow down; he slows down. You speed up; he almost pushes you off the road.

But you have taken an antikidnapping course.

You yank the gear into reverse and, with your wheels squealing, race back behind him. Then, with great cool, you do a 180, and take off in the opposite direction. Because you also know what to do in a skid, your next turn off the highway at an unreal speed is done flawlessly. You pull into a quiet hedge-lined driveway, put off your lights, and wait.

The kidnapper? When he finally stops and does a three-point turnaround, you have slipped out of his range. He drives right past you, naturally.

Originally designed for diplomats' and executives' drivers, this course is now open to anyone who thinks he or she might need a little extra protection, especially on the road.

Bob Bondurant School of High Performance Driving
P.O. Box 51980, Phoenix, Arizona 85076-1980. 800-842-7223 (toll free); 520-796-1111 (tel); 520-796-0660 (fax). E-mail: inquiry@ bondurant.com; Web site: www.bondurant.com

"Executive Protection/Anti-Kidnapping is an intensive driver-training course that will teach you how to identify and evade threatening situations on the road. In addition to learning car-control techniques, you will learn advanced driving techniques and how to fine-tune your awareness and ability in night driving. You will experience lots of scenarios that will quicken your pulse and stimulate your reactions.

Four days in their Mustangs or Crown Victorias: about $4,000.

Bondurant's Personal Protection Course allows you to learn how to defend yourself in your own vehicle, by learning car handling and control, as well as knowing what to look out for. One session is with a law enforcement officer.

Four hours: about $400 per module (the second module includes driving exercises).

Safehouse Security   10221 Slater Avenue, Suite 112, Fountain Valley, California 92708. 714-968-0088 (tel); 714-968-3040 (fax). E-mail: info@safehouse.com; Web site: www.safehouse.com

This company offers a two-day Evasive Driving course for anyone who thinks he or she needs it. Around the Irwindale Speedway near Los Angeles, drivers will be taught bootlegger and J-turns, reverse escape maneuvers, rapid decision, and a host of other clever road techniques to keep you and your family safe.

Two days of driving and instruction: about $1,500.

CHAPTER **27**

SUBMERSIBLES

Twenty thousand feet under the sea is the ultimate depth of the ocean and the ultimate depth a MIR submersible can descend. In a fantasy straight out of Jules Verne, two passengers and a pilot cruise around and over wrecks, or examine thermal vents, deep (but not quite to 20,000 feet) in the Atlantic and other oceans. In territory inhabited only by blind and bioluminescent fish, the floodlights of the MIR pierce the total darkness and create a path that takes you through an environment more exotic than any planet.

In the Atlantic, you can visit the remains of the famous *R.M.S. Titanic* or explore the shelled and broken *Bismarck*, sunk by the British warfleet in 1941. Off the Azores, get close enough to the hydrothermal vents to see the bleached and blind species of life that have developed from the chemicals spewing out of the earth. In the Arctic Ocean, try to piece together the collapsed hull of the *H.M.S. Breadalbane*, crushed by Arctic ice while on a rescue mission in 1853. The MIRs also dive beneath the North Pole (see Chapter 2, "The Arctic"), in the Mediterranean on ancient trade vessels, and off Papua New Guinea.

INSIDE THE MIRs

Strong enough to withstand the pressure at 20,000 feet beneath the surface, the submersibles maintain a comfortable and constant one-atmosphere pressure inside the cabin. The interior, about seven feet in diameter and twenty-five feet long, uses recycled air, as in an airplane, and reaches an ambient temperature of about 54 degrees F. Three portholes allow passengers to view the scene and snap pictures. Outside the submersible, cameras record the journey, while instruments take samples and make measurements.

Voice contact is maintained with the ship above, the *Akademic Kheldysh*, a 400-foot Russian research vessel, which carries about a dozen scientists and as many passengers in addition to its crew of sixty-five. Nondivers can spend time in its library or visit some of its seventeen laboratories, and stay in touch with the rest of the world with e-mail. A chef makes memorable meals, too.

Not since Jules Verne. Two passengers and a pilot ride the MIR submersible, as a diver and a support boat make sure it is lowered safely into the ocean. The trip from there descends slowly into the deep. *(Sawyer/Deep Ocean Expeditions)*

GOING UNDER

From the *Akademik's* deck, a crane lowers the MIR into the ocean, pumps ballast water into its tanks, and makes sure it has a safe descent. The average descent, at 100 feet per minute, takes between two and three hours; dives last a total of ten to twelve hours. To ascend, ballast water is dumped, enabling the rise of the submersible to the ship above.

Deep Ocean Expeditions   64b Sunninghill Avenue, Burradoo NSW 2576, Australia. 011 +61 2 48623013 (fax). E-mail: info@deepoceanexpeditions.com; Web site:www. deepoceanexpeditions.com

Adventurer Mike McDowell, the first person to combine Russian icebreakers with commercial travel to Antarctica and the Arctic (Quark Expeditions), teamed up with Don Walsh, a U.S. Navy submariner during the Korean and Vietnam Wars and the first commander of the Navy's Bathyscaphe, *Trieste*. They were joined by retired Captain Alfred McLaren, President Emeritus of the Explorers' Club, and a Cold War submarine captain.

When they partnered with Dr. Anatoly Sagalevitch, of the Russian P. P. Shirshov Institute of Oceanology, which was doing underwater research in the submersibles *Mir I* and *Mir II*, they asked: Why not take paying passengers? A descent provides a unique, educational experience, and in the process, passengers help fund scientific research. Ships master/dive master Belinda Sawyer joined them from New Zealand to help with operations.

WHAT YOU NEED TO KNOW

To descend in a submersible, you do not need a diving certification. But you must:

- Be nimble enough to get in and out of small spaces, and not freeze up during long hours of sitting.

- Have no history of cardiac or cardiovascular disease or events.
- Not have asthma.
- Not have diabetes.
- Not be subject to claustrophobia.
- Have a healthy urinogastric system.

There are no traditional bathroom facilities aboard the subs, but the chef has devised a "special diet" to minimize need for a bathroom, and passengers are given a urinal cup like those used by pilots, which can be used very discreetly.

Prices

The Rainbow Vents are about 280 miles southwest of the Azores, some 8,000 feet deep in waters full of twenty-three species of dolphins and whales. Sixteen days, from Ponta Delgado, Azores, including lectures, one dive, lodging, meals, and after-dive land tours of geysers, craters, and springs in the Azores: about $22,000; nondivers: about $5,000. Weather dependent.

H.M.S. *Breadalbane* is 350 feet below the ice; dives are in a two-passenger sub with a clear hemispheric dome. Starting in Ottawa, fly to Resolute then Ice Station Beechey. Ten days, including lectures, multiple dives, lodging (on Ice Station Beechey), most meals, and flights between Resolute and Ice Station Beechey: about $10,000; nondivers: about $5,000. Weather dependent.

The *Bismarck* is located south of Ireland, 700 miles west of Brest, France, some 14,000 feet deep. Sail out of Ponta Delgado, Azores. Fourteen days, including lectures, lodging, meals, and one dive: $28,000; nondivers: about $4,300. Weather dependent.

R.M.S. *Titanic* went down about 300 miles southeast of Newfoundland. Start from Saint John's, Newfoundland and cruise to the site. Eleven days, including lectures, one dive, lodging, and meals: about $36,000; nondivers: about $5,000. Weather dependent.

The following companies also offer some of these tours:

Wildwings　577-579 Fishponds Road, Bristol BS16 3AF, United Kingdom. 011 +44 0117 9658 333 (tel); 011 +44 0117 9375 681 (fax). E-mail: wildinfo@wildwings.co.uk; Web site: www.wildwings.co.uk

The Explorers Club　46 East 79th Street, New York, New York 10021. 800-856-8951 (toll free); 603-756-4004 (tel); 603-756-2922 (fax). E-mail: ectravel@sover.net; Web site: www.explorers.org

Space Adventures　4350 North Fairfax Drive, Suite 840, Arlington, Virginia 22203. 888-85-SPACE [857-7223] (toll free); 703-524-7176 (fax). E-mail: info@spaceadventures.com; Web site: www.spaceadventures.com

CHAPTER **28**

SURVIVAL TRAINING

If you have ever been haunted by worst-case fantasies, the what-ifs
that crop up from time to time—if you ever imagine drifting for
days on the ocean clinging to the shreds of the boat, or being completely lost in the desert with no oases in sight, or being forced to
spend the night outdoors in the rain with a small group of ornery
people—then read on. The following companies offer opportunities to learn some skills that might help you deal with difficult
situations.

THE TEXAS DESERT

David Alloway's Skills of Survival   P.O. Box 1777, Alpine,
Texas 79831. 877-371-2634 (toll free); 915-837-5146. E-mail:
David@skillsofsurvival.com; Web site: www.skillsofsurvival.com

Your plane crashes in the middle of the desert. There you are,
nowhere, with a small group of strangers, the survivors. Like yourself, they are not badly wounded. However, the plane smolders; it is
unbearably hot; no food; no water. Is it hopeless?

Of course not.

If survival dynamics appeal to you, try this Three Day Survival
Camp. The pitch is this: You and a small group of passengers are
the only survivors of a plane crash somewhere in the Chihuahuan
Desert.

Hot sun, the middle of the desert. A group of survivors has gathered wood, dug a firepit and lit a fire, and now is preparing the desert plant *lechuguilla* both to eat and to make cordage. *(David Alloway/ Skills of Survival)*

You and your group are transported to a desert and deposited, blindfolded. The van drives off, you remove the blindfold, and all you see is desert.

The first thing you have to do is prioritize finding a water source, building a shelter for protection from the blazing sun, making a fire, and establishing a place to send a signal for help. You also have to deal with the group dynamics, and make sure everyone is engaged in a positive way.

Your resources will be limited; but group instructors, acting as a search-and-rescue team, will find you sooner or later. (You will have a two-way radio for any real emergencies.)

Three days: about $400.

The prerequisite for this course is the Desert Survival Workshop. This is three days and two nights at a base camp in the desert area of Big Bend, Texas, with intensive hands-on learning, field exercises, as well as classroom instruction. You will cover the basics—fire, water, shelter, and food—as well as the psychology of survival, and the dynamics of surviving alone and in a group.

Three days at base camp: $350.

David Alloway has taught desert survival tactics to the U.S. Air Force, among others. "Don't panic," is his mantra. Learn the ABCs of survival: A: accept the situation you are in (don't blame); B: build a fire (this engages you in calming activity and creates a signal for help); C: consider your options (do an inventory of your resources); D: decide on a plan; and E: execute it.

"It ain't over 'til you're buzzard chow," says Alloway, who should know.

THE COSTA RICA JUNGLE

Incredible Adventures, Inc.   6604 Midnight Pass Road, Sarasota, Florida 34242, 800-644-7382 (toll free). E-mail: info@incredible-adventures.com; Web site: www.incredible-adventures.com

Incredible Adventures' Special Operations training in Costa Rica will give you ten days of hands-on instruction in how to survive the tropical jungle. Your instructors are former Green Berets. In a blend of enjoying Costa Rican beaches and doing serious work which includes trekking in the Osa Peninsula, at the end of this trip you will know how to read maps and a GPS, how and what to pack in a survival kit, how to find and prepare food in the wild, do wilderness first aid (with a written exam to receive certification), and learn jungle survival.

The beauty of the place, the opportunity to dive with hundreds of little tropical fish and dolphins in the Cano Island marine sanctuary, the ability to hike to the rainforest canopy, plus the promise of a resort and a complete spa at the end of the trip make this one easy way to learn how to survive.

Or at least you might think it's easy when it's over.

Ten days: about $3,500.

The Ocean and Jungle—Maui and Oahu, Hawaii

Incredible Adventures' Radical Sabbatical combines Hawaii-type vacation things (Haleakala crater hike, a downhill volcano bike ride) with some real Schwartzenegger, Bruce Willis survival techniques like surfing, powered hang gliding, and skydiving. Along the way, you learn how to read maps of the earth, ocean, as well as celestial navigation.

All of this in eight days, including lodging, meals, intraisland transport, and two helicopter flights: about $4,000.

Mountain Forest in Wales

UK Survival School   Seymour House, 24 East Street, Hereford HR1 2LU, United Kingdom. 011 +44 (0) 1432 376751 (tel); 011 +44 (0) 1432 357113 (fax). E-mail:info@uksurvivalschool.co.uk; Web site: www.uksurvivalschool.co.uk

The basic two-day introductory survival course is given in a mountain forest location in Wales. Practice satisfying the "human essentials": oxygen, water, food, shelter, and fire, by collecting and purifying water, trapping small animals and fish, and using flint to start a fire. You will also learn ropes and knots, how to cross a river, prepare natural medicines, navigate by day and by night, and evacuate medical emergencies.

Two days: about £100 ($150).

Jungle in Borneo

UK Survival School offers a thirteen-day jungle survival school in the dense and tropical rainforest of Borneo. This endurance test includes climbing Mount Kinabalu, trekking in the jungle, and a "bicycle adventure."

Two weeks: about £900 ($1,350), plus international airfare.

Desert in Utah

Boulder Outdoor Survival School   P.O. Box 1590, Boulder, Colorado 80306. 800-335-7404 (toll free); 303-444-9779 (tel); 303-442-7425 (fax). E-mail: info@boss-inc.com; Web site: www. boss-inc.com

BOSS's 10-Day Desert Navigator gives you the basic skills, then sets you loose in the desert for five days to live without modern technology.

In a two-day intensive, you will learn basic living skills: how to make or get water, shelter, fire, food, and air; then you learn how to read maps and compasses, everything from trail selection to the declination of the sun and magnetic fields.

Then they put you in the field with coordinates by which you navigate in the wilderness. If your orienteering skills are good, you will find the food, water, and coordinates for the following day that are there waiting for you at the next stop.

For the final three days, you go on a solo expedition, acting on BOSS's "Know more. Carry less" motto, testing not only your smarts but your physical endurance. With a poncho and a blanket, you walk about ten miles a day over rugged terrain. BOSS gives you daily food packs of staples containing about 1,500 calories; but the name of the game is survival.

At the end of the course, "proficient in all aspects of map reading," as well as knowing how maps and compasses should be used on the trail, you should never feel lost again.

Ten days: about $1,500.

CHAPTER 29

TRAINS

Excursion trains are like cruises without the ocean and the activity director. Passengers meet each other in the dining and bar cars, and on excursions when the train stops. But if your stateroom is comfortable, you never have to leave it.

Trains are naturally full of intrigue and a kind of sad excitement, like being in love with the right person at the wrong time. Maybe it's the reliable sound of the train on the tracks, or the poignant speed at which the countryside disappears, or the familiar strangers you pass in the corridors. Train travel is unique.

Today many excursion trains are renovated, some from a hundred years ago. *Luxury* is the operative word. Many are private and open to your group for personal charter; some, for a single person.

THE ORIENT EXPRESS, EUROPE

Abercrombie & Kent, Inc.   1520 Kensington Road, Oak Brook, Illinois 60523-2141. 800-757-5884 (toll free for brochures); 800-323-7308 (toll free); 630-954-2944 (tel); 630-954-3324 (fax). E-mail: info@abercrombiekent.com; Web site: www. abercrombiekent.com

The Orient Express is the train that inspired Agatha Christie's famous murder mystery. Traditionally, the train that crossed borders, rode through northern snows and southern villages, and at times, served in wars, was the principal transport between West and East. Compartments smelling of Gauloise cigarettes were filled with passengers who kept to themselves.

The Orient Express gradually fell into disuse, replaced by short-flight airlines and compromised by the Cold War. Twenty-odd years ago, when it was bought, refurbished, and reborn as the Venice Simplon-Orient-Express, it expanded its rail line to include Asia and Australia. But you can still travel Europe and see it from vistas you haven't seen before.

Europe, East and West follows the intrigue route. It starts in Paris with a couple of days to get acclimated. Then you put on your beret, fasten the belt of your trenchcoat, and settle into a private compartment, before the train begins to head east. During the night, you pass through darkened villages and stations with unknown names, across Germany and Austria into Hungary.

When you arrive in Budapest, a car takes you to your hotel for dinner; and the next day, you tour Buda and its castles and Pest and its shops. Back on the train, travel toward Romania and Bucharest, with a short stop at the mountain medieval town of Sinaia for a visit to Peles Castle (Dracula country), the first stop of the Orient Express in 1883.

Then race toward the Black Sea through Bulgaria, leaving the West behind. Your final destination, Istanbul, is on another continent.

Ten days, including first-class hotels, three nights onboard, some meals, and sightseeing: about $7,350 to $7,600 per person, double occupancy; about $9,900 to $11,000, single occupancy.

THE ROYAL SCOTSMAN, SCOTLAND

Abercrombie & Kent (see above) also offers brief one- to two-night tours aboard the luxurious Royal Scotsman. The Isle of Bute Tour, for example, begins in Edinburgh, heads north, stops in Dalmally at the Inverawe Smokehouse for a taste of smoked fish and a glass of wine, then spends the night at Loch Lomond. Next day take the train to Wemyss Bay to catch the ferry to the Isle of Bute for lunch and a tour of Mount Stuart, the Third Marquess of Bute's architectural fantasy. Then a stop at Stirling, and back to Edinburgh.

Two nights: about $2,600.

The Royal Scotsman is not your average train. A Scottish bagpiper pipes you aboard, and you are one of only thirty-six guests on a luxury train with mahogany and marquetry paneling; cabins with private bathrooms, wardrobes, and dressing tables; a viewing verandah at the rear of the car; and a restaurant with a reputation of being one of the best in the whole of the United Kingdom. At night, even the train goes to sleep, tucked into some quiet station. For more information, see: www.royalscotsman.com.

THE UNITED STATES

American Orient Express   800-320-4206 (toll free). Web site: www.americanorientexpress.com

The Oregon Rail Corporation refurbished fifteen vintage railcars from the 1940s and 1950s to form the American Orient Express, a sleek dark blue and gold train that runs through the best of the United States at the best seasons. The sleeping cars are renovated Pullmans, with a shower compartment at the end of each car. The wood-paneled dining car serves gourmet food, and the comfortable lounge car has a baby grand to entertain passengers who gather after dinner.

Running regional seven- to ten-night trips, the American Orient Express offers, for example, a fall foliage tour of New England, traditionally a bumper-to-bumper experience for drivers. The train goes from Boston to Quebec, stopping at Bar Harbor, Maine, for a whale watch. Then it cruises into Quebec and the Saint Lawrence River Valley to Quebec City before turning south through leaf country in New Hampshire and Massachusetts, with stops in the Berkshires at the Norman Rockwell Museum and Tanglewood.

Eight days, including lodging, meals, and excursions: about $3,200. Book early.

Sleek and straight, a luxury train speeds along the coast on its Pacific Coast Explorer Route. *(Courtesy of American Orient Express)*

The Rocky Mountains

Trains Unlimited Tours   P.O. Box 1997, Portola, California 96122. 800-359-4870 (toll free); 530-836-1745 (tel); 530-836-1748 (fax). E-mail: tut@psln.com; Web site: www.trainsunlimitedtours. com. *In the United Kingdom:* GW Travel Limited, 6 Old Market Place, Altrincham, Cheshire WA 14 4NP, United Kingdom. 011 +44 0161 928-9410 (tel); 011 +44 0161 941 6101 (fax).

"It takes a railroader to know how railroads operate" is the motto of Trains Unlimited, a company run by active and retired railroaders. Specializing in the rails of Latin America, Trains Unlimited also runs tours through the United States, Canada, and Russia. Their tours are graded for *tourists*, who like the idea of train travel; *railfans*, who are hardcore railroad lovers; and *railfan/tourists*, either the casual or the fanatic rider on sightseeing/photography tours.

THE TOURIST TOUR, COLORADO

Rocky Mountain Train Splendors

This is one of the most adventurous ways to see the best of the West. Traveling on Amtrak routes on trains restored from the Golden Age of Rail, when streamliners with names like the California Zephyr and the Empire Builder carried first-class passengers across the country, the trip runs from Oregon through spectacular scenery, such as the Columbia River Gorge, to Pike's Peak in Colorado. Interspersed with motorcoach transport and a combination of diesel and steam locomotives, some parts of the trip are short hops on historic trains.

The cog railway, once a coal-burning steam-driven engine but now a diesel-electric cog, ascends 11,000 feet of the 14,110-foot crest of Pike's Peak at a 25 percent grade. The trip takes about three hours.

Sixteen days, including first-class hotels and some meals: about $3,200. You will receive a bound trip guide, containing a daily itinerary, maps, and advertisements from the Golden Age of Rail.

THE RAILFAN TOUR, CUBA

Cuban Rail Historian Adventure

Cuba used to import American trains to run its sugar product to the docks. When relations went cold, Cuban rail workers, unable to buy replacement parts, made their own. Railfans have a chance to see these sugar steam rails, as well as the Hershey Cuban Electric Railroad, and other trains that comprise the "time warp of American-built rail transportation from another era."

Sponsored by Global Humanitas of Los Angeles, which makes the trip approved by the U.S. Treasury Department, the trip flies from Miami to Havana, then engages in thirteen solid days of rail talk.

Fifteen days, including all lodging, some meals, charter flights, motorcoach, lectures, escorts, and all permits: about $3,900.

COPPER CANYON, MEXICO

Rail Travel Center. 802-387-5812 (tel); 803-387-4350 (fax).
E-mail: railvt@together.net; Web site: www.railtravelcenter.com

The Sierra Madre Express has been put together with restored American railcars from the 1940s and 1950s, such as the North Coast Limited and the Domeliner trains. The observation car and the Dome dining car are perfect for sightseeing. The train is comfortable, but dated (read: no showers). The hotels where you stay in Mexico are classed as luxury, but the bumpy routes to them from the train may be dusty.

Nevertheless, this train was made for travel south from Tucson, through the Sonoran Desert, to the breathtaking panorama of the Copper Canyon. As you ascend around a series of loops, through 87 tunnels, and across 35 bridges that span chasms 8,000 feet below, you will see the vegetation change from tropical desert to the pines of the highlands. Stop at mountain towns and visit the Tarahumara Indians, who will show you their mission church and sell you handicrafts.

On the way down, the train stops for an overnight at a seventeenth-century mission village. Here you have the chance to go to Gallegos Overlook, to see the river winding its way through the canyon 6,000 feet below.

Eight days, including transport to and from the train, meals, and sightseeing: about $3,000.

THE TRANS-SIBERIAN RAIL LINE, RUSSIA

Mir Corporation   Off the Beaten Path Small Group Tours, 85 South Washington Street, Suite 210, Seattle, Washington 98104. 800-424-7289 (toll free); 206-624-7289 (tel); 206-624-7360 (fax). E-mail: info@mircorp.com; Web site: www.mircorp.com

The Trans-Siberian Rail Line is the longest in the world, stretching 6,000 miles. It crosses two continents, and brooks eight time zones.

On this small-group trip, board the train in Moscow, then begin an amazing journey through the Ural Mountains to Siberia, stopping at Irkutsk and Lake Baikal, which you will travel around on a special train. The lake, one of the bluest in the world, is so deep it is classified as the fifth largest body of water on earth; and it's growing. You will see species of fish and wildlife here not seen elsewhere.

From there, push through Mongolia, past towns and villages that seem to have been left in another time, until you reach a nomadic camp. Here, near the Buddhist Gandan monastery, the big three-day Mongolian Naadam festival takes place. This is a serious competition in archery, horseback riding, and wrestling for two days, with serious celebrating on the third. The final lap is to Ulaanbaatar.

Fifteen days, Premier Series (first-class), including lodging on the train and in start and end cities, meals, and excursions: about $3,700. International airfare is not included.

ROVOS RAIL, SOUTH AFRICA

American Museum of Natural History   Discovery Tours, Central Park West at 79th Street, New York, New York 10024-5192. 800-462-8687 (toll free); 212-769-5700 (tel); 212-769-5755 (fax). E-mail: info@amnh.org; Web site: www.discoverytours.org

Rovos Rail is a collection of nineteen coaches built before 1970, rescued from dereliction and scrap heaps throughout South Africa, refurbished, and put together with either a steam, diesel, or electric locomotive. The dining car, built in 1924, has seven pairs of carved wood arches and pillars. The observation car, originally built in 1936, was reconstructed in glass. Today guests enjoy air-conditioning, private baths, and space—two royal suites are each 172 square feet.

All of this is available for sixty-four passengers on a tour that begins in Cape Town, rides past the beaches, then heads up into vineyards, deserts, forests, and waterfalls. You will also visit Chobe National Park in Botswana for a safari, and fly to Zimbabwe for a priceless look at Victoria Falls.

Fifteen days, including hotel, train, meals, local transport, and a guest lecturer from the American Museum: from about $8,500 to $9,400.

EUROPE AND AFRICA

Travcoa   2250 SE Bristol, Newport Beach, California 92660. 800-992-2003 (toll free); 949-476-2800 (tel); 949-476-2538 (fax). E-mail: requests@travcoa.com; Web site: www.travcoa.com

This trip is a twenty-six-day bonanza of the best trains in the United Kingdom, Europe, and South Africa.

Start in New York, fly to London, and stay at Claridge's. Next day take the British Pullman, one of the most comfortable forms of transport around, for a tour around southern Britain, Winchester Castle, Stonehenge, and Southampton.

Then fly to Rome, board the Venice Simplon-Orient-Express, check in to your polished wood-and-gleaming-brass stateroom, then have dinner with the finest crystal and china.

Stop at Florence to see Michelangelo's *David*, then on to Venice for a gondola ride.

There is little time for sentimentality on this trip. Say goodbye to Venice and fly north to Edinburgh, then spend three days before picking up the Royal Scotsman (see above), where you will take a tour of castles into the Highlands, finding time for a sporting clay pigeon shoot. Travel on the Royal Scotsman south to Aberdeen, Dundee, cross the Firth of Forth, to Edinburgh, where you catch a plane for . . .

Johannesburg. Here you will pop on the Rovos Rail for a two-day excursion around Cape Town, then drive south to see the Cape of Good Hope and spend some time with penguins.

Back in Cape Town, board the Blue Train, South Africa's other luxury train, and ride through wine country to the Indian Ocean and the dramatic sandstone promontories above the Knysna Estuary. Gaze in wonder.

After this explosion of love for trains and train travel and going to the ends of the earth, spend a day or two in Cape Town, then fly back to New York, refreshed.

Twenty-six days, including hotels, most meals, all trains, and excursions: from about $16,000.

Travel Safely

KNOW BEFORE YOU GO

If you had to leave suddenly and could take only basics with you, what would they be? Someone once said that a passport, money, and soap were all any traveler needs.

But besides practical items, probably the best thing you can take is knowledge of where you are going. Carved in a frieze above Union Station in Washington, D.C., is a quote from Samuel Johnson, who was remembering a Spanish proverb:

> He who would bring home the wealth of the Indies must carry the wealth of the Indies with him. So it is in traveling, a man must carry knowledge with him if he would bring home knowledge.

Country Facts

You can get detailed information about any country in the world from the U.S. Department of State Consular Sheets (see www.travel.state.gov), including the level of danger involved in going there. For detailed political as well as demographic information, take a look at the CIA Factbook site (see www.cia.gov/cia/publications/factbook).

Documents

Passport

Make sure your passport will not expire while you are in the middle of the Sahara Desert. Take extra passport pictures with you in case you need further identification papers. Make a copy of your passport's main page before you go, in case you need to prove your lost or stolen passport was yours. Also, take along a second picture ID (e.g., a driver's license).

Visa

Check with your tour company or with the Department of State to see if you need a visa or visas. For all the countries mentioned in this book, you will need a visa, *except* for:

Botswana, France, Greece, Hungary, Iceland, Indonesia, Morocco, Namibia, New Zealand, Peru, Portugal, Seychelles, South Africa, Spain, Switzerland, Thailand, Tunisia, the UK, and Vanuatu.

Americans can get visas at the airport in Cape Verde, São Tomé, Tonga, Zambia, and Zimbabwe.

Health

Find out what's happening in health in the country of your visit by checking with the Federal Centers for Disease Control (CDC). See www.cdc.gov; or call: 877-394-8747 (toll free, automated), to receive a fax with details of a country's health problems, with a list of recommended inoculations and medications before you go.

Also check the World Health Organization at www.who.int/ homepage, for detailed health information by country. Both these sites list current disease epidemics as well as ongoing health problems.

Mosquito-Borne Diseases

Malaria is endemic throughout Africa, parts of Asia, Central and South America, and the South Pacific islands, especially Vanuatu.

It is spread by the female anopheline mosquito, which does not buzz and which sits on a wall, backside in the air.

There are about six antimalarial medications you can take to avoid the disease. None is perfect, and most of them require that you start taking them before you go on your trip, and continue after you return. Since people react differently to malarial medication, check with your physician to figure out the best one for you.

Dengue fever ("breakbone fever") is endemic in countries from 40 degrees South latitude to 30 degrees North latitude. It is spread by the aedes mosquito, which bites only in the daytime. It rests parallel to the wall (like the average summertime mosquito), but it has black and white legs.

Classic dengue fever lasts about a week, and is characterized by muscle pain and high fever. Tylenol is the simplest medication that works. Once gone, you'll never get it again.

Avoid Mosquitoes

Prevent bites. That is the only way you will avoid disease, including West Nile virus, and a host of other mosquito-borne problems. The standard advice is: Don't go out at dawn or dusk, when mosquitoes swarm. Wear light-colored long pants and long-sleeved shirts and avoid perfume.

DEET, also known as N,N-diethyl-m-tolumide, is the best general insect repellent. Try to apply it over all exposed skin (it's amazing how a hungry mosquito will always find the microspot you missed), and be prepared to reapply.

According to the CDC, the percentage of DEET in an insect repellent makes a difference: 23.8 percent gives an average of 5 hours protection; 20 percent gives 4 hours; 6.65 percent gives 2 hours; 4.75 percent and 2 percent soybean oil give 1½ hours.

In places where there are more mosquitoes than people, sleep within a mosquito net.

Food-Borne Diseases

Nothing is more of a bother, but all travelers know that the chances of getting diarrhea or dysentery are higher than getting malaria.

The best way to deal with this is to attack it symptomatically with over-the-counter medications such as Pepto-Bismol, Imodium, or Lomotil, or whatever your physician has prescribed before the trip.

These days some bacteria and parasites linger, and can settle nicely in your digestive system, occasionally acting up. Chronic dysentery is on the rise. It's a good idea to check with your health-care provider when you finish traveling.

Frostbite

In the polar cold, the trick to staying warm is to keep dry, wear layered clothing, and move around a lot.

If you sweat from wearing too many clothes, you increase the sense of being cold. If you hike, do so in as few clothes as you can, and some advise that you carry extra clothes with you so you can change into a dry outfit when you arrive. Outdoors outfitters can advise on the best fabrics to meet your needs. At the Poles, most tour operators provide heavy-weather parkas, as do some aurora borealis watching tours.

Don't drink alcohol in the cold; it lowers your temperature.

The Sun

Protect your skin from the sun, especially anywhere near the Poles. The ozone layer is thin to nonexistent at the Poles, and very thin in some places in the mid-latitudes as well. The sun's ultraviolet rays are unfiltered without the protective ozone layer.

Make sure that your sunscreen protects against not only UVB (the ultraviolet light that darkens skin), but UVA (the rays that go the lower layers of skin and do not darken it). In the ingredients of the lotion or cream, look for oxybenzone, avobenzone, titanium oxide, or zinc oxide, for protection against UVA.

Apply early, and apply often, even if it is "waterproof." SPF 15 will protect you as long as you have enough on at any given time. The advice is to stay in the shade from 10 A.M. to 3 P.M., but if that's unrealistic, at least wear a hat, and cover your skin.

Insurance

Things being what they are these days, trip cancellation insurance is a good investment. Lost Luggage insurance will tide you over until your suitcase turns up again, and will give you more compensation than the airline.

The most important insurance coverage you should consider is medical coverage appropriate to the country where you are going, as well as coverage for medical evacuation.

If you rent a car, it's a good idea to get all the insurance that goes with it. And buy flight and travel accident insurance that will provide extra coverage above your personal life and health insurance policies.

Toys

You might prefer getting away from your e-mail, but all kinds of PDAs will connect you, no matter where you are, as will some cell phones. The choice is yours. Also, check with your cell phone company to find out how you can call from wherever you will be.

In another part of the world, the best toys are a good GPS (shop around to find the one that really works for you), and an altimeter watch that counts the vertical feet up and down, gives barometric readings, temperatures, and compass readings.

Getting Through Security

Yes, you can carry a bowling ball aboard; no, you cannot take golf clubs. Yes, you can take knitting needles; no, you cannot take a screwdriver. Ask if you are not sure about something. The logic eludes.

Airport detection systems are very sensitive, and will go off easily, which means you and your carry-on bags might be searched with the wand. You might be asked to open and start up your computer, and to let guards look through your camera lens. Expect occasional random searches either at the initial screener or at the gate. These have nothing to do with you personally. It's the luck of the draw.

Wear slip-on shoes, leave your silver eagle belt buckle at home, and expect to wait. The screener will not harm the media in your digital camera; nor affect the hard drive on your laptop. But if you have to go through several checkpoints, it might be a good idea to pass them through to the guard.

Be especially vigilant of your personal belongings when they disappear into the screener. Wait until the passengers in front of you have cleared, so the belt is relatively empty when you put your stuff on it. If you are detained for a wand search, make sure you have your purse or wallet in hand, and keep a keen eye on your carry-ons.

In foreign airports when you leave the country, you might have to pay an exit fee. It is usually about $15 or $20 and payable in U.S. dollars. Find out when you land, and put the money in a special place so you will have it when you leave.

Bon Voyage!

Buon viaggio! (*Stephanie Ocko*)

Index

Abercrombie & Kent: African safaris, 218; Antarctica cruise, 6–7; Greek islands and Turkish coast cruise, 231; luxury concierge service, 168–69; Orient Express, 268–70
Absolute Adventures, 236
Ace Study Tours, 24–25
Adrift Adventures, 199
Adventure Network International, 11–12
Africa: ballooning, 52–54; cruises, 180, 182; overland trek, 183–84; safaris, 208–18; wingshooting, 124. *See also specific destinations*
African Shark Eco Charters, 237–38
Air combat planes, 130–34
Air Combat USA, 132–33
Airport security concerns, 281–82
Air tours: Arctic Circle, 20; around the world by private jet, 187; South Pole, 11–12
Air Ventures Hot Air Balloon Flights, Inc., 52–53
Akademic Kheldysh, 259, 260
Alaska: aurora borealis, 48–49; grizzly bears, 224–25
Aldrin, Buzz, 241–42
Alfa Romeo, 73, 74
Allen, Thomas B., 252–53
Alloway, David, 57, 263–65
Alojargentina, 200–201
Alpine Adventure, 191

Alps: ballooning, 50–52; motorcycling, 191
Amateur Chamber Music Players, 196
Amboseli National Park, 211
American Museum of Natural History: Kentucky Derby, 159; Rovos Rail, 274–75; Viking history cruise, 139
American Orient Express, 270
Amundsen, Roald, 10, 15, 17–18
Anasazi Indians, 30
Ancient art tour, 38–39
Ancient Caravan Route, 184–86
Ancient history tours, 136–39
Anderson, Scot, 237
Andrew, Christopher, 252
Anguilla Arts Festival, 30–31
Anniversary Inn (Salt Lake City), 171–72
Anossov, Ilia, 30
Antarctica (South Pole), 3–13; air tour, 11–12; cruises, 5–8, 11; eclipses, 44–46; meteorites, 12–13; Shackleton tours, 8–10
Antarctica Meteorite Expedition, 12–13
Antikidnapping courses, 256–57
Antique planes, 134–35
Anti-terrorism seminars, 255–56
Archetours, Inc., 21–23
Architecture tours, 21–25
Architours, 24

Arctic, the (Arctic Circle), 4, 14–20; air tour, 20; aurora borealis, 47–49; icebreakers, 17–18; icehotel, 178–79; submersible dives, 16–17
Arctic Char fishing, 120–21
Arctic Ocean: kayaking, 19
Argentina: tango, 200–201
Arizona: cowboy school, 101–2; driving school, 65, 67; eco-hotels, 172–73; motorcycle tours, 190–91
Arizona Cowboy College, 101–2
Arkansas: Urban Ops, 255
Art, 26–39; faux finishes, 26–29; frescoes, 29–30; painting, 31–34; pottery, 30–31; tours: in Europe, 37–39; in the U.S., 36–37
Arts in the Wild, 32–33
Art Trek, 31
Art Workshops in Guatemala, 35–36
Astronaut training, 242–46
Astronomical Tours, 41–42
Astronomy, 40–49; aurora borealis, 47–49; lunar eclipses, 44–47; observatories, 107–8; solar eclipses, 42–44; transit of Venus, 41–42. *See also* Space
Atlantic islands, 182–83
Augusta Heritage Workshops, 203
Aurora borealis, 47–49
Australia: biplanes, 135; camel treks, 61
Austria: music tours, 196, 197–98
Autos, 62–75; luxury makers, 73–75; off-road tours, 69–71; racing schools, 62–67; rallies, 68–69; rental insurance, 281; tours of races, 72–73
Autumn foliage tours, 189, 270
Aviation, 126–35; air combat planes, 130–34; biplanes, 134–35; warbirds, 127–29. *See also* Air tours

Baffin Island, 18–19
Baja California: off-road tours, 71
Ballooning, 50–54
Bandhavgarh National Park, 219–20
Barnstorming Adventures, Ltd., 128, 130
Barque Picton Castle Voyages, 228–29
Barron, Rosemary, 89–90
Bartle, Christopher, 158

Basque cooking tour, 88–89
Battlefields, 145–47
Beach's Motorcycle Adventures, Ltd., 191
Bears: grizzly, 224–25; panda, 220–21; polar, 15, 20, 223–24
Bengal tigers, 192, 219
Berlin: spy tour, 253
Bermuda: painting classes, 33
Bespokes Classic Limited, 74–75
Best of Morocco, 58–59
Betchart Expeditions, 219
Bev Gruber's Everyday Gourmet Traveler, 86–87
Bhutan: motorcycle tours, 192–93
Bicycle Adventures, 95–96
Bike Riders, 86
Bike tours: California wineries, 95–96; French cuisine, 86; Russian volcanoes, 110–11
Biplanes, 134–35
Birdwatching: Alaska, 224–25; Antarctica, 4; Arctic Circle, 18–19; Botswana, 212–13
Bismarck, 258, 261
Blackhawk Adventures, Inc., 102
Black Hawk Down (movie), 255
Blanc, Raymond, 82, 85
Blixen, Karen (Isak Dinesen), 209, 217
Bligh, William, 141–42, 166
Bluegrass music, 199
Boat cruises: around the world, 169–70; Africa, 180, 182; Alaska, 224–25; Antarctica, 6–8, 11, 45–46; Arctic Circle, 17–18; Atlantic islands, 182–83; Captain Bligh tour, 141–42; eclipses, 42, 45–46; French barges, 175–76; Greek history tour, 136–38; music, 198–99; Pirate Lafitte tours, 143; *Sea Cloud*, 230–31; spy, 251–52; Viking history tours, 139. *See also* Icebreakers
Boating. *See* Sailing
Bob Bondurant School of High Performance Driving, 65, 67, 256–57
Bombard Society, 50–52
Boojum Expeditions, 161–62
Borneo: orangutans, 221–23; survival training, 266

Botswana: safaris, 211–13
Boulder Outdoor Survival School, 267
Boulders, The (Scottsdale), 172–73
Bounty, H.M.S., 141–42, 230
Branson, Missouri, 79–80, 104
Branson, Richard, 163–65
Brazil: cooking tours, 89
Brazilian Academy of Cooking, 89
Breadalbane, 258, 261
Bridge to the Tango, 200, 201–2
British Virgin Islands: luxury hotel, 163–65
Bronco riding, 105–6
Bucharest: architecture tour, 24–25
Buddy Bombard Balloon Vacations, 50–52
Buenos Aires: tango, 200–201
Bull riding, 104–6
Bushtracks Expeditions, 213
Butel, Jane, 90–91
Bwindi Impenetrable National Park, 215
Byrd, Richard, 10, 15

Cabo San Lucas: off-road tours, 71
Cajun/Creole dance, 203
Cale Yarborough's Executive Racing School, 62–64
Calgary Stampede, 205
California: air combat planes, 130, 132–33; architecture tours, 24; circus school, 76–77, 79; flying warbirds, 128; garlic festival, 93–94; horseback riding, 154; Renaissance Faires, 140; shark diving, 235–36; wine tours, 95–96. *See also specific destinations*
California Pop, 24
Camel treks, 55–61
Campbell Travel Service, 149–50
Camp Jeep, 71
Canada: aurora borealis, 48; fishing, 120–21; painting classes, 32–33; polars bears, 223–24
Canoeing: Soper River, 18
Cape Town, South Africa, 94–95, 133–34, 237–38, 274–76
Cape Wineland Tours, 94–95
Caravans. *See* RV caravans

Caribbean: luxury yachting, 231; music cruises, 198–99
Carnegie Club, 165–66
Carolina Motorcycle Tours, 188–89
Cars, 62–75; luxury makers, 73–75; off-road tours, 69–71; racing schools, 62–67; rallies, 68–69; rental insurance, 281; tours of races, 72–73
Casablanca Air, 134–35
Castle hotels/rentals, 165–66, 173–74
Cattle roundups, 102–4
C Diamond C Ranch, 102
Celtic silversmithing, 35
Centers for Disease Control (CDC), 278, 279
Centre For Counterintelligence and Security Studies, 251–52
Chamber music, 194, 196
Chamber Music Holidays and Festivals, 194, 196
Charters: fishing, 116–20. *See also* Sailing
Chateau Saint-Paterne, 175
Chateaux & Hotels de France, 174–75
Cheetah Conservation Fund, 216
Cheetahs, in Namibia, 216
Chena Hot Springs Resort, 48–49
Cherry Hill Vineyard and Wine Camp, 97
Chianti, 94
Chiavaroli, Angelo, 84–85
Chihuahuan Desert, 263–65
China: Orient Express, 268–69; panda bears, 220–21; Silk Road trip, 184–87
Chobe National Park, 212–13, 274
Chrome Caballeros Tours, 190
CIA Factbook, 277
Circus, 76–80
Circus Center of San Francisco, 76–77, 79
Circus Space, 77–78
Cirque du Soleil, 80
City Breaks, 171
Civil War battlefields, 146–47
Classical art and history tours, 38–39, 136–38
Classical Cruises: Africa, 180, 182; Homer's *Odyssey,* 137–38

Climate change, the Poles and, 4
Clipper Adventurer, 7–8
Clipper Cruises, 7–8, 139
Clipper Ventures PLC, 226–28
Cloud tours, 115
Cloud 9 Tours, 114
Clown Conservatory, 78
Clown schools, 78–79
Cobblestone Small Group Tours, 88–89
Cold War, 252–53
Colorado Plateau, 109
Combat missions, 255
Cook, James, 10
Cooking schools/tours, 81–91
Copper Canyon, 205, 272–73
Copper Creek Cattle Round Ups, 103–4
Cordon Bleu, 81, 83–84
Costa Rica: survival training, 265; volcanoes, 111–12
Counterintelligence, 249, 251–53
Cousteau, Jean-Michel, 166
Covert operations, 254–55
Cowboys, 99–106; bull riding, 104–6; cattle roundups, 102–4; Posse Week, 99–101; school, 101–2. *See also* Horseback riding
Crow Canyon Archaeological Center, 30
Crow Indians, 104
Cruises. *See* Boat cruises
Cuba: salsa, 201–2; trains, 272
Cuisine International, 89
Czech Republic: architecture tours, 21–23. *See also* Prague

Dance Traveler, Inc., 200, 201–2
Dance workshops, 200–203
Danum Valley Conservation Area, 223
David Alloway's Skills of Survival, 57, 263–65
Davis and Elkins College, 203
D-Day battlefields, 145–46
Deep Ocean Expeditions, 16–17, 260–61
Deep-sea fishing, 116–18
Dengue fever, 279
Diarrhea, 279–80
Dinesen, Isak (Karen Blixen), 209, 217

Diseases, 278–80
Dives, shark, 234–38
Documents for entry, 278
Domenica: luxury yachting, 231
Douglas-Dufresne, Helen, 60
Dracula, 147–51; tours, 149–51
Dreamweaver Travel, 57–58
Dressage training, 157–58
Driving 101, 64
Driving schools, 62–67, 256–57
Druxngooland Country House & Equestrian Center, 155–56
Dublin: silversmithing classes, 35
DuneHopper, 53–54
Dysentery, 279–80
Dzanga-Sangha Special Reserve, 213

Earle, Sylvia, 231
Earth tours, 107–15
Earthwatch Institute International, 216
Eastern Trekking Associates, 154–55
Eclipse cruises, 42, 45–46
Eco-Expeditions: Borneo, 222–23; Botswana, 211–12; Mongolia, 161
Eco-hotels, 172–73
Eco-tours, in Patagonia, 109–10
Eco-volunteering, in Mongolia, 159–61
Edinburgh Artbreaks, 33–34
EduVacations, 193, 202
Egypt, 182; transit of Venus, 42
Elephant Island, 5, 9
Ellesmere Island, 19
Ellsworth, Lincoln, 10, 15
Endeavor, 5, 6, 8, 182–83
England: cooking classes, 82, 85; dressage training, 158; sports cars, 74–75. *See also specific destinations*
Equestrian Vacations, 156–57, 158
Equitours, 152–53, 157–58
Espionage. See Spying
Espionage and the Spy Capitals of the World, 252–53
Explorer, 6–7
Explorers Club, 262
Explore the Outback, 61
Extra 300Ls flights, 131–32
Extreme horsemanship, 102

Falconry, 161–62
Fall foliage tours, 189, 270

Fantasuite Hotels, 172
Fantasy Bull Riding Adventure, 104–5
Fantasy of Flight, 129–30
Fantasy RV Tours, 204–6
Farallones Islands: shark diving, 235–36
Farmhouse rentals, in Tuscany, 176–78
Faroe Islands, 47, 139
Fathom Expeditions, Inc., 8–9
Faux finishes classes, 26–29
Faux Finish School, 27, 28
Ferrari, 74–75
Fighter Combat International, 131–32
Fightertown Aviation, Inc., 129
Fiji Escape Travel, 166–67
Fiji Islands: luxury hotels, 166–67
Fishing, 116–21; Arctic Char, 120–21; deep sea, 116–18; shallow water, 118–20
Fishing International, Inc., 119–20
Flamenco, in Spain, 202
Flam Railway, 20
Flattmann, Alan, 33
Fleming, Ian, 253–54
Florence: art tours, 37; painting classes, 29; rental properties, 176–78
Florida: aviation museum, 129–30; biplanes, 134–35; driving school, 62–64; NASA space center, 246–47; warbirds, 127–29
Fly fishing, 118–21
Flying, 126–35; air combat planes, 130–34; biplanes, 134–35; warbirds, 127–29. See also Air tours
Flying Tigers Warbird Restoration Museum, 129
Food, 91–94; cooking schools/tours, 81–91; culinary tour, 98; garlic festival, 93–94; mushroom hunting, 92–93; olive picking, 91–92; truffle hunting, 92
Food-borne diseases, 279–80
Fort Bragg, California, 154
Four-wheeling, 69–71
4-Wheeling America, 70
France: ballooning, 52; barge cruises, 175–76; battlefields, 145–46; chateaux, 174–75; concierge service, 168–69; cooking classes, 81, 83–84, 86; luxury hotels, 167–69; painting classes, 31–32; truffle hunting, 92. See also specific destinations
France Cruises, 175–76
Franz Josef Island, 16
French Polynesia: painting classes, 31
Fresco painting classes, 29–30
Frostbite, 280

Gabon: lowland gorillas, 213–14
Garland Farms, 158
Garlic festival, 93–94
Gaudi, Antoni, 23
Gauguin, Paul, 31, 141
Gehry, Frank, 22, 23, 88
Genghis Khan, 161, 186
Geographic Expeditions, 218
Georgia: dressage training, 158
Germany: castle hotels, 174; spy tour, 253
Gettysburg: battlefields, 146–47
Giant Panda Breeding Center, 221
Gila National Forest, 99–101, 103–4
Gilroy Garlic Festival, 93–94
Glacier climbing, in Antarctica, 9–10
Global climate change, the Poles and, 4
Gorillas, in Africa, 213–15
Gough Island, 182, 183
Grand Prix Tours, 72
Grape and Grain Tour, 206
Great white sharks, 234–38
Greece: cooking classes, 89–90; history tour, 136–38; luxury yachting, 231
Green Berets, 254, 265
Greenland, 20, 138–39
Grizzly bears, 224–25
Grodsky, Lawrence, 193
Groth, Lawrence, 234, 236
Gruber, Bev, 86–87
Guatemala: weaving classes, 35–36
Guggenheim Museum Bilbao, 23
Gulet, 232

Habsburg Heritage Cultural Tours, 196
Halloween tours, in Romania, 149–51
Harley-Davidsons, 188, 190–91
Havana, Cuba, 201–2, 273
Hawaii: earth tours, 107–8; survival training, 266

Health concerns, 278–80
Hemingway, Ernest: in Key West, 144–45; safaris, 207, 209–10, 211
Hermitage Farm, 159
High-performance vehicles, 65–66
Himalayan Roadrunners Motorcycle Tours and Expeditions, 192–93
Hirsch, Martin Alan, 27, 28
Historic hotels, 170–71
Historic Hotels of America, 170–71
History of Food & Wine, 98
History tours, 136–51
Hole in the Sky Tours, 46
Holt Tours Limited, 145–46
Homebase Abroad, Ltd., 177–78
Homer, *Odyssey*, 137–38
Hopi Indians, 36–37
Horizons to Go, 35
Horseback riding, 99–104, 152–56
Horses, 152–62; dressage training, 157–58; eco-volunteering, 159–61; Kentucky Derby, 158–59; polo, 156–57
Hot-air ballooning, 50–54
Hotel Meurice (Paris), 167–68
Hotels, 163–79; castles, 165–66, 173–74; chateaux, 174–75; eco-, 172–73; historic, 170–71; icehotel, 178–79; luxury, 163–69; in space, 240–41; theme suites, 171–72
Houston Space Center, 247
Hudson River Valley Art Workshops, 33
Human Odyssey, 38–39
Hungary: Dracula tours, 149–51; wild boar hunting, 121–23
Hunting, 121–25
Hunting Navigator.com, 122–23

Iban tribe, 222–23
Icebreakers, 11, 16, 17–18, 20, 45–46
Icehotel AB (Sweden), 178–79
Iceland, 20, 139; eclipses, 46–47
ICSCIS, Inc., 31–32
Ilia Anossov, True Fresco, 30
Incredible Adventures, Inc.: air combat planes, 133–34; covert operations, 254–56; orbital flight program, 246; shark dives, 236–38; survival training, 265–66

India: tigers, 218–20
India Wildlife Safari, 219
Information sources, 277
Inniemore School of Painting, 34
Inn on the Lake (Yukon), 48
Innovations in Travel, Inc., 42
Insurance, 281
International Expeditions, Inc., 223–24
International Ghost Hunters Society, 146–47
International Space Station (ISS), 241, 242, 245–46
International Spy Museum, 253–54
Intra-Canal Waterway, 205
Intrav, 187
Inuit Indians, 17–19
Ireland: horseback riding, 155–56; needlework classes, 34–35; polo, 156–57; silversmithing classes, 35
Isla Guadalupe: shark diving, 236–37
Isle of Mull: painting classes, 34
Italy: concierge service, 168–69; cooking classes, 84–85; cooking tours, 86–88; opera tours, 197–98; painting classes, 29; rental properties, 176–78; sports cars, 73–74; wine tours, 94. *See also specific destinations*
Ivor Wigham's European Rally and Performance Driving School, 69

James Caird, 5, 9
Jane Butel Cooking School, 90–91
Jazz Cruise, 198
Jeep jamborees, 71
Jemez Caldera, 109
Jiler, James, 219
Johnson Space Center, 247

Kalahari Desert, 212
Kamchatka Volcanoes, 110–11
Kapitan Khlebnikov, 11, 17–18, 45–46
Kaprielian, Aram, 44–45
Kathmandu, 192–93, 220
Katmai Coastal Bear Tours, 224–25
Katmai National Park, 224–25
Kayaking: Arctic Ocean, 19; Canada, 32–33
Kayenta Scientific Investigations, 108–9

Kelly S. King Institute of Decorative Finishes, 28–29
Kennedy Space Center, 246–47
Kentucky Derby, 158–59
Kenya: ballooning, 52–53; safaris, 208, 209–10, 217–18; camel trek, 60
Keoladeo Ghana National Park, 219
Key West, Florida, 144–45
Kidnapping, 256–57
Kilauea volcano, 107–8
Kilimanjaro, 184; safaris, 211
Kinabalu National Park, 223
King, Kelly, 28–29
Knight Inlet Grizzly Bear Adventure Tours, 224
Koh Samui Island, 90
Kosi Tappu Wildlife Reserve, 192
Kruger National Park, 206

Lafitte, Jean, 143
Lamborghini, 73, 74
Lancaster, Karen, 156–57
Languedoc: painting classes, 31–32
Lapland, 20
Last Great Overlanding Challenge, 183–84
Las Vegas: art tours, 36; driving school, 64
Learning Adventures, 120–21
Le Cordon Bleu, 81, 83–84
Le Manoir Ecole de Cuisine, 82, 85
Le Ponant, 232–33
Les Liaisons Delicieuses, 92
L'Etoile, 175–76
Lewis and Clark expeditions, 142–43
Lexington, Kentucky Derby, 158–59
Lindblad Expeditions: Antarctica, 6; Atlantic islands, 182–84; Costa Rica, 111–12; Lewis and Clark, 142
Live music. See Music
Lodore River: rafting, 199
Loire Valley: ballooning, 52
London: circus school, 77–78; spy tours, 252
Lope Wildlife Reserve, 214
Lord of the Rings (movie), 135
Lorill Equestrian Center, 101–2
Los Alamos, 109
Los Angeles: architecture tours, 24; fresco painting, 30

Lowland gorillas, in Gabon, 213–14
Lunar eclipses, 40, 44–47
Luxury hotels, 163–69

McDowell, Mike, 260
Madra Dubh Fabrics and Threads, Ltd., 34–35
Malaria, 278–79
Manoir aux Quat' Saisons, 85
Marbleing classes, 26–29
Marchettis, 132–33
Marker, Laurie, 216
Marlin University, 118
Marquesas, 31
Marrakesh, 59, 98
Mars, 247–48
Mars Society, 247–48
Martha Hopkins Struever, 36–37
Martin Randall Travel, Ltd.: opera tours, 197–98; Spain, 23; Vienna, 38
Masai Mara Reserve, 52, 208, 209–10
Mauna Kea, 107–8
Mayhugh Travel, 45–46
Mesa Verde Black-on-White Pottery Workshop, 30
Messina Hof Winery & Resort, 96–97
Meteorites, in Antarctica, 12–13
Meurice Hotel (Paris), 167–68
Mexican Mushroom Tours, 92–93
Mexico: mushroom hunting, 92–93; shark diving, 236–37; trains, 273
Miami: luxury hotel, 167
Micato Safaris, 209–10
Midnight sun, 14, 120
MiG flights, 133–34
Mille Miglia, 73
Minnesota: clown school, 79; theme suites, 172
Mir Corporation, 184–86, 241, 273–74
Mir submersibles, 16, 258–62
Monet, Claude, 31–32
Mongolia, 186; falconry, 161–62; horse vacation, 159–61
Monteverde Cloud Forest, 111–12
Montgolfiades Internationales de Tunisie, 53
Montreal: circus, 80
Moosecamp, 79
Moremi Game Reserve, 212–13

Morgan Tours, 197
Morocco: camel treks, 58–60
Mosquito-borne diseases, 278–79
Motorcycle tours, 188–93
Mountain gorillas, in Uganda, 214–15
Mountain Travel Sobek: Antarctica, 7; Arctic Circle, 19; camel trek, 59–60; India, 219–20; Mount Kilimanjaro, 211; Silk Road tour, 186
Mount Kilimanjaro, 184; safaris, 211
Mozart, Wolfgang Amadeus, 197–98
Mushroom hunting, 92–93
Music, 194–203; chamber, 194, 196; cruises, 198–99; flamenco, 202; salsa, 201–2; tango, 200–201; tours, 196; opera, 197–98; zydeco, 203
M/V Fathom Discovery, 9
M/V Waters, 224–25
Myths and Mountains: China panda bears, 220–21; Vietnam battlefields, 146

Namibia: ballooning, 52–54; cheetahs, 216
Nansen, Fridtjof, 16
Napa Valley, 95–96
NASA, 40, 241; International Space Station, 241, 242, 245–46; space centers, 246–47
NASCAR, 65–66
National Auto Sport Association, 66
National Geographic Expeditions: Antarctica photography, 8; Caribbean cruise, 231; spy tour, 252–53; World War I battlefields, 145
National Severe Weather Center, 113
National Trust for Historic Preservation, 170–71
Navajo Indians, 36–37
Necker Island, 163–65
Needlework classes, 34–35
Nepal, 192–93, 219–20, 220
Neutral Buoyancy, 243, 245
New Circus, 76–78
New Hampshire: dressage training, 158
Newman, Paul, 65

New Mexico: cattle roundups, 103–4; cooking classes, 90–91; earth tours, 108–9; horseback riding, 102
New Zealand: biplanes, 135; concierge service, 169; motorcycle tours, 191; tall ship sailing, 229
New Zealand Hideaways, 169
Neys Provincial Park, 32–33
Ngorogoro Crater, 210
Normandy battlefields, 145–46
North Carolina: motorcycle tours, 188–89
Northern Italy Viva Verdi, 197
North Pole, 4, 14–20; aurora borealis, 47–49
North Pole Dive, 16–17
Northwest Passage, 17–18
Norway, 20; motorcycle tours, 191
Nunavut Territory, 18, 19, 120–21

Observatories, 107–8, 112
Odyssey (Homer), 136–38
Odyssey Learning Adventures, 18–19
Odyssey Tours, 142–43
Odzala Game Reserve, 213
Offoue River, 214
Off-road four-wheeling, 69–71
Off the Beaten Path, 104
Oklahoma: tornadoes, 112–15
Olive picking, 91–92
Open wheel race cars, 64
Opera tours, 197–98
Orangutan Foundation International, 222
Orangutans, in Borneo, 221–23
Orbital flight qualification preparation, 245
Oregon: trains, 270; wineries, 97, 206
Oregon Brewers' Festival, 206
Oregon Rail Corporation, 270
Orient Express, 268–69
Orlova, 20
Orvis Travel, 124
Orvis Wingshooting Schools, 124–25
Ouro Preto, Brazil: cooking tours, 89
Outback (Australia): camel treks, 61
Overland Experts, 70–71

Painting classes, 31–34; faux finishes, 26–29; fresco, 29–30

Painting in Provence, 32
Palio Tours, 94
Panama: fishing, 116–18
Panda bears, in China, 220–21
Panoz Racing School, 66–67
Paris: cooking classes, 81, 83–84;
    luxury hotel, 167–68
Parker, Steve, 72
Parker Company, 176–77
Passports, 278
Patagonia: earth tours, 109–10
Patagonia Research Expedition, 109–10
Peary, Robert, 15
Penguins, 4, 6, 7, 8, 182
Personal safety seminars, 255–57
P-51 Mustang flights, 127–28
Phoenix: motorcycles, 190
Picton Castle, 228–29
Pike's Peak, 272
Pinas Bay Resorts, 116–18
Pionair Adventures, Ltd., 135
Pitcairn Islands, 141–42
Pittendrigh, Vivienne, 194, 196
Planning tips, 277–82
Polar bears, 15, 20; in Canada, 223–24
Polar Bear Tundra Safari, 223–24
Poles, the: frostbite, 280. *See also*
    Antarctica; Arctic, the
Polo, 156–57
Portugal: dressage training, 157
Posh Journeys, 73, 220
Posse Week, 99–101
Pottery classes, 30–31
Prague: architecture tours, 21–23;
    ballooning, 51
Pride of Safaris, 217
Professor Multanovskiy, 7, 10
Provence: bike tours, 86; painting
    classes, 32
Przewalski Horse Reintroduction,
    159–60, 161

Quark Expeditions, Inc., 11, 17–18
Queen Elizabeth II, 251–52
Queen Elizabeth National Park, 215
Quilting classes, 34–35

Racetracks, 62–67, 72
Rafting, 199
Railroads. *See* Trains

Rail Travel Center, 272–73
Rainbow Tours, 214–15
Rallies, 68–69
Ranches, 99–101, 102, 154
Randall, Martin. *See* Martin Randall
    Travel, Ltd.
Ranthambore National Park, 219
Rapid Weather's Guided Weather
    Expeditions, 115
Recreational vehicles (RVs), 204–6
Renaissance art tours, 37
Renaissance Faires, 140
Rental properties: Italy, 176–78;
    Scotland, 173
Reykjavik, 20
Ricochet Ridge Ranch, 154
Ride America Motorcycle Tours, 190–91
Rift Valley, 184, 209–10
Ring of Fire Expeditions, 46–47
RiverBarge Excursions Line, Inc., 143
River Explorer, 143
Road racing, 66–67
Roadtrips, 72–73
Robertson, Sally, 31
Rock Boat, 199
Rocky Mountains, trains, 271–72
Rodeo schools, 104–6; for clowns,
    79–80
Rogers, Lynn, 224–25
Romania: architecture tours, 24–25;
    Dracula tours, 149–51
Roman ruins, 24–25, 38, 197, 198, 232
Rosemary Barron's Greece, 89–90
Ross Island, 11
Rovos Rail, 274–75
Royal African Safaris, 218
Royal Bardia National Park, 220
Royal Chitwan National Park, 192
Royal Scotsman, 269–70
Ruaha National Park, 210
Russia: air combat planes, 133–34;
    astronaut training, 242–46; trains,
    273–74; volcanoes, 110–11
RV caravans, 204–6
RV Caravan Tours, 206

Safari Drive Limited, 217–18
Safaris, 207–25; African, 208–16;
    design your own, 216–18;
    non-African, 218–25

Safehouse Security, 257
Safety tips, 277, 278–80
Sahara Desert, 55, 183; ballooning, 53; camel treks, 57–58
Saharan Dream, 57–58
Sailing, 226–33; around the world, 226–29; gulet, 232; luxury yachting, 230–32; Seychelles, 232–33
Salsa, in Cuba, 201–2
Salt Lake City: theme suites, 171–72
Salzburg Festival, 197–98
Samar Magic Tours Co. Ltd., 159–60
Sami people, 20, 178
San Francisco: circus school, 76–77, 79
Sankey Rodeo Schools, 79–80, 104–6
Santa Claus, 15
Santa Fe Trail, 102
Santorini: cooking classes, 89–90
SCCA Performance Rally Dept., 68
Schoenburg Castle, 174
Schubert, Franz, 196
Scotland: castle hotels/rentals, 165–66, 173; concierge service, 168–69; painting classes, 33–34; trains, 269; Viking history tour, 139
Scott, Robert F., 10, 11
Scotts Castle Holidays, 173
Scottsdale: cowboy school, 101–2; eco-hotels, 172–73
Scuola Del Pettirosso, 84–85
Sea Cloud, 230–31
Security concerns, airport, 281–82
Selous Game Reserve, 210
Serengeti Plain, 52, 208, 210
Seychelles: fishing, 119–20; sailing, 232–33
Shackleton, Ernest, 5, 8–10, 11, 182
Shallow water fly fishing, 118–20
Shark dives, 234–38
Shea, Lari, 154
Shore Club (Miami), 167
Sicily: cooking tours, 87–88
Siemer & Hand Travel, 212–13
Silk Road trips, 184–87
Silver Lining Tours, L.C., 114
Silversmithing classes, 35
Skibo Castle, 165–66
Sky and Telescope, 44–45
Sleeping Beauty Castle, 174
Smithsonian Study Tours, 36, 74

Society Expeditions, 141–42
Society for Creative Anachronism, 140
Sokol Tours, 110–11
Solar eclipses, 40–44
Sonoma Valley, 95–96
Soper River: canoeing, 18
Soren Larsen, 229
South Africa: air combat planes, 133–34; shark diving, 237–38; trains, 274–75; wine tours, 94–95; wingshooting, 124
South Georgia Island, 5, 8, 9–10, 182
South Pole. See Antarctica
Southwest: art tours, 36–37; cattle roundups, 103–4; cooking classes, 90–91; cowboy fantasies, 99–102; earth tours, 108–9; four-wheeling, 70; horseback riding, 99–104; motorcycle tours, 190–91; pottery classes, 30; survival training, 267
Soyuz simulator, 243–44, 245
Space, 239–48; astronaut training, 242–46; hotels in, 240–41; Mars, 247–48. See also Astronomy
Space Adventures: Antarctica, 12; astronaut training, 240, 241–46; Hawaii, 107–8; Russia, 133–34, 242–46; submersible dives, 262
Space centers, 246–47
Spain: architecture tours, 23; cooking tours, 88–89; flamenco, 202
Sporting clays, 125
Sports cars, 73–75
Spy Cruise, 251–52
Spy Drive, 249, 251
Spying, 249–55; covert operations, 254–55; museum, 253–54; tours, 249, 251–53
Stallion 51 Corporation, 127–28
Stargazing. See Astronomy
State Department, U.S., 277, 278
Stenciling classes, 26–29
Steve Parker Off Road Entertainments Ltd., 72
Stock car racing, 63–64
Stoker, Bram, 147–48
Storm Chasing Adventure Tours, 112–14
Storm-chasing tours, 112–15

Struever, Martha, 36–37
Stuart Castle, 173
Studio Brandini, 177
Submersible dives, 258–62; North Pole, 16–17
Suborbital flights, 244
Sun Bay I, 180, 182
Sun Bay II, 137–38
Sun protection, 280
Sunrise International, 18
Survival training, 263–67
Sweden: icehotel, 178–79
Swiss Alps: ballooning, 50–52; motorcycling, 191

Tahiti, 141–42; painting classes, 31
Tall ship sailing, 229–30
Tania Vartan Academy of Trompe L'oeil Painting, 29
Tanjung Puting National Park, 222
Tanks, 72–73
Tanzania: safaris, 210
Tasting Places Limited, 90
Tasty Tuscany, 91–92
TCS Expeditions, 20, 38–39, 98, 186
TC Tango, 201
Tempest Tours, 114–15
Terrorism seminars, 255–56
Texas: camel treks, 57; survival training, 263–65; winery, 96–97
Texas Camel Corps, 57
Thailand: cooking classes, 90
Theme suites, in hotels, 171–72
Thomson Safaris, 210
Tigers, in India, 218–20
Titanic, 258, 261
To Grandmother's House We Go, 87–88
Tornado tours, 112–15
Torres del Paine National Park, 109–10
Tortella, Mario, 84
Tourist information, 277
Track Time, Inc., 64
Trains, 268–76; Copper Canyon, 272–73; in Cuba, 273; Orient Express, 268–69; Rovos Rail, 274–75; Royal Scotsman, 269–70; Trans-Siberian Rail Line, 273–74; in the U.S., 270–72

Trains Unlimited Tours, 271
Transit of Venus, 40, 41–42
Trans-Siberian Rail Line, 273–74
Trans Wales Trail, 155
Transylvania, 24–25, 149–51
Transylvania, Inc., 150–51
Travcoa, 275–76
Travel insurance, 281
TravelQuest International, 44–45, 48
Trepanier, Cory, 32–33
Tristan da Cunha, 182, 183
Trompe l'oeil classes, 26–29
Tropic Star Lodge, 116–18
Truck Africa, Ltd., 183–84
Truffle hunting, 92
Tsavo East National Park, 211
Turkey: luxury yachting, 232
Turtle Island, 166
Tuscany: art tours, 37; olive picking, 91–92; painting classes, 29; rental properties, 176–78
Tuscany Tours: Welcome to the Renaissance!, 37

Uganda: mountain gorillas, 214–15
UK Survival School, 266
Ulaanbaatar, 160, 161, 162, 186, 274
United Four-Wheel Drive Association, 70
Uqqurmiut Centre for Arts and Crafts, 19
Urban Ops, 255
USA Adventure Center, 187, 214
Ushuaia, 6, 8, 9, 10
Utah: survival training, 267

Vampire tours, 147–51
Varga VG-21s, 130
Vedel, Ulrik, 19
Venice, 275; cooking tours, 86–87; opera tours, 197
Venice Carnivale, 86–87
Venus, transit of, 40, 41–42
Verdi, Giuseppe, 197, 198
Verdun, 145
Verona, 197, 198
Victoria Falls, 182, 206, 212, 274–75
Vienna: art tours, 38
Vietnam War battlefields, 146
Vikings, history tours, 138–39

Virgin Islands: luxury hotel, 163–65
Vineyards, 94–98, 175, 206
Visas, 278
Vlad the Impaler, 147–48, 149–51
Volcanoes, 107–8, 110–12
Voyage of the Vikings, 139

Wales: horseback riding, 154–55;
    survival training, 266
Walsh, Don, 260
Wanglang Panda Reserve, 221
Warbird Adventures, Inc., 128–29
Warbirds, 127–29
Washington, D.C.: spy museum,
    253–54; spy tours, 249, 251
Weather tours, 112–15
Weaving classes, 35–36
Weddell Sea, 5
Weightlessness (zero-gravity), 242–43
West, Nigel, 252
West Virginia: Zydeco, 203
Wide Open Baja Off Road Adventures,
    71
Wigham, Ivor, 69
Wild boar hunting, 121–23
Wilderness Travel, 232
Wild Frontiers, 60
Wildlife RV Safari, 206
Wildwings, 237, 262

Wiltsie, Gordon, 7, 8
Wine and vineyards, 94–98, 175, 206
Wingshooting, 123–24
Wings Over Botswana, 212–13
Wisconsin: theme suites, 172
World air tour, 187
World cruise, 169–70
World Dracula Congress, 149
World Health Organization, 278
World Of ResidenSea, 164, 169–70
World War I: battlefields, 145
World War II, 253; battlefields,
    145–46; flying warbirds, 127–29
Wyoming: cattle roundups, 103, 104;
    horseback riding, 152–53

Yachting. See Sailing
Yamal, 16
Yampa River: rafting, 199
Yarborough, Cale, 62–64
Yukon, 17, 48
Yuri Gagarin Cosmonaut Training
    Center, 242, 243

Zane Grey Reef, 116–18
Zegrahm Expeditions, 232–33
Zero-gravity (weightlessness), 242–43
Zhurkovsky Air Base, 133–34, 242, 245
Zydeco, in West Virginia, 203